MUSIC, FILM, AND ART

MUSIC, FILM, AND ART

Haig Khatchadourian
University of Wisconsin
Milwaukee

WIPF & STOCK · Eugene, Oregon

Wipf and Stock Publishers
199 W 8th Ave, Suite 3
Eugene, OR 97401

Music, Film, & Art
By Khatchadourian, Haig A.

ISBN 13: 978-1-60899-572-1
Publication date 6/16/2010
Previously published by Gordon and Breach, 1985

To
Vicken Abie & Sonia Sue
and Sasha

CONTENTS

Preface

The present volume brings under one cover thirteen selected essays on aesthetics and philosophy of the arts, which together exhibit both unity and variety. The first nine essays deal with important aesthetic issues in a number of major art forms and genres: music, painting and sculpture, literature, dance, theatre, and film. The central issues are the identity—or ontological status—and the nature—or some important features or aspects—of the particular art form or genre. The essays attempt to formulate fresh insights and conclusions, as well as fresh arguments for certain established conclusions. Some important interrelations between and comparisons of the major art forms and genres are also highlighted.

The last four essays concern various philosophical and other problems touching all art without exception, not least contemporary art. "The Need for Art in the Modern World" and "Artistic Freedom and Social Control," as well as "Humanistic Functions of the Arts Today," explore various facets of the roles of the artist and of art in present-day society, while "Art: New Methods, New Criteria" explores fundamental theoretical problems facing the aesthetician and the art critic as well as the general public in categorizing or classifying "avant-garde art" as *bona fide* music, painting, sculpture, literature —or as *bona fide* art. The same problems crop up in the evaluation of such productions as *good* or *poor* music, painting, literature, and so on. The article also considers the difficulties that face contemporary audiences in their endeavor to understand and appreciate or enjoy contemporary, particularly avant-garde, art.

As their titles generally indicate, two or more essays that concern a particular subject or art form are either complementary or are otherwise closely related. On the other hand, one of the aims of "Remarks on the 'Cinematic'/'Uncinematic' Distinction in Film Art'' is to stress the nature of film as a multimedia art form, as against the widespread tendency in recent writings on film art to overemphasize the cinematographic (visual) qualities of film. To that extent, it endeavors to rectify the same tendency in ''Film as Art'' and provides a necessary modification of some of that essay's central claims.

The present collection complements my general aesthetic views developed in my other publications on aesthetics and the philosophy of art, particularly my detailed analysis of the ordinary concept of art as a whole set forth in *The Concept of Art*. It should be useful to the student of the arts as well as to students of aesthetics and professional aestheticians and critics. Indeed, it can be of considerable use to the serious general reader. For although all the essays are intended to make original contributions to their particular subject, they eschew as much as possible technical philosophical jargon and highly specialized philosophical concepts. This is in line with the general philosophical treatment or method used throughout, a treatment that adds an element of methodological coherence to the substantive unity of the collection.

HAIG KHATCHADOURIAN

Acknowledgments

Grateful acknowledgment is made to the following persons and publishers who have kindly granted permission to reprint the essays in this volume:

Gordon and Breach and F. Joseph Smith for permission to reprint "The Identity of a Work of Music-I," *Music and Man*, Vol. 1 (1973) and "The Identity of a Work of Music-II," Vol. 2 (1978).

Basil Blackwell and Stephan Korner for permission to reprint "About Imaginary Objects," *Ratio*, Vol. 8 (1966) and "Fictional Sentences," Vol. 20 (1978).

Wayne State University Press and John Fisher for permission to reprint "Film as Art," *The Journal of Aesthetics and Art Criticism*", Vol. 33 (1975) and "Movement and Action in the Performing Arts," Vol. 37 (1978).

Redgrave Publishing Company and Ronald Gottesman for permission to reprint "Remarks on the 'Cinematic/Uncinematic' Distinction in Film Art," *Quarterly Review of Film Studies*, Vol. 3 (1978).

Thomas & Hudson Ltd. and Harold Osborne for permission to reprint "On the Nature of Painting and Sculpture," *The British Journal of Aesthetics*, Vol. 14 (1974) and Oxford University Press and T.J. Diffey for permission to reprint "Movement and Action in Film," Vol. 20 (1980).

University of Illinois Press and Ralph A. Smith for permission to reprint "Art: New Methods, New Criteria," *The Journal of Aesthetic Education*, Vol. 18 (1974), "Artistic Freedom and Social Control," Vol. 12 (1978), and "Humanistic Functions of the Arts Today," Vol. 14 (1980).

Milan Damnjanović for permission to reprint "The Need for Art in the Modern World," *Proceedings of the IX International Congress of Aesthetics*, Dubrovnik, Yugoslavia, August 25–31, 1980.

PART ONE

Chapter 1

The Identity of a Work of Music—I

I

In "The Artist and the Community,"[1] R.G. Collingwood maintains that "the work of artistic creation is not a work performed in any exclusive or complete fashion in the mind of the person whom we call the artist."[2] Again,

> This [the aesthetic activity] is a corporate activity belonging not to any one human being but to a community. It is performed not only by the man whom we individualistically call the artist, but partly by all the other artists of whom we speak as "influencing" him, where we really mean collaborating with him. It is performed not only by this corporate body of artists, but (in the case of the arts of performance) by executants, who are not merely acting under the artist's orders, but are *collaborating with him to produce the finished work*. And even now the activity of artistic creation is not complete; for that, there must be an audience, whose function is therefore not a merely receptive one, but collaborative too. The artist . . . stands thus in collaborative relations with an entire community; . . . the actual community of fellow artists from whom he borrows, executants whom he employs, and audience to whom he speaks. By recognizing these relations and counting upon them in his work, he strengthens and enriches that work itself; by denying them he impoverishes it.[3]

Collingwood, therefore, in effect (though he does not use the phrase as such) maintains that a work of art is an *incomplete object or thing* as it issues forth from what we call the artist or creator.[4] In this section I shall be mainly concerned to show, first, that the putative sense of "complete" and "incomplete" or "finished" and "unfinished" Collingwood has in mind is (must be) different from any ordinary meaning these English words have as applied to art; and second, to show that there is no real need to think or advantage in thinking of art in the way Collingwood does and, in effect, recommend that we do. The present inquiry is, I believe, particularly relevant to contemporary developments in the arts since I agree with Collingwood that "there are many indications that they [artists] are more willing than they were, even a generation ago, to regard their audiences as collaborators."[5] I think this is true of young audiences too, and that this tendency is probably greater now than it was when Collingwood wrote the foregoing essay (1945). The discussion that follows generally applies to all art, and almost everything I say applies to all the performing arts, though our main concern will be music.

A. It can be readily seen that the "incompleteness" Collingwood attributes to a work of art is not, cannot be, incompleteness in any of the following ordinary ways:

(1) in the sense in which a work may be what I can conventionally incomplete, e.g., a "sonnet" consisting of only eight or nine lines, left unfinished by its author;

(2) in the sense in which a work may be a fragment or has become incomplete by losing some part or parts; e.g., "Venus of Milo" as we have it at present; or even

(3) in the sense in which a work may be said to be aesthetically incomplete, meaning that the overall effect or impression it leaves on qualified judges is one of incompleteness: when it lacks a well-rounded effect. In this third sense Schubert's "Unfinished Symphony" is complete, though as a classical symphony it is (conventionally) incomplete, unfinished. If we omit the last stanza of, say, Keats' "Ode To A Nightingale," the poem would be aesthetically incomplete; so also if Keats had not composed that stanza at all, or anything else in lieu of it. But this sense of incompleteness, though closer than either sense (1) or (2) to what Collingwood has in mind (which I shall call sense 4) is not identical with it either. For even what we ordinarily call a (an aesthetically) complete poem, painting or work or music, such as the entire "Ode To A Nightingale" as composed by Keats, Picasso's "Guernica" or Bartok's First Quartet, would be incomplete in Collingwood's putative sense of "incomplete."

To say that some but not all works of art are incomplete in any of the foregoing ordinary senses, hence to say that some (most) of the works we actually have are complete in all three senses, has important implications. One is that on the ordinary conception the "contributions" of performers and audiences, and of other artists, are not the completion of something otherwise incomplete or unfinished. It implies that the creative process is completed when the work it results in is (correctly said to be) complete in senses (1)–(3); or the contributions of other artists, performers, and audiences are not instances of (co-)creation in any ordinary sense. Collingwood's departure from this conception is closely connected with, though as we shall see not logically entailed by, his idealism; i.e., his conception of a work of art as a mental entity or experience. Since this is most clearly true with respect to the audience, I shall concentrate on it here.

Collingwood's theory can be briefly expressed thus. (A) The work of art is an ideal object existing (initially) in the artist's mind, and (B) is reconstructed by the audience in the light of the artist's sensuous "recording" of it; what we call the painting, the sculpture, etc. But even at its best, Collingwood holds, (B) is only partial and imperfect. This view, particularly (A), removes a basic conceptual barrier which the ordinary conception of a work of art as at least partly sensuous or physical erects between the work and its perception, interpretation and enjoyment by others. For if (A) is assumed the work would enjoy the same kind of reality as the audience's "imaginative experience" of it. This experience can then literally be a reliving or reconstruction of the artist's original experience (limited only by the empirical difficulty of duplicating it in others) as well as the addition to it of ideal elements contributed by the audience. It is not, as on the ordinary conception, an impact or effect produced by a qualitatively different kind of cause, viz. a partly or wholly physical thing. The painting, the poem or the work of music as we ordinarily use these terms *are* physical, and are the immediate cause of this imaginative experience; but they are not themselves the work of art, and the experience they give rise to is an experience of the work of art only in the degree in which they are adequate sensible "records" of it. The real source of the experience is the ideal object in the artist's mind.

Since the above applies, *mutatis mutandis,* to the contributions of performers and of other artists, it follows that if the ordinary concept of a work of art as at least partly sensuous or physical is retained, Collingwood's recommendation regarding the participation of performers, audiences and other artists cannot be always accommodated. It cannot be accommodated at all with regard to wholly sensuous works of art, such as some so-called geometrical abstractions, or even works that include certain ideal elements, such as works of literature and program music, to mention only obvious examples. For as will be emphasized in Section II, the ideal elements of works of art, whenever they obtain, are on the ordinary conception just as objective as the sensuous elements themselves; whereas a mentalistic conception of these elements is needed to render the I-thesis more readily acceptable. In short, this thesis would be *prima facie* plausible if one considers a work of art (as, for instance, Samuel Alexander does) as a physical object into which certain ideal elements (''tertiary qualities'') are so to speak ''infused'' by the perceiver's imagination or mind. But this view coincides neither with the ordinary nor with Collingwood's conception of art. Hence on the former view what the performer's or the perceiver's imaginative experience ''contributes'' cannot be an addition to, a process of completing (or, rather, of making less incomplete) the work's ideal components.[7]

I said above that the acceptance of Collingwood's idealistic conception of art makes the I-thesis more plausible than otherwise. I did not say that it logically commits us to it—for aesthetic idealism is perfectly compatible with the ordinary view that a work of art may be and often is complete, in some or all of our three ordinary senses of the word. This is well illustrated by Croce's aesthetic theory, from which Collingwood derived proposition (A) above, for I find no evidence that Croce thinks of a work of art as something incomplete as it is ''intuited'' and ''expressed'' by the artist; indeed, all the evidence points in the opposite direction. Yet this is perfectly consistent with Croce's idealism. In other words, none of the three ordinary senses of ''complete'' and ''incomplete'' commit us to the view that a work of art cannot be wholly mental.

On the ordinary conception, the *interpretation* of a work is not literally a form of collaboration between artist and audience. For if the heard tones, the painted canvas or the hewn marble is the work of art it follows that the attempt to understand the work's meaning can only be the understanding of something whose meaning, like the object itself, is independent of the audience's account or conception of it, and is the yardstick of the latter's adequacy or inadequacy, its correct understanding or misunderstanding of it. Indeed, this view of the relation of interpretation to the work is perfectly consistent with the indealist view itself; i.e., the mental or physical character of the work is immaterial to it; provided we draw a logical distinction, as both ordinary language and Collingwood do, between a person's understanding and that which is understood. It is true that:

> There is no sense in putting the dilemma that a man either understands it [the work] or does not. Understanding it is always a complex business, consisting of many phases, each complete in itself but each leading on to the next. A determined and intelligent

> audience will penetrate into this complex far enough, if the work of art is a good one, to get something of value; but it need not on that account think it has extracted "the" meaning of the work; for there is no such thing. The doctrine of plurality of meanings, . . . is in principle perfectly sound.[8]

The point is that the plurality of meanigs is perfectly explicable on the ordinary view of art. The diversity of a work's, especially a good work's possible meanings, hence the possibility of a plurality of equally adequate but different accounts of these meanings, can be accounted for by, e.g., the imaginative, conceptual or emotional richness or "density" of (especially good) works and the possibility of utilizing different concepts and conceptual schemes, such as different philosophical, theological, scientific or political concepts and theories, for understanding them. Further, many of the elements or aspects of a work that occasion interpretation, e.g., symbolism, figurative meaning, and connotation are not fixed or determinate like the printed text of a poem or the color scheme of a painting. The author's own explanation—even if not an account of what he *intended* to do, whether or not he succeeded in doing so—is just one possibly adequate account of their meaning. Any interpretation, however novel or unorthodox, is adequate to the extent to which it is, first, logically consistent and in agreement with the work's text or score, or the painting, sculpture, etc., as the artist has produced it; and second, if it is properly comprehensive, does not leave out any facts it is intended to explain. Understanding a work is not, as Collingwood supposes, making "that entire experience [the artist's experience, which Collingwood equates with the work as it is created by the artist] *his own,*"[9] in any but a figurative sense of "make his own." To interpret a work is not literally to experience it or part of experiencing it; though an adequate understanding is certainly helpful in properly enjoying the work (in Collingwood's misleading language, experiencing it).

Again, it is often true, particularly with regard to the works of dead artists, that "the audience as understander, attempting an exact reconstruction in its own mind of the artist's imaginative experience, is engaged in an endless quest."[10] Indeed, this quest is also frequently futile if we adopt the Croce–Collingwood recommendation of speaking of a work of art as an "imaginative experience" or an "image" in the artist's mind. For then there is no guarantee that what the audience attempts to understand is the work itself, since the latter would be a mental entity to which we have no direct access. Contrary to Collingwood's claim, we would have no guarantee that what the audience thinks it understands is not some subjective transmogrification of it in their minds. For we cannot be sure that the artist was successful in "recording" his intuition-expression. Or if certain parts of it adequately reflect his intentions, we cannot be sure what they are. In discussing centain interpretations of Eliot's "Sweeney Among the Nightingales," Collingwood assumes that he has at least a partial understanding of it; since he assumes—without warrant for an idealist—that the conventional meanings of the words constituting the poem coincide with Eliot's (intended) meaning. But if understanding the poet's (intended) meaning or even the work's meaning—assuming that the two are distinguishable on the idealistic theory—is all that interpreting a work consists in for Collingwood, anything added or otherwise literally contributed by the audience would be merely subjective, adventitious fantasy, not part of understanding it. The "collaboration" and hence partial "completion" of the work in which this allegedly consists dissolves into thin air.

The *influence* of the audience on the artist is another facet of what Collingwood regards as the "collaboration" between them. The artist may be (a) the spokesman of his audience; he may try to express emotions "not peculiar to himself, but shared by his audience."[11] As a result, (b) he will be open to its judgment of the work's value. This may in turn influence his future productions. However, no kind or amout of influence can be properly regarded as a form of completion; or the existence of some influence in a particular case does not entail that in its absence the work would be "incomplete." The influence is incorporated in the work, whether the latter is complete or incomplete in any sense. Without it the work may not exist at all; or what is created may be a different work. But neither has anything to do with its completeness or incompleteness in any ordinary sense or any sense remotely like it.

The same remarks apply to the *influence of one artist on another*. It too does not entail any form of "completion" of an otherwise "incomplete" thing; or the possible influence of the audience or other artists does not provide a good reason for calling it a form of completion. The differences between it and the completion of an incomplete thing in any ordinary sense are too great, while the similarities, if any, are too small, to justify the move.

The situation is quite different with *performance* in the case of music and the other performing arts: performance at its best is a form of artistic collaboration between artist and performer in an ordinary, literal sense. The most general form this collaboration takes is quite obvious. As Collingwood states, "the book of a play or the score of a symphony, however cumbered with stage-directions, expression-marks, metronome figures, and so forth, cannot possibly indicate in every detail how the work is to be performed."[12] The significant question is whether these features of the notation we call the text or the score of the work, even if regarded as a form of incompleteness, constitute or entail any kind of incompleteness in the *play* or the *music* itself. Or the question is whether the collaboration between performer and artist here consists in the former's helping to complete the work in some sense. Collingwood thinks so, since he says that the performer's role is not merely to "fill in the details" in the text but to fill in the details in the work. Yet in agreement with the ordinary conception he distinguishes the work from its text. Is he then justified in his inference? I believe not. For leaving aside numerous complexities in the notion of a perfectly adequate performance, the ordinary notion of identity or sameness as applied to objects, events and situations no less than works of art in general, admits of a certain variable degree of qualitative latitude. A large though finite number of qualitatively different performances, whose differences are partly or wholly due to the necessarily sketchy character of the text, are normally considered performances of the same work provided they agree in a broad or general way in reproducing the "letter" of the text, however sketchy or indefinite it may be.[13] Indeed, the less determinate it is the greater the latitude, within limits, allowed by the ordinary concept of sameness. But of course the concepts of sameness and difference are not completely open textured; or there are limits to the freedom they allow the performer as such.

Perhaps the most essential point is that the performer's artistic rendition of a work does not constitute any kind of addition to it. A performer who plays a good piece of music skillfully, with understanding, and expressively, moves the sensitive and discriminating listener intensely and profoundly, and, like the good critic, gives him insight into its aesthetic qualities and merit. In short, the performer at his best is a creative artist in a somewhat different way from the good composer, poet or painter. He has affinities to the latter, but also to the good critic.

It is worth noting that *improvisation* poses no problems for the ordinary conception of art. The composer or poet is the musical or literary improviser, the improvisation is the (conventionally or aesthetically) complete or incomplete work. The same is true of the composition of variations on a theme by another composer, though as with improvisation, but understandably more so, some credit is normally given to the composer of the original theme.

There is a certain special case in which the performer does add to and so completes an otherwise incomplete work. This is the soloist's improvisation of a cadenza in some classical concertos. However, a classical concerto without a cadenze may be incomplete in sense one, and sometimes also in sense three. But neither of these is what Collingwood has in mind; and I can see no reason why we must entertain some other, nonordinary sense of the word as allegedly involved in this case.

A different type of situation obtains in relation to some contemporary avant-garde music. In one such work of chamber music I have heard, the composer gives the individual performers the option of starting and stopping at any point in the score they wish; thus chance plays an important role in each performance, and no two performances can be alike. A similar element of deliberate indeterminacy, this time *vis-à-vis* the audience, obtains with respect to, e.g., novels printed on a stack of separate, unmarked cards, which can be shuffled and read in any order the particular reader desires. But in neither type of case or in other cases where chance plays an aesthetic role, can we call the works incomplete in any ordinary sense or any sense remotely like it, since the special part played by the performer or the audience cannot be considered an activity of completing the work. The kind of determinacy which the performer or the audience brings to the work is qualitatively different from, e.g., filling in details, adding a theme, section or movement, supplying a cadenza, and so on. There *is* here a type of literal collaboration between artist and performer or audience absent from works, or the performance of works, of a more conventional nature; but this, like many other types of collaboration, does not constitute or entail the completion of something allegedly incomplete.[14] The upshot of the discussion in this section is, I think, this. First, Collingwood ill-advisedly lumps a host of heterogeneous activities or processes together under the name of "completion," when by virtue of their heterogeneity, if nothing else, it would be desirable to keep them distinct, as they are in ordinary discourse. This means that Collingwood fails to give "completion" and "incompletion" in the relevant sentences a clear and unified meaning clearly distinguishable from the ordinary uses of these words as applied to art. Second, the discussion shows that the ordinary conception of art can readily handle the types of situations that he thinks necessitate the acceptance of the I-thesis. The need to change our normal way of talking is thus shown to be nonexistent.

All this notwithstanding, it is not unlikely that the ordinary Western concept of art itself *will* actually change along the lines of the I-thesis, if the present emphasis of avant-garde artists and their audiences on the collaborative character of art in its production, performances and enjoyment persists for an appreciable time. Certainly this may occur in relation to the performing arts. But if it does happen it will not be because Collingwood proposes it. Notoriously, changes in the linguistic habits of a people are not a result of recommendations by philosophers; any more than such counter-recommendations as I have made would deter nonphilosophers from effecting them. Still, if these changes do come about our discussion will have hopefully shown some of the *additional* changes that must be concurrently made in the current ordinary Western concept of art. One of these, which I mention only because I did not deal with it in this section, is the new ways in which works of art as well as artists, performers and audiences will have to be aesthetically evaluated, assuming that the practice or even the concept of aesthetic valuation is not completely dropped.

II

On another occasion[15] I maintained that a work of music is at least partly a physical, sensible thing, being at least partly a sequence of sound patterns[16]—and I may add, in agreement with Margaret Macdonald, "ordered by common conventions . . . ."[17] The partly or wholly physical character of a work of music is an essential component of the ordinary concept of music. For the medium of music, which is of necessity physical (and so, as Macdonald says, public) is an integral part of what we ordinarily call a work of music. The same is true, *mutatis mutandis,* of the other arts, or of the ordinary uses of "work of art," "poem," "painting," "sculpture," etc.[18] Consequently, as noted earlier, the idealist (e.g., Crocean) view that a work of art is a wholly mental entity, a cluster of integrated images, is essentially a revisionary conception, for it altogether leaves out the medium from the concept of a work of art or "aesthetic object."

The interesting philosophical problems begin rather than end with the admission that a work of music is at least partly a sequence of sounds ordered by common conventions. In what follows I shall attempt to bring out some of the complexities involved in this view and to show how, by implication, the ordinary view attempts to steer away from (1) Platonic Realism, (2) Idealism (Crocean), (3) Phenomenalism and Sense-Data theories, and (4) Epistemological Dualism, thereby avoiding the assorted and well-known ills they face in general and particularly as aesthetic theories. But anything like a final judgment on its success in this attempt cannot be reached in this essay.

A. Our basic proposition (1) "A work of music is at least partly a sequence of sound patterns . . ." implies the following things, among others:

[1] First, that a work of music is not a congeries of Platonic universals, since for one thing the latter are supposed to be wholly nonsensible, perceived by the mind and not the senses. Further, Platonic universals may or may not be "exemplified" by any particulars (here particular sounds), whereas a work of music on the ordinary view necessarily involves a sensible medium, is a phenomenological object. On the other hand the ordinary view agrees with Platonism in at least two important ways. (a) It conceives of a work of music (of a work of art in general) as something objective, not something sujective (mental) as idealism holds. (b) It conceives of it as consisting of sounds (tones), generically speaking. (But see later for important qualifications of these statements.) Each of the notes—C flat, D sharp, E natural, and so on—in a musical score stands for an indefinite number of individual musical tones, which can be repeatedly sounded on different occasions and in different places; just as the word "book" can occur in many books, newspapers and magazines.[19] The view that they are (Platonic) universals is thus fairly attractive; and it seems to receive support from the fact that a work of music is distinguished from its performances,[20] individually and collectively.[21]

[2] Since a work of music is at least partly sensuous, it is at least partly nonmental. Again, a mental image or any other kind of mental entity or experience consists of elements or parts that are specific in character. Thus the auditory images in which a work of music consists for Croce is of necessity a sequence of "sounds" the composer "hears" in his head; whereas, as pointed out under [1] the sounds that we ordinarily refer to in speaking of the elements of a work of music are "generic" sounds. The "sounds" the composer "hears" in his head are but one (and on Croce's view necessarily unrepeatable) mental rehearsal or performance, so to speak. The fact that this happens in the privacy of the composer's head is immaterial for our purposes.

[3] Again, on the ordinary conception a work of music is not an interconnected set of sense data, whether mental or physical[22] (cf. G.E. Moore's view that sense data are physical, existing with material objects in physical space and somehow related to them), this despite the fact that it is at least in part a sensible thing. The reason is that sense data theories, including those forming part of phenomenalism, are alternative "languages" intended to replace ordinary perceptual language in philosophical thinking. Sounds are not sense data on the ordinary conception, any more than colors or shapes are, or objects are bundles of them (or logical constructions out of them). Again, the sense data I am supposed to have while listening to, say, Stravinsky's "Italian Suite after Pergolesi" are particulars, not sense data in the generic sense, kinds of sense data. If a work of music is more plausibly conceived as a set of sense data, generically speaking, the question of whether they are Platonic or Aristotelian universals, and so on, again crops up.

[4] I stated earlier that although a work of music is at least partly sensuous, it is not subjective in the sense of something mental, a concatenation of "ideas" (Locke). It is also not a physical occurrence in the perceiver's brain or central nervous system, generated by the putative causal action of sound waves on the perceiver's sensory mechanism. At the same time a work of music on the ordinary view can and does exist, or continues to exist, when not actually heard. Indeed, it exists even if it is never heard, provided that it is possible to hear it, e.g., by virtue of the existence (or continued existence) of its score. Nevertheless, the sounds that constitute a work of music are not identifiable with the putative material objects, or the physical waves, which for epistemological dualism (and for science) are the physical causes of the sensations (or "ideas") of sound and other "ideas of secondary qualities" (Locke) we have. For as has been widely recognized for a considerable time, the ordinary "commonsensical" view (or Naive Realism) is a form of epistemological monism and does not bifurcate nature as epistemological dualism does. This does not mean, however, that on the ordinary view the actual tones we hear when someone plays a Chopin waltz somehow continue to exist unheard, when the playing stops! Further, when we speak of the waltz at times when it is not played by anyone, we do not refer to "unheard sounds" in the sense of "completely inaudible sounds"; meaning by this sounds that are too faint to hear without the aid of, say, electronic amplifers.[23] The latter, like sound waves, are "particulars," not the waltz as a work of music itself. What "the waltz as music exists

whether or not it is heard" does mean is that the tones we actually hear on the occasions on which it is played do not exhaust it as music: they only constitute particular performances of it; whereas the waltz is something that can be played over and over again, endlessly.[24]

Lastly, the sound waves that exist independent of the perceiver, unlike sounds, colors, etc., on the ordinary conception, are not perceived at all, being unperceivable in principle. What we perceive is always their alleged subjective effects on (and in) us.

B. With this, we turn to a closer look at the positive features of the ordinary conception of music.

[1] We must begin by distinguishing two familiar uses of "performance": a process and a product use, or "performance_1" and "performance_2", respectively; i.e., the activity or event of performing (presenting) a work of music, and that (the sequence of sounds) which is thus presented or performed, respectively. On the ordinary view a work of music is distinct from (a) its performances_1, both individually and collectively, but not from (b) its performances_2[25]; though the latter statement must be later qualified in important ways. The truth of (a) is easily established, e.g., by noting that a performance_1 of, say, Beethoven's Fifth Symphony by the Berlin Philharmonic is an occurrence, event or activity, while the Fifth Symphony itself is not (cannot be) an event, etc.: a category mistake would be committed if we talk about it in that way.[26] Also, as stated earlier, the events which constitute performances_1 of the Fifth Symphony occur intermittently, in particular places; but on the ordinary view the Fifth Symphony, once created, exists continuously, even when not performed_1 and independent of its performances_1, e.g., even when it is, as we say, actually lost. It makes no sense to ask *where* it is, in the sense in which it makes sense to ask where the Fifth Symphony is being performed_1 at a given time, and where the painting called the "Mona Lisa" is at this moment. Performances_1 are auditory renderings of the antecendently existing work; the latter is a necessary condition of its performances_1. Obvious absurdities or other difficulties relative to the ordinary aesthetic framework as a whole would arise if a work is identified with its performances_1 even all actual and possible performances_1. For instance, (a) the loss and later recovery of a work, and (b) its destruction, would mean something quite different—if "getting lost," "being recovered," etc., retain any meaning at all—if a work is identified with its performances_1. Note that a person recovering a lost work would have to be called a "co-creator" or even a "creator" of what would be then a numerically "new" work—and so on. These

oddities of speech would be unobjectionable, however, if one is willing to refashion aesthetic (musical) language as a whole in accordance with the new way of talking about a work of music. Whether it is advantageous to do so is another matter. On the positive side the ordinary way of talking about a work of music as enjoying uninterrupted existence, barring its destruction (e.g., by the destruction of all extant copies of its score and the death of all those familiar with the work), has all the advantages, such as the simplicity or conceptual economy, of our everyday way of talking about physical objects, events, qualities, etc.

I said that a work of music is logically distinct from its actual or possible performances$_1$. In this sense of the word or of "interpretation" Macdonald is therefore mistaken in holding (in *AICA*) that "there seems to be no work [e.g., *Hamlet*] apart from *some* interpretation"[27] and "my reading of *Hamlet* is not an 'instance' of *Hamlet* though it is one of a vast number of more or less similar performances without which . . . it would make no sense to speak of the play."[28] On the other hand, her statements are true if "performance" is understood as "performance$_2$"; likewise if "interpretation" is taken in the same sense. For then her statements express the ordinary view (which is presumably what she wished to express) that the sounds which, generically speaking, constitute a work of music, cannot exist apart from the particular sounds constituting correct performances of the work. She expresses this very clearly when she says: "The idea of a 'work of art-in-itself' which can never conceivably be experienced is as mythical as a 'material object-in-itself' which can never conceivable be perceived."[29] The concept of music—of art as a whole—is inextricably bound up with heard sounds, with phenomenological objects. It is not connected with something unperceivable, or even something perceivable *but only insofar as it is unperceived.* When we speak of a composition that no one has actually heard, not even the composer, the phrase "unheard composition (music, etc.)" does not refer to any putative unheard *sounds* existing independent of any sentient being; e.g., (as we would ordinarily describe it) sounds made by someone on a musical instrument but not heard by him or anyone else, e.g., because he is deaf or wearing earplugs and no one is around to hear the music.[30] The very same waltz or symphony which is unheard at a given time because it is not performed *is* what is heard when the score is correctly performed. On this view no ontological wedge can be driven between the music as a particular set of *repeatable* sequences of sound and that which is heard in any correct performance$_1$ of it. We say "I had the occasion to hear Beethoven's 'Eroica,'" and "there were many occasions on which I heard the 'Eroica.'" In either case what we heard (if the statements are true) *was* the symphony *as performed* by a particular orchestra on a certain date in a certain place.

In the light of the above we can say, as I did in *WAPR,* that:

> Beethoven's Symphony No. 3 ... seems to be what all the actual and possible interpretations, performances or renderings of a particular score will have in common as sequences of sound patterns ..., if the interpretations of the notation in the score are all made in conformity with the conventions established by musicians.[31]

We can say this provided it is correctly understood, for a problem arises when we try to ascertain in which of the two uses of "performance," etc., it is true. Clearly the first will not do: that which is common to a set of qualitatively similar or identical occurrences can only be a kind of *occurrence.* It would be true in use two provided we do not interpret it in either of the following ways, the first of which we have cautioned against; I mean as implying that what is common to these performances$_2$ is a transendent entity existing over and above the individual performances$_{1,2}$. On the second, likewise inadequate interpretation, a work of music would be construed as a logical construction of some sort, whether à la phenomenalism or otherwise. The latter is exemplified by Macdonald in *AUCA.* She says:

> One might suggest that "same" here [in the statement "Different ages or even different persons in any age evaluate the "same" work of art"] is used analogously to its use in "same function". *Hamlet* is a function of which individual interpretations are values as "X is a man" is a function of which individual men are values.[32]

But she warns:

> If the work of art is such a construction as I have suggested, it is unique and not to be identified with any others with which it may be compared. The history of the arts, of criticism and evaluation, does seem to show that "work of art" is not used for simple, identifiable objects which can be indicated like a pebble on a beach or a book on a shelf, but rather for something like a set of variations on a basic theme.[33]

Among the constructions from which she wishes to distinguish a work of art is the alleged construction of a physical object from sense data, on the phenomenalist thesis.[34] Although she is right in dissociating herself from phenomenalism in her account of music (art), the notion of a construction can be misleading; since it may be construed to entail that a work of music is some kind of abstraction—which is not, I think, what Macdonald wished to claim. For as I have emphasized, a work of music is a concrete existing thing, and partly or wholly sensuous. Moreover, if it is construed as an abstraction, it is easy to slide into some form of subjectivism on the one hand or metaphysical realism on the other hand.[35]

III

In Section II I reiterated that a work of music is *at least partly* a sequence of sounds (tones), for it is my view that on the ordinary conception it may also be partly nonsensuous, may include certain ideal elements or aspects. In this final section I shall therefore deal with two connected questions: (1) What are these ideal elements or aspects, or in what sense(s) of "ideal" may music have such components?, and (2) How are they related to the structured tones which constitute the sensuous component of music? Because of limitations of space the discussion will be necessarily sketchy.

It is I think undeniable that successful works of "program music," such as good symphonic and tone poems, operas, musicals, oratorios or masses, as well as most music composed for the dance or for films, convey more or less definite or specific (a) images and (b) ideas,[36] as well as depict or suggest (c) feelings, emotions, mental states or experiences; by virtue of the theme, story or program they (in some way) present to the audience. This is quite frequently due to the verbal (literary) or plastic (e.g., pictorial) components that some of these works have; e.g., operas and oratorios in the former case, films and dances in the latter case. But even if, like Edward Hanslick,[37] we refuse to regard such "composite" kinds of art works of music proper (whatever "proper" may mean here)[38], there are purely instrumental works, such as symphonic and tone poems as well as some symphonies, which are also descriptive and as such convey more or less definite ideas and imagery as well as more or less specific feelings or emotional states.[39] Hanslick would naturally reply that these things are not part of any work of music proper, since they are merely associated with its descriptive title or the subtitles of its various sections,[40] for the title of a work or its subtitles are not part of the music itself. Granting the truth of the latter statement, and granting that a descriptive title such as "Pastoral Symphony" or "In the Steppes of Central Asia" does convey ideas and imagery, it is nonetheless true that if the title is appropriate to the music the latter must reflect, even if only by suggesting, the conceptual or imaginative as well as emotional content or overtones of the title itself. If Beethoven's sixth Symphony is not utterly misnamed, there must be a "pastoral" quality about it, however indefinite and elusive this may be, and however difficult to pinpoint it precisely in the individual themes or in the harmonization and orchestration. Clearly a work does not become "pastoral" simply by the composer's labeling it so. For instance, the "Pastoral Symphony" contains definite representational elements, such as the (notorious) cuckoo song. (Compare and contrast the "Moonlight Sonata.") Only some pieces of music have the character, e.g., the atmosphere or *ambiance,* of a "pastoral symphony"; though there can be tremendous differences in the specific characteristics, including the emotional and other aesthetic qualities, of different "pastoral" works.

If it is granted that ideas and imagery may be conveyed by purely instrumental program music, it will also be granted that musical tones and their combinations do not do so because of any existing (social) conventions, unlike verbal expressions or conventional signs and signals in the ordinary meaning of these terms. In other words, they lack signification in all of the diverse ways in which the foregoing have signification.[41] This is, *a fortiori,* also true of "absolute" music, since by definition words of the latter description do not contain or convey any imagery or ideas in the usual sense, or at best contain or convey indefinite ideas. To the extent that the latter is true, however, they include ideal elements in the same sense as program music. In the way we ordinarily think and talk of a work of music, images no less than ideas are an objective part of the work: in the same way in which (certain) ideas and imagery may form part of any other kind of art.[42] In order to see this we must be careful not to confuse the ideas and the imagery in a work with those which they, or the work's sensuous part, may evoke in a listener's mind by personal or even conventional (cultural) associations. This confusion is easy to fall prey to because the latter may be confused with the conceptual or imaginative connotations that these tones and their combinations (in some cases due to their instrumental quality or timbre) may have for the particular culture or subculture. For the latter are just as much part of the ideal content of a work as the connotations of (certain) words are part of the poem or novel in which the latter occur. These connotations, though not meanings themselves, particularly in the sense of signification, are similar in important ways to the signification of words, as Isabel Hungerland has clearly shown.[43]

Although musical tones do not have conventional meaning in the sense of signification, whether in the way words, conventional signs, or conventional signals have it, they can obviously function as symbols and so have *symbolic meaning.* In this they are not different from colors, visual forms or other sensible phenomena which can be made to stand for something else by means of a convention. Since musical tones, sounds in general, in contrast to visual things, have had little symbolic content in Western culture as a whole, it is difficult to ferret out whatever symbolic meaning an absolute work of music may have—or even know whether it contains any symbolism—without going outside it; e.g., without the composer's provision of verbal explanations. The essential thing here, however, is that symbolism is a vehicle for conveying ideas or imagery; or that a relation between the sensuous and intellectual or imaginative aspects of a work of music may be symbolically established.

In addition to these ideal elements, works of music, both absolute and program, clearly possess emotional and other aesthetic qualities (A-qualities). They may be cheerful, whimsical, humorous, sad, melancholy, elegaic or nostalgic, elegant, graceful, cold, as well as dynamic, agitated, flamboyant, and so on. All these qualities are mentally noted or observed; though one must hear the musical tones in order to able to notice them. This does not mean that they are somehow subjective, mental, hence not part of the work, in contrast to its nonaesthetic qualities (N-qualities),[44] any more than the ideas and mental images that a symphonic poem or an opera may communicate are subjective because mentally apprehended.

The formalist's retort is predictable: all descriptive, anecdotal or representational elements a work of music may include (assuming for the sake of argument that he would concede their existence in some works of music)[45] are irrelevant to it as art. Only its formal features—more precisely, the musical tones in their various combinations[46]—constitute the work of art.

It may be replied, as I have done elsewhere,[47] that this involves a recommended departure from the ordinary descriptive use of "work of art," and that this departure is unwarranted even if "form"—or rather, "significant ("expressive") form"—could be given a clear and noncircular meaning. But we are not here concerned to show the failings of formalism or to defend the ordinary nonformalist conception but merely to note that the two views are different. On the latter view a work of music may possess, as art, various sorts of ideal components in addition to sensuous components.

In addition to symbolic meaning the sensuous and ideal elements of a work of music and the work as a whole many have meaning in quite a different way; viz. in the sense of *significance*. In *The Concept of Art* I distinguished two forms of *significance* which in some sense or other the impact of a work (*qua* art) may have. Correlatively, these two forms of significance can be distinguished in the work whose qualities are responsible for its aesthetic impact. As a matter of fact we can characterize one of these forms of significance, what I call "specifically aesthetic significance" or $significance_2$, independently of the work's impact, since we can define "$significance_2$ of impact" itself in terms of the $significance_2$ of its phenomenological features. This will be seen from the way I shall characterize "$significance_2$." (a) An idea, image or symbol in a work of art X, or some sensuous feature, aspect or part of it, is $significant_1$ or possesses "human significance" in the degree in which it has "significance for man in his total setting, reality as a whole."[48] Correlatively, X as a whole may (and if organic, will) possess $significance_1$ insofar as some or all of its components have $significance_1$. The moral, social, political, religious or "existential" significance of a work exemplifies this type of significance. Since it is directly or indirectly due to the work's intellectual, imaginative and/or emotional content discussed earlier, it is a "referential" or "designative" type of meaning; though in a sense of "designative meaning" different from those encountered in relation to language, conventional signs and conventional signals. But note that it is a work's sensuous elements-in-relation which are ultimately designative insofar as they have meaning in the present way, since they convey the ideas or imagery, and/or exemplify some or all of the emotional qualities that possess moral, social, political or other forms of $significance_1$. Insofar as they are ideas and imagery *of* something or other, ideas and imagery themselves are intrinsically referential, whether or not they are $significant_1$. (b) The ideal elements of a work possess $significance_2$ to the extent to which they contribute to or enhance the work's specifically aesthetic value, e.g., its beauty. Consequently the meaning of an element here (and only the elements of a work can have meaning in this way) consists in its organic relation to other elements of the work, hence the work as a whole.[49] The more intimately related the elements the more $significant_2$ they are. This means that only coherent or organic—hence to that extent good—works can have significance$_2$ in an appreciable degree. Clearly this sort of meaning is not directly designative; and it need not be even indirectly so; but, e.g., the human meaning of an idea may be enhanced by its logical relation to other, similarly meaningful ideas.

Significance$_2$ is in some ways similar to what Leonard Meyer calls "embodied meaning." He says

> But even more important than designative meaning is what we have called embodied meaning. From this point of view what a musical stimulus or a series of stimuli indicate and point to are not extramusical concepts and objects but other musical events which are about to happen. That is, one musical event (be it a tone, a phrase,or a whole section) has meaning because it points to and makes us expect another musical event.[50]

There are, nonetheless, a number of things wrong with this passage if taken as a description of meaning in the sense of significance (significance$_2$)[51], and with Meyer's, following Morris Cohen's, general account of meaning. For one thing, Meyer wrongly makes "embodied meaning" dependent on the listener's expectations. He says: "Embodied musical meaning is, in short, a product of expectation. If, on the basis of past experience, a present stimulus leads us to expect a more or less definite consequent musical event, then that stimulus has meaning."[52] If this is so, the wonder is that he also maintains that this meaning is objective, for the listener's expectations may or may not be satisfied by the work's particular elements-in-relation, or what is a product of expectation is something psychological, hence variable, whereas significance$_2$ is independent of expectation. But a trained and experienced listener, who, listening to a symphony or quartet for the first time, *perceives* the aesthetic interrelations of its earlier themes or movements, may successfully anticipate its later developments as it unfolds. It all depends, of course, on how consistently or inconsistently, conventionally or unconventionally, etc., the composer develops his musical ideas.[53]

Meyer appears to me to confuse either (1) "X is (not) meaningful for me" or (2) "I can (not) see some (any) meaning in X" (or "I find [do not find] it chaotic, without rhyme or reason") with (3) "X is (not) meaningful (significant$_2$)." Both (1) and (2) describe variable phenomena, and (2) states a putative psychological fact. Further, any kind of temporal relations that exist between musical tones, melodies and the like can arouse expectations of what is to come, whereas significance$_2$ lies in the phenomenological (tonal and/or ideal) interdependence of these elements, which is a special, intimate, and perfectly objective kind of relationship. In (1) and (2) "meaningful" and "meaning" do not mean "$significant_2$" and "having $significance_2$," respectively, though they could mean "$significant_1$," etc. On the other hand we say: (4) "I fail to see the unity of X," which means that the speaker fails to perceive the $significance_2$ of its parts.

Again, Meyer following Cohen appears to be too much under the unfortunate influence of the referential theory of meaning, which is seen even in his definition of "embodied meaning," since he locates meaning in this sense too in an element's indicating or pointing to something beyond itself.[54] If we insist on using these words in relation to an organic (or "internal") relation between two elements A and B, we can only do so in an ontological, not, as with Meyer's understanding of this relation of indication or pointing, in a noetic or psychological sense. Further, Meyer, like Cohen, mistakenly supposes that meaning in the sense of *signification* is necessarily designative; hence his "designative meaning" is not really identical with "signification." For it is commonplace that some words, such as "is," "and," "if ... then" have signification but no reference. Reference is not meaning, and not even part of meaning; though in the case of nouns and adjectives, and verbs which have a reference, meaning logically determines reference. On the other hand reference can exist without meaning (signification), as with many proper names.[55]

Since meaning in any sense, including $significance_2$, is not some kind of entity, whether logical, mental or physical, the $significance_2$ of a musical work does not provide any ideal elements or kinds of elements over and above those discussed earlier.

NOTES

1. In Frank A. Tillman and Steven M. Cahn, eds., *Philosophy of Art and Aesthetics* (Harper and Row, New York, 1969), pp. 484–495.
2. *Ibid.*, p. 495.
3. *Ibid.*, italics mine.
4. For convenience I shall call this Collingwood's I-thesis.
5. *Ibid.*, p. 487.
6. See Section II.
7. *Ibid.*, p. 486.
8. *Ibid.*, p. 486.
9. *Ibid.*, Italics mine.
10. *Ibid.*
11. *Ibid.*, p. 489.

12. *Ibid.*, p. 493.

13. There are special complexities in the case of the dance, where collaboration between artist and dancer is at a maximum. But I am not concerned with that art form here.

14. This can be seen, for example, in the case of John Cage's aleatory music.

15. In "Works of Art and Physical Reality," *Ratio*, Vol. II, No. 2 (February 1960), pp. 148–161. Hereafter referred to as *WAPR*.

16. *Ibid.*, p. 153.

17. "Art and Imagination," in Melvin Rader, ed., *A Modern Book of Esthetics*, 3rd ed., (Holt, Reinhart And Winston, New York, 1961), p. 221.

18. Cf. *WAPR, passim.*

19. Although the analogy to the type/token distinction in semiotic theory is useful to some extent (and I have used it in *WAPR*, along with Margaret Macdonald and others), it can be misleading if pressed too far; as, e.g., Jay E. Bachrach shows in "Type and Token and the Identification of the Work of Art," *Philosophy & Phenomenological Research*, Vol. XXXI, No. 3 (March 1971), pp. 415–420. Perhaps it is, therefore, best to avoid it altogether in talk about art. (See also later.)

20. But as we shall later, only in one use of the word.

21. Cf. *WAPR* and *AI, passim.*

22. Cf. my *The Concept of Art* (New York University Press, New York 1971), Chapter 1. But the fact that sounds, unlike most visual qualities, are not qualities of any substances or objects but are merely made or emitted by them, makes sense datum theories and phenomenalism *prima facie* more plausible in their case. This is a different matter, however.

23. This appears to point to an important difference between works of music and plastic art, due to differences in the use of "sound" and "color" ("line," "form," etc.). The color patterns that constitute a painting in the aesthetically important use of "painting" are ordinarily thought to exist, when unperceived, *in exactly the same way as when perceived.*

24. A corollary of the above is that the words "waltz," "symphony" and the like have a double use in ordinary discourse, not usually distinguished except contextually. They refer both to a work of music ($waltz_1$, symphony) as such, and to the individual renditions of it ($waltz_2$, $symphony_2$). The same appears to be true of "music." This is connected with the dual use of "performance" explained above, and is probably one reason why some aestheticiams erroneously believe that a waltz or symphony as a *work of music* is an event.

25. This disinction is not drawn either by Macdonald in *AI* or by me in *WAPR*: hence our categorical denial that a work of music is identical with any and all performances of it. But cf. Macdonald's earlier view in "Some Distinctive Features of Arguments Used in Criticism of the Arts," in William Elton, ed., *Aesthetics And Language* (Basil, Blackwell and Oxford, 1954), pp. 114–130, hereafter referred to as *AUCA*.

26. Yet the view that a work of music is an event is widely held; e.g., by Monroe Beardsley, Richard Rudner, Leonard Meyer. Cf. also Jay E. Bachrach, "Type and Token and the Identification of the Work of art," *Philosophy and Phenomenological Research*, Vol. XXXI, no. 3 (March 1971), pp. 418ff.

27. *Ibid.*, p. 126.

28. *Ibid.*, p. 128.

29. *Ibid.*

30. The ordinary conception of unheard sounds is not, therefore, in conflict with the scientific account of the way sounds are produced. That is, the ordinary view does not suppose that sounds exist in the physical world in the absence of sound waves.

However, the concept of unheard sounds is considerably more complex than indicated in these brief remarks. For example, in Keats' "Heard melodies are sweet, but those unheard are sweeter," the phrase "those unheard" does not mean that the melodies are not being played at the time. Yet here "unheard" has a perfectly good (metapherical?) meaning. But I shall leave a consideration of this usage for another occasion.

31. Macdonald, *op. cit.*, p. 128.

32. *Ibid.*

33. *Ibid.* As seen from *AI*, she later abandoned this view, adopting a position with which I am essentially in agreement.

34. *Ibid.*

35. Cf. Jay E. Bachrach, *op. cit.*, p. 418, regarding the adoption of the universal/particular scheme in relation to the identification of a work of art.

36. In the same sense of "idea" in which a poem or novel, or an everyday statement, conveys ideas; not in the sense of "musical idea," i.e., a melody, musical theme or conception. In the latter sense all works of music contain or consist or ideas.

37. In "The Beautiful in Music," in Frank A. Tillman *et al.*, eds., *Philosophy of Art and Aesthetics* (Harper and Row, New York, 1969), pp. 389–396.

38. To my mind this would be arbitrary; indeed, as maintained by formalists or isolationists, such as Hanslick himself, it is issue begging—but no matter.

39. If Hanslick were able to free himself from the classical expression theory of art, with all its confusions, he could have maintained (more adequately than he does) that feelings, including specific feelings, can form part of a work of music. He could have then rejected the view that music "represents" feelings without being forced to maintain that it nonetheless "expressed" them.

40. Cf. Hanslick, *op. cit.*, *passim*.

41. Or what Leonard Meyer, in "The Meaning Of Music," Tillman, *op. cit.*, pp. 466 ff., though not altogether correctly, calls "designative meaning."

It is important to note that "signification" or "meaning" in the present kind of use means something different in each case. Cf. my "Words, Signs, Signals and Symbols," *The Philosophical Forum*, vol. I, No. 4 (New series), (summer 1969), pp. 493–508.

42. See *WAPR*, pp. 157ff.

43. "Language and Poetry," *op. cit.*, pp. 155–189.

44. On this I am in agreement with Frank Sibley, *op. cit.* In *The Concept of Art* I attempted to show precisely how a work's N-features are responsible for its A-features. See also Isabel Hungerland, "The Logic of Aesthetic Concepts," Tillman, *op. cit.*, pp. 595–616, and "Once Again, Aesthetic and Non-Aesthetic," *Journal of Aesthetics and Art Criticism* (Spring 1968), pp. 285–295.

45. But contrast Hanslick, *op. cit.*, *passim*.

46. Cf. Clive Bell. However, I was mistaken in *WAPR* in not recognizing the objectivity of "emotional qualities" and admitting only the feelings and emotions (which are clearly subjective) evoked by a work's N- and A-features, either directly or as a result of our awareness of "their rightness and necessity" (Bell). See *The Concept of Art* for an attempt to rectify this error; also Ronald W. Hepburn, "Emotions and Emotional Qualities: Some Attempts At Analysis"; Tillman, *op. cit.*, pp. 561–571.

47. *The Concept of Art*, Chapter 2. See also Morris Weitz, "The Role of Theory in Aesthetics," Rader, *op. cit.*, pp. 199–208, where he points out that "significant form" constitutes an honorific (essentialist) redefinition of "art" in the descriptive sense. See also Beryl Lake, "A Study of the Irrefutability of two Aesthetic Theories," in Elton, *op. cit.*, pp. 107–113.

48. *Ibid.*, p. 225.

49. Cf. *op. cit.*, p. 225f. The above facts are not recognized by Meyer in his distinction between "designative" and "embodied" meaning. See above.

50. *Op. cit.*, pp. 467–468.

51. Otherwise, this alleged type of meaning is, I think, a myth; or more correctly, Meyer confuses the phenomenon he describes with meaning in some sense.

52. *Op. cit.*, p. 468.

53. For example, such anticipation is well nigh impossible with regard to chance music.

54. Cf. Cohen's general definition of "meaning" in *A Preface to Logic*, p. 47, quoted by Meyer. (Meyer, *op. cit.*, p. 466)

55. See my *A Critical Study in Method* (Martinus Nijhoff. The Hague, 1967), Chapter 4.

Chapter 2

The Identity of a Work of Music—II

I

In an earlier essay[1] I presented, among other things, an outline of my views concerning the identity of a work of music, as conceived in the way in which we ordinarily apply such expressions as "work or music," "musical composition," or, say, "Beethoven's 14th Quartet." A number of important distinctions were made there. They included the distinction between (1) a work of music on the one hand, and, on the other hand, its score as well as its live and recorded performances or renderings; and between (2) a performance as the event or activity of presenting a work of music, or performance$_1$, and that (the seqence of sounds) which is thus presented or performed, or performance$_2$. Further, I maintained (3) that a work of music is "what all the actual and possible interpretations, performances or renderings of . . . the particular score will have in common as sequences of sound patterns . . . if the interpretations of the notation in the score are all made in conformity with the conventions established by musicians"[2]; and (4) that a work of music is "at least partly a sequence of sound patterns"[3]; indeed, that it is identical with its (actual or possible) performances$_2$, if this statement is properly qualified or understood. Finally, (5) I argued against the identification of a work of music with (a) a congeries of Platonic universals, (b) any mental entity, (c) any interconnected set of sense data, (d) any cerebroneural occurrences in the listener's body, or (e) any sequence of sound waves existing in physical space. It is something objective and at least partly sensuous.

In this section I propose to develop and clarify some of the basic ideas in *IWM*, particularly propositions (3) and (4) above, by providing a fuller positive account of the nature and mode of existence of a work of music. In Section II I shall compare works of music and films, paintings and sculptures, ontologically speaking. I shall start with the central question: What is the ontological status of a work of music, and in what way is it that which is common to all adequate or faithful $performances_1$—and I should add here, mental readings—of the score? Or in what sense is it identical with the performances of its score, whenever they are the logical product of the score's adequate $performances_1$?

The following are a partial answer to the preceding question.

(1) In the ordinary view, a work of music as an empirical, partly or wholly sensuous particular, i.e., as a sequence of *heard* sound-patterns, *exists in and only in* (a) each and every one of the faithful $performances_1$, and (b) the adequate mental readings, of its score. The former is what I meant in *IWM* in saying that "a work of music is a concrete existing thing, and partly or wholly sensuous."[4] With regard to (b), we should add that a work of music, as an empirical particular, can also be a "quasi-sensuous" thing, as a sequence of sound patterns heard mentally by a musician reading the score. An analogous situation arises with regard to other sensible qualities, such as colors and shapes. In philosophical terminology, we can say that a work or music exists in (and only in) adequate $performances_1$ and readings of its score in the sense of being exemplified or instanced in them just as the "universal" redness for Plato and Aristotle is exemplified or instanced in red apples and sweaters, etc. (But the term "realization," which William E. Webster uses in "A Theory of the Compositional Work of Music,"[5] is perhaps better than "exemplification", since it avoids the latter's traditional associations with philosophical theories of universals.) As an empirical particular, a work of music cannot exist temporally prior to all (faithful) *actual* realizations of it, e.g., its adequate $performances_1$. It follows that each corresponding $performance_2$ of the score would be an instance or a realization of the work of music, similarly with adequate mental readings of the score. The important distinction between a realized work of music and the events that empirically realize it is thereby preserved.

There is, however, a crucial way[6] in which a work of music is not logically exhausted by its actual realizations; though it is, indeed, exhausted by all its actual and possible realizations. Insofar as both of these things are true, it resembles a congeries of universals as Aristotle conceives of the latter. Insofar as it cannot exist independently of all its actual and possible realizations, it differs singificantly from a congeries of universals as Plato conceived them. On the other hand, as I stated in *IWM*, it is not a logical construction in the way philosophers use the term.[7]

Another way of describing a work of music as something unrealized or as an "abstract particular," to borrow a term coined by Webster in the article alluded to above, is that it is a (nontemporal) sequence of sound patterns designated by the score; understanding by "sound" here not an individual sounding of the notes but the notes generically speaking, as C-natural, B-flat, F-sharp, etc. As an abstract particular, a work of music consists of the totality of these elements-in-relation—the sounds, whether actually heard or unheard, in their complex and multifarious melodic and harmonic interrelations—that are common to, e.g., all actual and possible performances$_2$ (hence all faithful performances$_1$) of the score.[8] As an abstract particular, a work of music consists of unheard sounds. In this sense it is always, to some extent, only potentially realized. But this also means that, whenever the appropriate conditions prevail, it is something that is actually heard. Unheard sounds are not sounds that cannot possibly be heard, for then they would not be sounds at all.[9] In Berkeleyan–Millsian terminology (but without its idealist–phencomenalist underpinnings) a work of music as an abstract particular is a "permanent possibility of (sensuous and mental) experience."

To sum up our discussion so far, the term "work of music" (or "a symphony," "a sonata," "Chausson's *Poeme*," etc.) refers both to (1) something that is always actually (and inescapably) only partly realized and therefore also partly unrealized, something always partly potential, i.e., an abstract particular, and to (2) a set of concrete particulars each of which is an empirical realization of a work of music as an abstract particular. Music as sound, whether heard or unheard, is the twofold referent of the musical notation (i.e., the signified). The latter are the conventional signs (the signifier) which, in a certain conventional order, refer to different parts of the work of music. This finds its essential analogue in literature, for in the corresponding sense, a literary work is that complex whole which is sequentially designated by the words and sentences, paragraphs, lines of verse, etc., of the text. A major difference is that whereas many words have conventional meaning in addition to conventional referents (and many words refer to what they do by virtue of their meaning), musical notation has no conventional meaning (sense or signification) but only conventional referents.

If the foregoing is true, it follows that my view in *IWM*, which (like the present account) is based on the conception of music as sound, was inadequate to the extent that it did not distinguish heard and unheard sounds, and therefore stated without qualification that the "concept of music ... is inextricably bound up with heard sounds, with phenomenological objects."[10] Correlatively, that account failed to make clear that in employing the term "a work of music" or the phrase "Bach's 'Partita No. 3 for Unaccompanied Violin,'" etc., in ordinary language, we refer to *two* ontologically related things, viz. (a) a partly unrealized sequence of sound patterns, an abstract particular, and to (b) empirical, partly or wholly sensuous entities, actual realizations of the abstract particular.

Earlier I used Berkeleyan–Millsian language in describing an unrealized work of music as a permanent possibility of experience. I should now add that I am not talking about it as a permanent possibility of, among other things, (aural) perception in Berkeley's or Mill's sense, or in the sense of any idealist or phenomenalist for that matter. For on the ordinary conception of sound—as with the "naive" realist view of sensible phenomena in general—sounds have objective physical existence, independent of all sentient beings. They are not (mental) sense impressions or data, and the like. Whether in the last analysis this view is philosophically tenable is of major consequence for metaphysics and epistemology in general and theory of perception in particular. But in the present discussion I am not concerned with even a preliminary examination of its merits or demerits.[11]

I said earlier that a work of music, as an abstract particular, is in some ways similar to a congeries of Aristotelian universals. But there are also some important differences between them. One such difference is that an Aristotelian universal, *qua actual* universal—as opposed to a potential universal, i.e., as the form inherent in an object, event, etc.—exists as a concept in the mind of whoever apprehends the form of the particular entity. But a work of music is not a concept, though we can and do think of a work of music in general and so have a concept or a number of concepts of it. It is a primary object of thought as opposed to a concept, which, in an obvious sense, is only a secondary object of thought. Again, individual works of music, such as Brahms' "Piano Concerto No. 2," can be thought about; but to have an idea about that work is to know or understand something about it. As a matter of fact, once it has been composed by Brahms, it enjoys a reality independent of anyone's thinking or knowledge of it.

A second major difference is that an Aristotelian universal is only one aspect of the particular of which it is the form in Aristotle's sense.

In contrast to this, a work of music is a particular of some kind—in Aristotle's terminology, it is a unity of form and matter—though not an empirical (sensible) particular. It is "form" and "matter" combined, not just the putative *essential qualities* of some kind of phenomenon.

But if so, would not works of music as abstract particulars be inevitably reduced to their realizations$_2$ (e.g., performances$_2$), and so open to obvious criticism? The answer is "No." Rather than being the set of all their adequate actual performances$_2$, a work of music consists of those interrelated features that are common to all actual and possible performances$_2$ (hence adequate performances$_1$) of its score.

An objection immediately arises. If a work of music is of necessity always partly unrealized, or its concept allows for its sometimes being unheard, how can it be said to have a sensuous medium? Is unheard sound sensuous? Further—especially if the answer to this question is "No"—how can a work of music be distinguished from the *conception* of a particular work of music, e.g., in the composer's mind as he creates it, before he has put it down on paper in the form of a score or played it on some instrument, and so on?

Starting with the latter objection or question, the answer seems to be this. This finished conception of, say, Schubert's "Ave Maria" in the composer's mind during its creation (or the conception in another musician's mind when he reads the score or goes through the work in his head after a concert) *is the work itself*. But that conception is logically distinct from the sequence of sounds that Schubert heard in his mind when he conceived the music. Here again we must distinguish the activity or process of Schubert's conceiving the work and that which he conceives, the conception or the work itself, though it must be noted that Schubert's conceiving of or creating "Ave Maria" is not a realization$_1$ of it in Webster's and my sense. The possibility of the music's actual realizations logically depends on Schubert's conceiving the work. On the other hand, the composer himself would be "silently" realizing the work whenever he goes through the score in his mind, after having written the music down or created it in his head. These mental realizations$_2$ have the same relation to actual performances$_2$ of the work and to the work as an abstract particular as actual performances$_1$ have to the latter. Consequently Croce's and Collingwood's (as well as Jean Paul Sartre's) conception of a work of music (as of art in general) as a mental entity confuses the mental realizations$_{1,2}$ of a work and the work itself, which is not mental.

The distinction between a work of music as an abstract particular and its realizations can also be seen as follows. We are accustomed to think of a work of music as a temporal entity, just as we think of a work of literature as a temporal entity. Nothing seems more plain, since the medium employed in each case, as heard sounds and as words, is temporal in an obvious sense. Consequently we speak of music and literature as temporal arts in contradistinction to the "spatial arts" of, e.g., painting and sculpture. Likewise we speak of cinema as both a spatial and temporal art. All this is true as far as it goes; but it does not go far enough. For first, a work of music as an abstract particular, as *unheard* sounds, is something all of whose parts coexist; similarly with a work of literature as Roman Ingarden sagaciously observes in *The Literary Work of Art*. But the performances$_1$ and mental readings of a work of music, like the realizations of a novel or a poem, are essentially temporal, since they are partly or wholly physical occurrences. Consequently, too, the experience of reading the score or listening to a performance$_1$ of it unfolds in time. On the other hand, the performances$_2$ of the work, or music as heard sound, being qualitatively or in content identical with it, are themselves nontemporal. Although a performance$_2$ comes into existence *in* an event we call a performance$_1$, it is not itself an event. The situation here is essentially no different from any other temporal process and its logical product, such as education, construction, or organization. For though the activity of getting or imparting an education is a certain kind of occurrence, the education one gets as a result of that process, the knowledge acquired, is a nontemporal phenomenon. Likewise, *mutatis mutandis*, with a construction—e.g., a building—as opposed to the process of constructing it.

Taking the score of a work of music as our point of departure, the latter as an abstract particular can be thought of as operationally defined by a set of directives, indicated in the score, whose executions consist of operations for producing certain sequences of actual sound by means of certain instruments, etc. Whenever these directions are properly followed, we have specific adequate realizations of the work in the form of so many performances$_2$. Consequently, starting with the score, to apprehend a work of music as an abstract particular requires (though it is not identical with) apprehending a usually complex set of directives having, e.g., the form: "Whenever you do such and such—play a certain sequence of notes on the piano—you will have a performance$_1$ of Beethoven's 'Appassionata Sonata' (say)." Another way of stating these directives would be: "If you wish to perform Beethoven's 'Appassionate Sonata,' play such and such a sequence of notes on the piano, as indicated by the score."

This is essentially the way I would be now tempted to analyse statements about all qualities, whether sensible or nonsensible, as "universals," viz. in terms of directions specifying operations that, if executed, would result in realizations$_{1,2}$ of these qualities.

I said that a work of music is operationally defined by, rather than consisting of, a set of directives, etc, for the latter are conventionally set down in the score (notation) of the work, and we must be careful not to slip into the mistake of identifying a work of music with its score. As I said earlier, the score, as setting forth a set of directions for performing the work, has the work as its referent. In semiotic terminology, it is the signifier, not the signified. (Of course some signifiers are reflexive; such as certain words, including the word "word" itself. But musical notation is not reflexive.) It would simplify matters tremendously, ontologically speaking, if we could yield to the nominalistic pull and equate a work of music with the musical notation that constitutes its score, i.e., with the directions for its performance. But that would be an error. In any event, it would be a different conception from the everyday conception of a work of music, in which alone we are here interested. This does not mean, however, that as philosophers we may not have to settle eventually for a nominalistic ontology as a whole, hence in relation to music. But the truth or falsity of the quasi-Aristotelian ontology implicit in the everyday conception of music is not under consideration in this paper, which is purely descriptive and anot reformatory. Nevertheless, it is clear that sooner or later the ontologist of music must come to terms with this age-long problem in the history of Western philosophy.

II

It is instructive to compare the ontological status of a work of music and a film. I shall ignore the dialogue and other linguistic components of sound films, which would require a separate treatment of the ontological status of a work of literature or of a piece of language in general, though it can be shown that a work of literature is an abstract particular of some sort, as an abstract particular it is partly a complex of "types" realized in the individual instances or "tokens" of a work's text.

If I am correct in maintaining that a work of music is an abstract particular, the musical component of a normal sound film consists of an abstract particular of the kind described in this paper. But what interests us here is the ontological status of a film as a whole, e.g., one that includes music in its sound track.

Perhaps the most striking thing about the ontology of cinema is that, ontologically speaking, a film resembles, in different respects, works of music and literature on the one hand and paintings, sculptures and works of architecture on the other hand.

The visual images in a film resemble a work of music as an abstract particular because the sequence of "moving" images on the silver screen wholly consist of a complex of visual qualities: those created by the play of light and shadow or of color on the screen, just as a work of music, as a sensuous phenomenon, consists of a complex of auditory qualities, namely sounds. Both differ from a painting or a sculpture, *in one common sense of "painting" and "sculpture,"* in not being partly or wholly *physical objects.*[12] Morever, neither is an event; though the screening of a film is an event, like the performance$_1$ of a work of music. On the other hand, an important difference between a film as a whole[13] and a work of music is that its screenings are disanalogous to musical performances in certain respects.[14] For example, all actual and possible screenings of a film, barring such things as changes in the film stock caused by wear and tear, are qualitatively identical, in contrast to the numerically distinct performances of a work of music, even by the same performers. Further, the reels of celluloid (which we also call "the film") and the sequence of images projected on the silver screen are related to each other in quite a different way from the way in which the score of a work of music is related to its actual or possible performances. And so on. (Again, compare the different *versions* of a film such as *The Hunchback of Notre Deme* or *King Kong*, say, and different performances of Beethoven's "Fifth Symphony," say, as conducted by Weingartner, Furtwangler or Solti.[15]) The question is whether these and other differences between the screenings of a film and the performances of a work of music entail that a film is *not* an abstract particular of some kind. For notwithstanding the preceding difference, some similarities between screenings and performances do exist. For one thing, the word "screening" too suffers a process-product shift of meaning. A screening may be either the event of viewing a film or that which is viewed; and so we can distinguish "screening$_1$" (event) and "screening"$_2$ ("product"). Utlizing this distinction, our question is whether the numerically distinct screenings$_2$ of a film can be regarded as some kind of *realizations* of it. If a film is identical with *each* of its actual or possible screenings$_2$ rather than being that which is common to them all, it would appear that a film is not, cannot be, an abstract particular of some kind; or that its various screenings are not realizations of it.

My view is that a film is indeed an abstract particular; though it is, qualitatively, quite different from the a work of music (or a work of literature) as an abstract particular. I mean that when we talk about *a film*, e.g., *Barry Lyndon*, we are talking about something that does not literally or strictly exist in any particular places or times (i.e., whenever and wherever it is actually screened), something that retains its reality and identity even if it is never actually screened. The strong temptation to think otherwise stems, I think, from the fact that all actual and possible screenings of a film (with the qualification made earlier) are qualitatively identical. As I see it, this is logically compatible with a film's being an abstract particular, just as much as the fact that no actual performances of a work of music are qualitatively identical is compatible with the proposition that a work of music is an abstract particular. This can be seen, perhaps, by noting that in principle or logically, it *is* possible for *all* performances$_{1,2}$ of a work of music to be absolutely identical. Their lack of identity is only due to contingent factors.

NOTES

1. "The Identity of a Work of Music," *Music and Man*, Vol. 1, No. 1 (Gordon and Breach Science Publishers, London, 1973), pp. 33–57. (Hereafter referred to as *IWM*.) Also in this volume, pp. 6–36.
2. *Ibid.*, p. 25.
3. *Ibid.*, p. 19.
4. *IWM*, p. 27.
5. *The Journal of Aesthetics and Art Criticism*, (Fall 1974), pp. 59–66.
6. But this does not involve a different meaning or sense of the terms "musical composition," "music," "work of music," or, e.g., "Vivaldi's "Four Seasons," etc. See later.
7. *Op. cit.*, p. 27.
8. Webster gives a precise technical description of a work of music as an abstract particular, in *TCWM*.
9. This is another way of saying that a work of music that is not empirically realizable in principle is an impossibility. Cf. Aristotle on universals.
10. *Op. cit.*, p. 24.
11. But see my "Toward a Critique of Idealism," in *Midwest Studies in Philosophy*. Vol. I, edited by Peter French and Ted Uehling (Morris, Minnesota, 1976), pp. 34–42, for a preliminary criticism of idealism.
12. There is another, aesthetically more important sense of "painting" and "sculpture," in which "a painting" at least partly refers to a two-dimensional colored

design painted, etc., on some surface, often giving the illusion of depth, and sometimes representing objective phenomena. Similarly, *mutatis mutandis*, "a sculpture" partly or wholly refers to a three-dimensional spatial design created in some physical material or materials. But I shall here ignore the implications of this sense of "painting" and "sculpture" for the ontology of paintings and sculptures.

13. This means that although the musical and linguistic components of a sound film are, as such, abstract particulars of certain kinds, the fact that they form part of a complex whole, a multimedia phenomenon called a film, gives them ontological characteristics not found in works of music or of literature (or language in general) as such, as ontological wholes in their own right. Thus they become ontologically transformed to some extent, this, apart from any aesthetic transformations that may occur in them as a result of becoming parts of a more complex whole; e.g. by, becoming organically related to one another and to the visual images, etc., in the case of some films that rise to the level of art.

14. I owe this point to my colleagues Professors Stefan Morawski and Ronald Gottesman of the Center for Twentieth Century Studies of The University of Wisconsin-Milwaukee.

15. Further, the different versions of *The Hunchback of Note Dame* are not *realizations* of the film's screen script(s) of Victor Hugo's novel, in our sense of "realization."

PART TWO

Chapter 3

About Imaginary Objects

INTRODUCTORY REMARKS

The mode of existence of a work of literature, like the corresponding question concerning music considered in Part I, is a fundamental philosophical question. But another important and related question is the subject of this essay. I refer to that which is involved in the way we ordinarily talk and think about imaginary objects, such as characters, places, events, etc., in works of fiction; e.g., the Prince of Denmark and Elsinore in *Hamlet* or Duncan and Macbeth's castle in *Macbeth*. Since we also talk about such imaginary things as centaurs and golden mountains, a comparative analysis of the ordinary uses of "about" in statements about them is in order.

I

The aim of this essay is to analyze the ordinary uses of "about" in statements which, as we say, are about imaginary objects. More precisely, I wish to inquire as to the sense or manner in which certain statements are about imaginary objects: what we mean and what is entailed by these statements; or how "about" refers to imaginary objects. In the first two sections I shall discuss some of the major aspects of the uses of this word in (a) statements referring to imaginary objects which might possibly exist in the universe (e.g., centaurs, unicorns or golden mountains), and (b) statements referring to (i) fictional, or (ii) historical characters (such as Mr. Pickwick or Macbeth, respectively), or other objects that occur in imaginative literature. In the last section I shall consider some fundamental similarities and differences between statements of type (a) and statements of type (b).

1. We should note first of all that there is a perfectly good ordinary sense of 'about' in which we speak of talking or making statements about (also, imagining, or thinking about) imaginary objects; just as we speak of talking or making statements (also, thinking or imagining various things) about existent things.[1] Consider, for instance, the following exchange: A. "What were you talking about a little while ago, you and your son?" B. "We were talking about golden mountains: We were saying that we would certainly be happy to own one, if one existed." Thus Gilbert Ryle (and R.B. Braithwaite, who agrees with Ryle on his main point) is to my mind definitely wrong when he claims that a statement such as "Mr. Pickwick visited Rochester" is not really about Mr. Pickwick at all, but only seems to be about Mr. Pickwick—for the simple reason that there is no Mr. Pickwick for it to be about. I certainly agree with Ryle (and Braithwaite) "that there is no 'universe' of discourse outside the real world in which imaginary objects exist, and that to imagine one of these objects is not to presuppose its existence."[2] But it is also true that to *talk*, to make statements about any one of these objects is not to presuppose its existence! Ryle's view is that we cannot talk about imaginary objects because they are imaginary: his assumption is that we can only talk about real things. On the other hand, we do *not* ordinarily say that we are talking about nothing, that we are not talking about anything, when we make statements that purport to be about centaurs or golden mountains. We say that we are talking about something—about something unreal, imaginary, non-existent. Further, we do not ask or try to find out whether something, X, being (as we say) talked about, actually exists in order to decide whether it would be proper to say that X is indeed being talked about instead of only being apparently talking about. And as we said, when someone asks "What are you talking about?" and he receives the reply, "About centaurs," he does not automatically assume—falsely—that centaurs exist.

2. Despite the expected differences between statements about imaginary things on the one hand and statements about real things on the other hand, due to the fact that the former refer to something imaginary while the latter refer to something real, the word "about" has the same sense or meaning—though a *distinct* use[3]—in the two types of cases. This is shown, for instance, by the fact that the word does not change its meaning if something existent, X, which we speak or think about or otherwise refer to, ceased to exist; or when a nonexistent thing comes or were to come, into existence. Thus the statement

(a) "Dinosaurs are dying off by the thousands," which we can imagine a contemporary of these ponderous animals during the Ice Age to have said to his companions in skins, and (b) "Dinosaurs are now extinct," said in 1964, are both about Dinosaurs in the same sense or meaning of "about"; i.e., they both refer to something, unlike a nonsensical string of words which is not and cannot be about anything, whether real or imaginary. In other words, in speaking or thinking about something it does not make any difference, as far as the referential role of "about" is concerned, whether that thing is real or unreal; whether it has existed before but now no longer exists; or whether it has existed so far but will come into existence at some future date. It also makes no difference whether we know or are ignorant of the existence or non-existence of what we talk or think about; as when we talk about unknown but possibly real things; e.g., in scientific theorizing or in philosophy. These things can be stated otherwise by saying that statements of the form 'R' is a statement about something X," or of the form "A talks (or thinks) about something X," assert, entail, or imply nothing whatsoever about the existence or nonexistence of X. X's existence or nonexistence is always an additional—empirical—fact about X not included or in any other way involved in the foregoing statement-forms. The *meaning* of a statement (sometimes together with the context in which it is employed) *wholly determines* what the statement is *about*: but this is possible precisely because a statement's being about something real or about something unreal is an empirical, extra-semantic fact, external to the meaning of the statement and to the meaning or uses of "about." Ryle is therefore wrong in holding that "That a proposition is about something is a matter of fact external to the meaning of the proposition. We cannot know merely be understanding a sentence that it is true or false of something. To know this we have to know an extra matter of fact."[4] What Ryle says is true only if by "something" in the foregoing statement we (tautologously) understand something real or existent; not something that, as we ordinarily say, may be either existent or nonexistent. That is precisely how Ryle himself uses the word; as witnessed by the fact that he speaks of a proposition that *is* about, not merely seems to be about, *something*.

The trouble with Ryle's negative thesis is that he unwittingly *restricts* (but not quite successfully) the ordinary uses of "about" to contexts in which what is spoken about is something real, without convincingly showing that this is desirable. (This is not surprising, since he obviously does not consider his "view" as a linguistic recommendation.) The only point he makes which can be taken as an argument for this restriction is that "so long as it is confusedly felt that the proposition 'Mr. Pickwick visited Rochester,' or the philosophers' proposition 'Mr. Pickwick is an imaginary entity' are 'about' a Mr. Pickwick, so long will people continue to suppose that there is a Mr. Pickwick somewhere in Dickens's head, perhaps, or in a mysterious repository called an universe of discourse."[5] In point of fact, however, ordinary men do not get confused by the ordinary way or speaking about these things. It is only some philosophers who get, or used to get, confused by them—as they got confused by numerous other perfectly harmless and intelligible ways of speaking in daily life. This is not the fault of ordinary language itself but of the philosophers who are, or used to be, misled into assimilating the uses of "centaur" and "golden mountains" or "Mr. Pickwick," to the uses of expressions that name or otherwise refer to real things. And that is due to their taking statements about real things—and so the use of "about" in relation to these things—as their paradigm or model. Let me add that, so far as I know, no nonphilosopher (except perhaps a child) supposes or is in danger of supposing that "there is a Mr. Pickwick somewhere in Dickens's head, perhaps, . . ."—unless Ryle means by this the supposition that "Mr. Pickwick" refers to a concept in Dickens's mind and/or the minds of the readers of *Pickwick Papers*.

In a recent article, Nelson Goodman makes the following telling criticisms of Ryle's above-mentioned negative thesis. He says:

> If there is no such thing as Pickwick for the statement ["Pickwick fell"] to be about, neither is there any such thing for the statement to seem to be about. In the second place, to say merely that the statement seems to be about Pickwick glosses over the distinction between cases like this and very different once like
>
> Maine and everything else is material,
>
> Which may seem to be about Maine, or like a certain utterance of
>
> Paris is growing
>
> that is about a town in Maine but may seem to be about a city in France. Some more satisfactory account must be given of the sense in which (27) ["Pickwick fell"] is about Pickwick and not about Pegasus, centaurs, or Maine.[6]

Ryle does attempt to give a positive account of such statements as "*x* exists" and "*x* does not exist" by claiming that "In the proposition '*x* exists' or '*x* does not exist,' the term '*x*' which from the grammar seems to be designating a subject of attributes, is really signifying an attribute. It is a concealed predicative expression. And the proposition is really saying 'something is *x*-ish' or 'nothing is xish.' "[7] Thus "Ether exists" asserts that something real (Ryle omits the word "real," since—consistently with his negative thesis about "about"—he restricts the uses of "something" and "thing" to "something real" and a "real thing" respectively) has the quality of ethereality. On the other hand "Ether does not exist" denies that anything (real) has the quality of ethereality. Whether or not Ryle's paraphrase of "*x* exists" and "*x* does not exist" is correct I shall not here attempt to determine. Some of my later remarks will, however, indicate the degree of my agreement with Ryle's analysis.

Now it is true that we—or at least philosophers and scientists—talk about ethereality (the "quality" of being ether), and we—or at least students of literature—talk about Pickwickishness (the "quality" of being Pickwick). But talking about these things is not the same as talking about ether or Pickwick (about which we also talk) respectively. (In any event, the force of Ryle's own positive thesis essentially depends on supposing or assuming that to talk about Pickwickishness or ethereality is *not* to talk about Pickwick and ether respectively. For if Ryle does not assume this, he cannot validly suppose that "Pickwick visited Rochester" is about Pickwickishness (which has existence for Ryle) and yet hold that it is not (and cannot be) about Pickwick (who does not exist). We should ordinarily say that to talk about "Pickwickishness" is to talk about the (set of) *qualities* which the imaginary Mr. Pickwick *possesses* in *Pickwick Papers*; and we say that to talk about ethereality is to talk about the qualities which nineteenth-century scientists used to attribute to an alleged medium, called ether, that was supposed to fill "empty space." But just as the meaning of "about" is the same when used both in relation to real objects or persons and imaginary objects or persons, it is the same in relation to Pickwickishness or ethereality on the one hand and Pickwick or ether on the other hand. However, just as there are important differences between the uses of 'about' in relation to the former, there are important differences between the uses of the word in relation to the latter. And some of these differences are due to the fact that Pickwickishness or ethereality, and the like, is a set of qualities (and not merely because they exist in some sense)[8] while Pickwick and ether are a person and an object respectively (and not merely because they are imaginary). But we shall not consider these differences.

3. We shall next consider some fundamental similarities and dif-

ferences between statements about such things as centaurs or unicorns and statements about such things as (a) Macbeth and (b) Mr. Pickwick, made by actual people (in the latter case, say by readers of *Macbeth* or *Pickwick Papers*).

II

The truth of falsity of a statement such as "There are centaurs in the world" is a factual matter, determined by what the world contains and what it does not contain. (I am assuming that the concept of a centaur is not self-contradictory.) Similarly, the truth or falsity of the statement "Hamlet lived in Denmark, as the Prince of Denmark in Shakespeare's *Hamlet*" depends on whether there are empirical facts—here statements in *Hamlet*—to the effect that Hamlet was the Prince of Denmark, and lived in that country; or that he did not live there, etc. The same is true of the more complicated statement "Hamlet loved Ophelia in Shakespeare's *Hamlet*."

Now consider *historical* novels, plays or short-stories. These are, as we say, *about* some actual person or persons. An example is Shakespeare's *Antony and Cleopatra* which depicts, among other things, some highly dramatic episodes in the life of Julius Caesar, Mark Antony and Cleopatra. Note that in this work, as in all other historical novels, plays, etc., some though not all of the things which Cleopatra, say, is depicted as saying, doing or experiencing may be imgined, may not have been said, done or experienced by the real Cleopatra. Further, the utterances which the character Cleopatra makes about the character Mark Antony, say, may or may not also *fit* or be *applicable* to the real Mark Antony. Moreover, I think that even those utterances that fit the latter may or may not be ordinarily said to be *about* him, as well as about the former. Whether or not they are spoken of in this way depends, to my mind, on whether the work appears to indicate that they are *intended* (that Shakespeare intended them) *to be* about him. Nevertheless, even when they are not so intended, there may be, as a matter of fact, various statements, made by the real Cleopatra about him, some or all of which have the same meaning as these utterances. More obviously, whatever the character Cleopatra says about any *fictional* character in the play, cannot be attributed to the real Cleopatra, and clearly cannot be said to be about any real person or persons.

We must here distinguish the utterances made by the character Cleopatra about the character Mark Antony from those statements which historians, in their history books, make about the real Antony. Some or all of the latter may also be *true of* (or fit) the character Antony in, say, *Antony and Cleopatra*, and/or some other play, novel, etc. But even then they would *not* be also about any such character.

Now of course we can meaningfully (and truly) speak of seeing, talking with, touching, etc., Julius Caesar, Cleopatra or Joan of Arc. But when we say so we will be talking about or referring to the flesh-and-blood person whose experiences, utterances and deeds are depicted in a play by Shakespeare or Bernard Shaw, or some other author, as the case may be. But of course the character Julius Caesar, Cleopatra or Joan of Arc does not and cannot "inhabit" our would, "walk about" in our streets, and be seen or heard or touched by us. In this respect a historical (*a fortiori*, a fictional) character differs from such things as centaurs or golden mountains. For it is logically possible that someone may encounter a centaur on, say, the plains of Thessaly; but the character called "Julius Caesar" or "Macbeth" is not the *sort of thing* that can possibly be seen strolling down the streets of London or Copenhagen, or meditating on a bench in Hyde Park. Existing things can be imagined in other capacities than the one or ones they have in real life; but imaginary things cannot "be" in any other capacity than "their" capacity as imaginary things. One can of course imagine imaginary things as existing; but this is not the logical counterpart of imagining existing things as represented in a play, a novel, etc. For to do the latter is not to imagine them as imaginary, nonexistent.[9]

The historical character Julius Caesar occurs in a work of art or a number of works of art; but the person called "Julius Caesar" has or had existence in the actual world. Or to put it otherwise, Julius Caesar the person and Julius Caesar the character in a play are logically distinguishable. The fact that the latter is a representation of the former does not affect the distinction. As far as this is concerned, a historical and a fictional character are similar. Thus those actions, utterances, experiences, etc., of a historical character that fit the particular real person are part of the actions, utterances, and the like of the character in exactly the same way as the imaginary things he is made to say, feel, think or do in the work. They are in the work, part of the work, just as much as the latter.

What we have said about historical characters applies, *mutatis mutandis*, to the spatial and the temporal setting of a novel, play, short story, etc., whenever, as we say, this setting is an actual place or an actual time (i.e., whenever the setting *represented* in the work is an actual place or an actual time). This is true both in the case of historical works and non-historical works. It also applies to the incidents that may be depicted in a work, whenever these are actual happenings; as they are, for instance, in many historical works and in some non-historical works. For a work may certainly be of the latter description even if it has an actual spatial and/or temporal setting. Many novels, plays, etc.—and certainly the realistic or naturalistic ones among them—are of this description. They are properly classified as nonhistorical so long as none of the characters—in particular, none of the principal characters—is an actual person. For however great or striking the resemblance between a character and an actual person may be in any given instance, we will not normally identify the two so long as the particular author does not or did not *intend* the character to be any historical personage.[10] If one or more of the principal characters in a work represents an actual person, the work will be properly a historical novel, play, and the like. But however extensive, striking or faithful the resemblance between a given (including a principal) character and some actual person (including a well-known person) may be, we should still refrain from calling the work a historical novel, play, etc., unless the resemblance is expressly intended. In contrast to this, a work may be fictional even if its spatial setting is an actual place.[11]

Now of course we can imagine human beings, in the usual sense of this phrase, as having *all* the physical and all the psychological traits of Mr. Pickwick or any other *fictional* character in a novel, play, or other literary composition; or even as undergoing all the experiences, and performing all the actions that Mr. Pickwick undergoes or performs in *Pickwick Papers*.[12] But any actual person who possesses all these qualities will not be ordinarily regarded as (Dickens's) Mr. Pickwick himself, but a person who is *exactly like* him, who resembles him in every respect. Or stated figuratively, we may speak of such a man as a living image of him. We meet people who possess a considerable number of Mr. Pickwick's qualities; and then we say: "This man is like (or very like) Mr. Pickwick: he possesses some (or many) of Mr. Pickwick's qualities." We do not say—it would be nonsensical to say—that he is the same as Mr. Pickwick.

Now Mr. Pickwick is unique in the sense that there is only one *character* who can be correctly referred to as "Dickens's Mr. Pickwick." But this is only because Dickens wrote only one work (viz. *Pickwick Papers*) in which the character he called Mr. Pickwick occurs.

Dickens could have very well "reproduced" Mr. Pickwick in another work, as Shakespeare reproduced—though not exactly—the Falstaff of *Henry IV* in *Henry V* and *Merry Wives of Windsor*. Yet if he had done so, the character in the latter work called "Mr. Pickwick" would be *identical* with the Mr. Pickwick we know in *Pickwick Papers*, in *one* ordinary sense of "identical." But he would be undergoing new experiences, getting entangled in new situations; in the same or in a different setting, in the same or a different period of his "life." This is exactly the sort of thing, *mutatis mutandis*, that happens to Falstaff, say. (Cf. in this connection Lawrence Durrell's treatment of the characters and the plot in the four successive novels of the *Alexandria Quartet*.) The same thing would be true if the author who 'reproduces' Mr. Pickwick is some other author than Dickens.

I said that there is a (qualitative) sense in which one and the same character can occur in two or more distinct works. (I might add, in anticipation, that this will be true whenever the character traits that are given to the particular character in each case are qualitatively identical.) But there is a *second*—quantitative—sense in which we should say that there are *three* distinct characters, called "Falstaff," in Shakespeare's plays: *numerically distinct* like the three separate works in which they occur. Similarly with our hypothetical situation in the case of *Pickwick Papers*. Thus we may say: "Here we have two qualitatively identical characters: one of them occurs in *Pickwick Papers* and the other ('Mr. X') in a work entitled 'Y.'" Indeed, "Mr. X" and "Mr. Picwick" would be, numerically, two distinct characters even if both occurred in the same work—say *Pickwick Papers* —provided that, say, some of the things they said and/or did, thought, etc., were different. (If the latter is the case, it would not make any difference whether they have different names; though the use of the same name for both would be utterly confusing to the reader.) Clearly, "Mr. Pickwick" and "Mr. X" could be intended to be identical twins in *Pickwick Papers*.

One of the important things that emerges from the foregoing analysis is that we do *not* ordinarily understand by, say, "Mr. Pickwick" a (fictional) character who, in addition to "possessing" certain physical and psychological traits does, says and experiences *all* that Mr. Pickwick does, says and experiences in *Pickwick Papers*—and in the exact order in which they are depicted by Dickens. For if a name such as "Mr. Pickwick" were ordinarily thought of as having a direct or indirect reference to the sum-total of Mr. Pickwick's qualities, actions, utterances, etc., two plays, novels and the like would have to be exactly or very nearly identical in content in order that a character in the one may be correctly said to occur in the other. (But then we should not have two plays or novels, etc., but two copies of one and the same work; or two nearly identical *versions* of one and the same work.[13]) However, as we stated before, this is patently false: witness the way in which we talk about Falstaff in Shakespeare's *Henry IV*, *Henry V* and *Merry Wives of Windsor*, or any of the principal characters in Lawrence Durrell's *Alexandria Quartet*. It is true that Falstaff differs to some extent, in character-traits, in the three foregoing plays; and there are subtle or obvious changes or developments in the principal characters in *Alexandria Quartet*. But the essential point is that there would be no impropriety or contradiction in our speaking of Falstaff as exactly the same character in all of the foregoing plays, despite the fact that the plays themselves are quite different in content. Similarly with the tetralogy. Stated generally, the statement "Mr. X in novel A and Mr. Y in novel B are identical though A and B are two distinct (and therefore, by implication, qualitatively more of less different[14]) novels" is perfectly proper or self-consistent.

It is worth comparing the foregoing with the situation that we should get if the name of an actual human being, or of a centaur, sea-serpent or unicorn refers (or were to refer) to the particular person, animal, etc., in the same all-inclusive way as we imagined above in the case of names of characters in literary compositions. In the first place, it is logically possible for two distinct persons or two centaurs, sea-serpents or unicorns to be completely identical in personal qualities *and* in life history, and to exist simultaneously. In the second place, it is logically possible for them to be non-contemporaneous without everything else in the universe as a whole, or even in our world, being identical at the two times. This logically presupposes that the doctrine of identity of indiscernibles is false in the present kind(s) of cases: and this is indeed my view, as I have argued in another place.[15]

Let us now consider an interesting *similarlity* between statements about characters in novels, plays, etc. and statements about centaurs or golden mountains, respecting analyticity or nonanalyticity. Propositions expressed by statements about centaurs or golden mountains, unless they happen to be extremely vague, are either analytic or synthetic. Similarly with propositions expressed by statements about a fictional or a historical character in a play, a novel, and the like. For example, the proposition expressed by "Hamlet behaves in *Hamlet* as though he suffered from mother fixation" is (probably) true; and it is synthetic. Indeed, only tautologies, such as "Hamlet is Hamlet" express an analytic proposition: all other statements in which "Hamlet" (as the name of the Prince of Denmark in Shakespeare's *Hamlet* or of any other fictional object or character) is the grammatical subject express synthetic propositions. In this respect statements about Hamlet or Mr. Pickwick are in no way different from such statements as "Plato, the ancient Greek philosopher, is the author of the *Republic*" or "John Smith has been living in Dallas, Texas since 1960," where "Plato" and "John Smith" name some real person, dead or alive. This rests on what appears to me to be the fact that proper names, such as "Hamlet" and "Mr. Pickwick," or "Socrates," "Plato" and "Dwight D. Eisenhower," do not, in any ordinary sense, mean, and therefore are not "translatable" into, any (definite) description or set of descriptions. I have attempted to show this in another place,[16] through the detailed analysis of the ordinary uses of "meaning" and "to mean" in relation to proper names, and by detailed criticism of various forms of the connotative theory of the meaning of proper names.

Propositions about a character (fictional or historical) in a play, novel, etc., must be clearly distinguished from propositions about a play, novel, short story, etc., as a whole, or about its plot or some other aspect or quality of the work. I have in mind such true synthetic propositions as those expressed by "The plot of *Macbeth* is simpler than the plot of *Hamlet*," and "*Hamlet* is a tragedy." They are true by virtue of the fact that the plot of *Macbeth* is, as a matter of fact, simpler than the plot of *Hamlet*, and that *Hamlet* is a tragedy, respectively. Equally obviously, "*Hamlet* was written by Shakespeare between 1599 and 1601" expresses what is probably a true synthetic proposition. Similarly "*Hamlet* aims at portraying the tragedy of a superior person with a probing and powerful intellect plagued by a sensitive, refined temperament and a vacillating will" is synthetic; and a good deal of evidence can be given to show that it is true as well. At any rate, it can be known to be true or false by a careful analysis of the tragedy.

Now consider "Hamlet studied mathematics at Wittenberg, before he went ot Denmark at the beginning of *Hamlet*"; or "Iago, the villain in *Othello*, had dark hair and eyes." These have the appearance of being bona fide statements about Hamlet and Iago respectively. But, unlike such statements as "Hamlet was in love with Ophelia in Shakespeare's *Hamlet*," these cannot be properly said to express either analytic or synthetic propositions. Moreover, they are neither true nor false. I am assuming, of course, that there is no mention, or no indication at all in *Hamlet* that Hamlet either did or did not study mathematics at *Wittenberg*. Similarly, *mutatis mutandis*, with *Othello*. When a person who thinks that *Hamlet*, or *Othello*, states or suggests the foregoing things is shown that these plays are absolutely silent on these matters, he will admit error, his statements having no basis in fact. But he will not say that they are false; although he will correctly say that he thought they were true. To say that they are false is to imply that their contradictories: "Hamlet did not study mathematics at Wittenberg, before he went to Denmark at the beginning of *Hamlet*," and "Iago, the villain in *Othello*, did not have dark hair and eyes" are true. Whereas in point of fact these utterances, like their contradictories, are neither true nor false.

The reason, to my mind, why these utterances are neither true nor false is that they are not genuine statements at all. For to speak of Hamler or Iago in the above manner is somewhat similar to committing a category mistake. These utterances confuse the way we normally and correctly speak about Hamlet, Iago and other *characters* in novels, plays, etc., with the way we speak about actually existing persons or things. It is, in other words, to think of Hamlet or Iago as though they were real persons. These characters are wholly and completely delineated, once and for all, in the pages of *Hamlet* or *Othello*; they are and are only what *Hamlet* or *Othello* depicts them to be. Shakespeare could, if he wished, have depicted Iago as having dark hair and eyes; and he could have depicted Hamlet as having studied mathematics at Wittenberg. But the fact is that he did not. The situation would not have been materially different if he had originally conceived or imagined Hamlet or Iago as possessing these attributes, or even if he had written these things down in the form of notes or of a (lost) draft of *Hamlet* or *Othello*. It would make sense—and it would be either correct or incorrect—to claim that some historical figure (e.g., Napoleon or Hitler) had dark eyes or hair, say, even if his biographies or other historical portraits of him are silent about the matter. For then our statements about that person would be about an actual person, who either had or did not have dark hair (assuming that he had any hair on his head at all!) or eyes; who either studied or did not study this or that subject at some school or university.

In other words, the utterance "Hamlet studied (or did not study) mathematics at Wittenberg, before he went to Denmark at the beginning of *Hamlet*" is a well-formed and perfectly meaningful *sentence*; but it cannot express meaningful *statements* (and so utterance that are either true or false) if used in the context of *Hamlet*.

All this is true with regard to utterances about historical characters. But the oddness or impropriety of such utterances as "In Shakespeare's *Antony* and *Cleopatra*, Cleopatra is 5 feet 4 inches tall" is obviated or concealed by the fact that it does make sense to speak in this way of the *real person* who is, at the same time, a historical character; viz. Cleopatra in this particular instance. But it makes sense to speak of Cleopatra in this way, we must emphasize, only *qua* actual person, not *qua* (or not also *qua*) historical character. In other words, the utterance "In Shakespeare's *Antony and Cleopatra*, Cleopatra is 5 feet 4 inches tall" is not *true or false of* the character called "Cleopatra" in *Antony and Cleopatra*. But interestingly enough, this utterance can be sometimes said to be *about*, may refer to, Shakespeare's Cleopatra. Whether or not it will be so depends (over and above the fact that its grammatical subject is the word "Cleopatra") on the intention of the speaker or writer; on whether or not he means to refer to it. Nonetheless, even when it is so intended, we should still tell the speaker or writer that he is not making a proper statement about the character Cleopatra, anything that can possibly be either true or false.

I have analyzed at some length the ordinary uses of "about" in statements about imaginary objects, including those that occur in works of fiction. In the next essay I shall turn to works of fiction themselves for an examination of two main types of sentences that occur in them: authoral sentences and sentences "made" by a character in the work about itself or other characters.

NOTES

1. Cf. G.E. Moore, "Imaginary objects", *Proceedings of the Aristotelian Society*, supplementary volume XII, 1933, p. 59.

2. Braithwaite, "Imaginary objects," *op. cit.*, p. 44. Braithwaite's contribution to the symposium is on pp. 44–54.

3. This is an interesting example of how a distinction between two uses, U_1 and U_2, of an expression "X" may not mark a difference in "X's" meaning. It is to be noted, however, that our two uses of "about" above are merely distinct, not different.

4. "Imaginary objects," *op. cit.*, p. 26.

5. *Ibid.*, p. 23.

6. "About," *Mind*, Vol. LXX, No. 277 (January 1961), p.18.

7. *Op cit.*, p. 21.

8. An important question that arises here is: In what sense can Pickwickishness or ethereality be said to exist; or what are the logical implications of holding, as Ryle for

example implicitly holds, that they exist. But it does not concern us in the present discussion.

9. However, there is an ordinary sense in which a *particular* fictional or historical character is said *to be* or *not to be* in a particular fictional or historical play, novel, etc. Thus there is no character called Ivan Karamazov in *Antony and Cleopatra*; while a character by that name is found (or, there is a character by that name) in Dostoevsky's *The Brothers Karamazov*. But these latter locutions do not, of course, imply that Ivan Karamazov enjoys some sort of existence in the latter work, *in the sense* in which we have been using the words "existence" and "exist."

10. In other words, a *poor historical work* is one in which the resemblance between some principal character (or characters) and the actual person (or persons) with whom the former is (are) intended to be identified is very slight or superficial. It is not a work in which *no* character(s) resemble(s) any (known or relatively known) actual person(s).

11. On the other hand, the setting of a historical novel, play, etc., may be fictional. Similarly, some of the characters, and some or all of the incidents in it may be fictional. Let me add that some works are partly fictional, partly nonfictional, a "mixture of fact and fancy." Examples are the fictionalized lives of eminent artists, statesmen, scientists and the like. In these works the elements of fact and fancy are pretty well balanced, without the one predominating over the other. The principal character or characters is or are real; but there is so much fancy mingled with the facts of his or their life, including much filling of gaps in his or their known biography, that the work is not usually felt to be a historical work.

12. This fact has misled Ryle and Braithwaite into confusing Hamlet, say, as a fictional character, with actual or possible human beings who may resemble him in greater or lesser degree—with all the errors which this confusion carries in its train. At the very least, Ryle and Braithwaite confuse *fictional* characters, such as Mr. Pickwick with *historical* characters in novels, plays, biographies and so on.

13. See my "Works of Art and Physical Reality," Ratio, Vol. II, No. 2 (February 1960), pp. 148-61, *passim*.

14. *Ibid.*

15. *The Coherence Theory Of Truth: A Critical Evaluation* (American University of Beirut, Beirut, 1961), p. 94 f.

16. "The meaning of proper names," *International Logic Review*, No. 12 (December 1975), pp. 186–203.

Chapter 4

Fictional Sentences

Novels, plays and short stories abound with fictional sentences. They are of two major types. The first type is exemplified by "Emma Woodhouse, handsome, clever and rich, . . . seemed to unite some of the best blessings of existence," which is part of the opening sentence of Jane Austen's novel *Emma*, i.e., indicative sentences in which the author speaks about an imaginary character, object, occurrence or situation forming part of a particular work of fiction. (I shall henceforth refer to these sentences as authoral sentences or type A sentences.) The other type of fictional sentence (henceforth referred to as type B sentences) is exemplified by "Cldye! You really loved Roberta Alden at first, didn't you?"[1], i.e., indicative sentences which the author imagines some character to have made in a particular work of fiction, about himself or herself, some other character, or some object, occurrence or situation depicted in the work. In this essay I shall consider some aspects of the logical grammar of sentences of the latter type—about which, as far as I know, little has been written—as well as about sentences of the former type—about which a fair amount has been written. The term "fictional sentence" too is sometimes used by aestheticians only to designate sentences of the former type (cf. Margaret Macdonald). But there is little justification for not employing the phrase in the inclusive sense in which I am employing it here.

I

Type A Fictional Sentences

The main question that has engaged philosophers writing no fictional sentences of this type is whether they can be properly said to be either true or false. And this is, indeed, a convenient line of approach to their logical grammar. My own view on this matter is basically the same as the one Margaret Macdonald expresses in "The Language of Fiction,"[2] where she defends the thesis that (1) these sentences are neither true nor false; hence that (2) it is false that all such sentences express false statements (Moore and Ryle); and that (3) it is false that they express lies (Hume). My aim in this part of the essay will be to defend this view by adducing further evidence in support of (1), along lines Macdonald did not take or did not pursue far enough, and to attempt to meet some objections to it.

I shall criticize Ryle's and Moore's view before passing to the positive thesis I am defending.

(I) (A) Ryle's fundamental negative thesis in "Imaginary Objects"[3] is that we cannot really talk or think about—in general refer to—something nonexistent, because it is nonexistent.[4] Sentences ostensibly about nonexistent things are therefore really about something else. This raises the basic question as to the evidence or kind of evidence that can possibly be given for this view, in the light of the fact pointed out by Moore in his "Imaginary Objects,"[5] namely that a sentence such as "Mr. Pickwick went to Rochester' is about Mr. Pickwick" is a perfectly proper ordinary sentence. The same may be said about, e.g., "Centaurs do not exist." This linguistic fact is reiterated by Macdonald in her essay.[6] For in line with this fact that they are in ordinary use, we ordinarily consider *some* sentences about nonexistent things as true and others as false. For example, we say that "Centaurs are (imagined to be) half-horse half-man" is (analytically) true, but that "Centaurs exist" is (contingently) false.

Now there are all sorts of problems, into which I do not propose to enter, regarding the meaning of statements that state that the real or logical subject of a certain type of sentence, S, is other than its apparent or grammatical subject, that S is about something other than its grammatical subject. For one thing, the very meaning of such statements is far from clear. But one way in which the issue between Ryle and myself can be stated without getting entangled in all sorts of logical or metaphysical problems, is this: Can, and do, type A fictional sentences ever succeed in referring to imaginary objects? And by this I mean: Can, and do, we ever succeed in enabling our hearers to pick out or identify the imaginary object(s) or thing(s) we sometimes wish to talk about? For it is an empirical fact that we do sometimes—and writers of fiction do all the time in their novels, plays, etc.—wish to talk about something imaginary in the sense of a

Mr. Pickwick, a Raskolnikov or an Abram Bok. The answer to the *foregoing* question is I think definitely "Yes". (In Ryle's terminology in *SME*, the answer would be stated as: "Mr. Pickwick" is the real or logical subject of "Mr. Pickwick went to Rochester," not just its grammatical subject.) Indeed, it seems to me that unless the answer is "Yes," works of fiction as we ordinarily understand them would be impossible.

In order that a *speaker* may succeed in referring to something (whether existent or imaginary) X by means of a sentence S,[7] two conditions must be fulfilled. (1) He must intend to refer to X, and so must have X in mind in framing S; hence as a precondition there must be a concept or conception of X, if "X" is a general name, such as "centaur" or "mountain"; and (2) the expression he employs for the job, S, must be conventionally or contextually capable of doing this. It must have or be given the appropriate meaning or use. A further minimal condition must be fulfilled in order that the *hearer* may recognize or identify X as S's referent; viz. (3) he must know the conventional or contextual meaning of S. Where S is a singular or particular indicative (demonstrative) sentence, he must also know, independently of his understanding of S, (4) what the speaker intends S's subject—the proper name or pronoun—to refer to.

The presupposition of condition (1) accounts for the fact that such sentences-in-use as "The present king of France is bald" constitute a very important kind of exception to what I said in this section concerning referring and its relation to intention to refer. That is, it cannot possibly refer to anything, including anything factually possible though nonexistent, or anything fictional, if it is made in, say, 1980. It clearly cannot refer to anyone alive in 1980, since France does not, at present, have a king. More importantly, it cannot refer to something *nonexistent though factually possible* [and here the presupposition of condition (1) comes in], for there is no conventional concept or conception, or the speaker does not have a personal concept or conception in mind,[8] of something possible, correctly describable as "the present king of France." This is in contrast to the existence of one or more current concepts of, e.g., a sea serpent, and the existence of a traditional concept (and conception) of a centaur, properly describable as the concept of a (an imaginary) creature that is half-horse half-man.[9]

In his "Is Existence a Predicate?" Murray Kiteley says: "if what you are talking about is nonexistent, it must at least be a conversation-piece in some body of legend, fable or fiction, or some passé scientific hypothesis."[10] This is generally true; but it is taken care of by what I think is the crucial point here; viz. that in order to be able to talk about something nonexistent, you must have a concept or conception of that nonexistent thing. In many or most cases, this is actually ensured by the nonexistent thing's forming part of some body of legend, etc. If such a concept or conception exists, then one will be able to meet Kiteley's condition that "you must be able to make, if challenged, identifying references. . . ."[11] This does not mean, however, that what we refer to by "centaur," say, is the concept or conception of centaur itself.

In the case of, e.g., "The present king of France is bald" (F), uttered in 1973, we have a peculiar situation. As *intended* by a speaker who believes that France is currently a monarchy, F cannot be used to make either a fictional statement or a statement about something logically possible though nonexistent (like a unicorn, for example). But F as such *can* be used to make a statement of either type, depending on whether (a) its grammatical subject is intended to refer to some fictional character, or (b) to something logically possible but nonexistent. That is, it depends on the centext in which it is uttered, provided the speaker (or the hearer) has some concept or conception that can be said to be the concept or conception of "the present king of France." If such a concept or conception forms part of a work of fiction, i.e., if "the present king of France" refers to a fictional character, F will make a fictional statement. On the other hand, it will refer to something possible though imaginary if the said concept or conception does not form part of a work of fiction. In the absence of such a concept or conception, F will not be about anything whatsoever, whether possible but nonexistant, actual, or fictional; it will have no possible reference. Precisely because of this, it will not have point (as J.L. Austin puts it) if it is uttered, say, in 1973.[13] The implication of this analysis is that a sentence that is intended to refer to something real but fails to do so because its subject refers to nothing real or actually conceived by the speaker or hearer at the time it is uttered, is quite a different sort of sentence from one that refers to something, whether real or unreal (in the latter case, either centingently nonexistent, or fictional). Ryle's view leaves no room for this distinction.

One important point that emerges from this analysis is that a sentence that fails to refer to anything at all is quite a different sort of sentence from one which refers to something, whether that thing is real or unreal (in the latter case, either contingently nonexistent, or fictional). Ryle's view, it seems to me, leaves no room for this distinction.

(B) In *SME* Ryle explicitly considers the nonexistence of such things as Mr. Pickwick and centaurs as the reason for his view that statements apparently about them cannot be really about them. Thus he says: "Suppose I assert of (apparently) the general subject 'carnivorous cows' that they 'do not exist,' and my assertion is true, I cannot really be talking about carnivorous cows, for there are none. So it follows that the expression 'carnivorous cows' is not really being used . . . to denote the thing or things of which the predicate is being asserted."[14] Again, he says the following about such statements as "Mr. Pickwick is a nonentity," "Mr. Pickwick is an imaginary object," etc.: "None of these statements is really about Mr. Pickwick. For if they are true, there is no such person for them to be about."[15]

Now it may be retorted that this thesis leads to a paradox. Ryle says that if this statement is *true*, "Mr. Pickwick does not exist" cannot really be about "Mr. Pickwick." But, the critic may say, this statement can only be true if it is really and not only apparently about some nonexistent thing—whether Mr. Pickwick or something else is immaterial. For it asserts of its *real* subject, whatever it may be, that it does not exist; and this assertion can only be true of some nonexistent thing. But Ryle does in effect forestall this objection with his positive thesis, for he maintains that, e.g., "Mr. Pickwick is a fiction" "is really . . . about Dickens or else about *Pickwick Papers* [which are, of course, real]."[16] Thus according to him it means either something like "Dickens wrote a fable" (referring to *Pickwick Papers*) or "*Pickwick Papers* is a pack of lies." And these two statements are both true and about something existent. But note what this account means. It means that "does not exist," "is unreal," themselves are *not the real predicate* of "Mr. Pickwick does not exist" and "Mr. Pickwick is unreal," respectively: they are only the apparent predicate. The real predicate of the statement to which "Mr. Pickwick does not exist," say, is equivalent, asserts the existence, not the nonexistence, of its real subject (Dickens or *Pickwick Papers* in this case). Stated generally, it follows from Ryle's view that true statements of the form "X is not real (is imaginary, etc.)," (S), where "X" is e.g., "Mr. Pickwick," are really equivalent to some statement(s) which assert(s), or implies (imply),[17] the existence or reality of something that does exist (S'). Consequently, the negative particle, "not" is always in principle dispensable from statements of type S.

Now in *SME*, Ryle proposes a second view alongside his view of the correct analysis of statements of type S above; viz. an analysis of existential statements, on which the grammatical predicate of these statements is not the real predicate (the same applies, *mutatis mutandis*, to the grammatical subject of such statements). The reason is that he holds, with Kant, that existence is not a predicate. But this view does not really help Ryle avoid the conclusion that the real predicate of S is either the assertion or the implication of the *existence* of something (the real subject)—which certainly appears to me to be rather paradoxical. For what is actually entailed by Ryle's analysis of existential statements (call it thesis *ES*) is that in S "does not exist" is not a predicate *in the same way or sense* in which, e.g., "is bald" is the predicate of "Mr. Baldwin is bald" or even "Mr. Pickwick is bald." That is, it does not refer to a quality or attribute. It does not entail (or imply) that "is bald" is *not asserted of its real subject at all*, whatever that subject may be. In other words, it does not help eliminate what appears to be the negative character of S.

Again, it follows from the foregoing that "Mr. Pickwick" is not the grammatical subject of statement S in the same way as, e.g., "Mr. Baldwin" in "Mr. Baldwin was bald." It does not follow that it is not the real subject in any sense of "subject." To accept the latter view we must accept thesis *SIO* itself, which is precisely at issue here.

It is noteworthy that in everyday discourse, in contradistinction to what Ryle maintains, we would say that, at best, S only implies certain things about Dickens or *Pickwick Papers*. We would not say that it *is* really about—not even indirectly about—either. We would say that S is directly or explicitly about Mr. Pickwick himself.[18] Thus *SIO* erases the distinction between "is directly or explicitly about" and "only implies" in this particular type of case.

I attempted to show above that theses *SIO* and *ES* are logically consistent with each other. It can also be shown that *ES* does not entail or imply *SIO*; so that, supposing it is true, it does not constitute any logical support for *SIO*. We are therefore faced with the basic question as to whether there is any good reason for supposing that *SIO* is true, that it is impossible for a statement to be about anything nonexistent: especially as Ryle does not, either in *IO* or in *SME*, give us, strictly speaking, any argument for it.

Now Ryle's negative thesis has an undeniable air of commonsense plausibility about it. Nothing seems to be more commonsensical than to suppose that we cannot really talk about something nonexistent, for what is nonexistent is nothing. How can one talk about *nothing*? Yet we do talk—and just as commonsensically, it can be argued—as though we sometimes intended to refer to such nonexistent things as Mr. Pickwick or a centaur; and moreover, we seem to succeed in making our hearers think about (and so, *a fortiori*, "pick out") these very same things. What then is the source of this apparent contradiction, and what is its resolution?

One obvious way of explaining—and resolving—it would be to distinguish two different senses in which we talk and think about something: one way in which we speak of existent things, and another way in which we speak of nonexistent things. For then one could maintain that Ryle has been misled by the fact that we cannot talk (or think) about a nonexistent thing in the same way as we do about existent things, into thinking that we cannot talk (or think) about them in *any* sense. It is interesting that Moore himself (and in this he is followed by Miss Macdonald) thought that "about" is used in two different senses, in, e.g., "Dickens' proposition ['Mr. Pickwick went to Rochester'] was not about anyone" and in "Dickens' proposition was about Mr. Pickwick."[19] But I think that Moore is wrong. I think that in every case we understand "about" in the one and only sense involved when we hear statements of the form "statement about . . . ," "talking (thinking) about so-and-so (such-and-such)," etc., and we do so whether we know that what is being (or is apparently being) referred to is real or unreal. And when we find out or are told that what is being (or is apparently being) referred to is nonexistent, we do not feel that "about" takes on a different sense or meaning. Addressing ourselves specifically to Moore's two foregoing sentences, we might note that in "Dickens' proposition was not about anyone" and "It is not true that Dickens' proposition was not about Mr. Pickwick," what is used in two different ways is "anyone" rather than "about." In the first sentence "anyone" means "anyone existent," while in the latter sentence it is not restricted in this way: it means "just anyone, whether existent or nonexistent."

It is undeniable that "about" has different senses. For example, in "He pulled the gun without looking about him," the word is used in a very different way from the above. But this sense of the word is clearly irrelevant to our discussion.

Another, perhaps more plausible explanation is that we tend to think of talking and thinking about something on the analogy of pointing to it; for the obvious reason is that pointing out something is a common way of helping to identify it for our hearers. Clearly only that which exists can be pointed out in this way. But "bewitchment" by this picture cannot fully account for the disquietude one may feel when he thinks of talking about nonexistent things. For it does not seem to be puzzling—or, at least, as puzzling—to think of our talking about the past and the future or other possible events or things. [And yet it would seem that, if Ryle is right, we should be just as unable to talk about the latter as about Mr. Pickwick or Hamlet. See (E) below.] I think what causes this difference in feeling is that with respect to both past and future (possible) events or things we have some concept or conception: in the case of things past, in the light of the fact that they did exist and had a nature of their own. On the other hand it may be felt that this cannot be true with regard to things that have never existed and may never exist. But if this is a psychological source of the puzzlement, it is logically quite unfounded. For it is just as true that we have or can have a concept or conception of a centaur or Mr. Pickwick.

(C) Irrespective of whether we can refer to nonexistent things, such statements as "Mr. Pickwick went to Rochester" and "Mrs. Bardell fainted in Mr. Pickwick's arms" do not assert what Ryle believes they assert in *IO*. If Moore's statement of Ryle's view is correct—and I think it is correct—the following is what Ryle believes the latter statement asserts: "One man and one man only *was* called 'Mr. Pickwick' and Mrs. Bardell had fainted in that man's arms."[20] (Hence, according to Ryle, this sentence is false; since it is not the case that one man and one man only *was* called "Mr. Prickwick," in the sense that no such man existed.) Moore comments: "He [Ryle] believes, therefore, that Dickens's proposition ['Mrs. Bardell had fainted in Mr. Pickwick's arms'] says, as *part* of its meaning, that one man and only one was called 'Mr. Pickwick': that is to say he tells us, about the analysis of the proposition which Dickens expressed by 'Mrs. Bardell had fainted in Mr. Pickwick's arms,' that *part* of what it says is 'One man and only one man was called 'Pickwick'."[21]

I agree with Moore[22] that the proposition expressed by "*One man and one man only* was called 'Mr. Pickwick' " (the italicized words indicate the crucial point here) is not part of what Dickens' sentence expresses. But this is not what interests us here. We are interested in what appears to be Ryle's view that "Mrs. Bardell fainted in Mr. Pickwick's arms" in part means or states that there was a *real* man who had all the qualities which Dickens "attributes" to Mr. Pickwick, the complex predicate Pickwickishness. It seems perfectly clear to me that Ryle is wrong. What we ordinarily suppose the sentence to mean (express), which is also what it does mean, is not, even in part, the foregoing. No one who knows that "Mrs. Bardell fainted in Mr.

Pickwick's arms'' was written by Dickens in *Pickwick Papers*—a work that was clearly intended as a work of imagination—who knows that ''Mr. Pickwick'' was intended as the name of a fictional character, would suppose the sentence to mean (or to state) in part that there actually was a person, either at the time of Dickens or before, called ''Mr. Pickwick.'' Again, only if Dickens himself believed that he was writing about some actual person—which, as a matter of fact, is not what he believed—would it be correct to say that he intended his sentence about Mr. Pickwick to refer to some real person. But even then it would be incorrect to say that the *statement* itself means, or asserts, that its subject exists. On the other hand, if Dickens was only pretending to be writing about some real person (as Ryle appears to believe), he could not have seriously intended to assert that there *was* a real man called ''Mr. Pickwick.'' In any event, the sentence ''Mrs. Bardell fainted in Mr. Pickwick's arms'' does not mean in part, and so does not state, *either that there was or that there was not* a real man called ''Mr. Pickwick.'' There is nothing in this sentence, or any similar fictional sentence of type A, which either means or states—or even implies in any sense of ''imply''—that what it refers to either exists or does not exist; though, of course, that which it refers to either exists or does not exist. The writer generally makes it clear (and intends to make it clear) to his readers, by various conventional devices, especially from the character of the context in which his type A sentences occur, that he is talking about something fictional. Thus we can say, if we like, that *Dickens*, in speaking of Mr. Pickwick in the way he does in *Pickwick Papers as a whole, implies* that he is talking about something fictional. (It is common knowledge, however, that it is not always easy or even possible to know whether or not the author intends us to suppose that he is implying this.) Again, it is the context in which a sentence occurs—this time an everyday situation—which enables us correctly to infer that the speaker intends to refer to something existent. In both types of cases, whether we are right or wrong in our inference, it is not the sentence as such but the context or kind of context in which the sentence-in-use occurs, which indicates that he is or is not talking about something existent.

If this is true, the argument which logically supports the thesis that type A sentences are all (necessarily) false falls to the ground. This paves the way to some extent[23] for the view that this type of sentence is neither true nor false.

It is noteworthy that Moore shares Ryle's fundamental assumption that type A sentences in part mean or state, that what they refer to—in

Moore's case, the fictional character or object itself—exists.[24] This common element in an otherwise different analysis of type A sentences logically leads Moore to the same conclusion as Ryle regarding the truth value of these sentences; namely, that they are all false. Therefore, to the extent to which our preceding criticism of Ryle's analysis of type A sentences is valid, it is also valid against Moore's analysis of them.

(D) Ryle's analysis of type A sentences is, I believe, mistaken in another fundamental respect. Ryle supposes, in Miss Macdonald's words, that Jane Austen—

> is writing about a number of properties, signified by the general term she uses [here "Emma Woodhouse"], and asserting that they belonged to someone [existent].... A work of fiction is, or is about, "one big composite predicate" and is so understood by readers who need neither to know nor believe that any subject was characterized by it. If, however, there had been, by chance, and unknown to Jane Austen, a girl called Emma Woodhouse who conformed faithfully to all the descriptions of the novel, its propositions would have been about and true of her and Jane Austen would have "accidentally" written biography and not fiction.[25]

Or as Moore puts it, Ryle's positive view appears to be that "Mr. Pickwick," in, e.g., "Mr. Pickwick went to Rochester," is "a concealed predicative expression" or "is really signifying an attribute."[26]

This view seems to me to be mistaken even if we grant the thesis that "Mr. Pickwick went to Rochester" is not really about Mr. Pickwick. The sentence does not state or even imply in any sense anything (hence cannot be) about "Pickwick's" purported qualities. And which of those qualities which Dickens ostensibly attributes to Pickwick is a (any) sentence whose grammatical subject is "Mr. Pickwick," about? All the qualities which Dickens "attributes" to "him," both explicitly and indirectly? Or only some of them? If the latter, which ones and why? Is Ryle saying or implying that "Mr. Pickwick" is equivalent to a definite description listing all or certain of "Mr. Pickwick's" imagined qualities? If this is what he means[27] (cf. Moore on Ryle, *op. cit.*, pp. 61–62), then I think he is definitely wrong. For no proper name, whether of an existent or a nonexistent thing, is "shorthand" for any definite description, however detailed or complete.[28]

If "Mr. Pickwick went to Rochester" does not state or imply anything about Pickwick's purported qualities, *a fortiori* it does not assert or imply that, e.g., the man who was so-and-so or did such-and-such went to Rochester. Only sentences such as (2) "Mr. Pickwick was a serious-minded person" assert or imply—in this instance attribute—a specified personal quality to the logical subject. Similarly, (3) "The man in the iron mask was imprisoned on a solitary island" does state the subject's possession of some "attribute." Ryle's view is true, if at all, only of fictional sentences that fall under (2) or (3), not ones that fall under (1) above.

(E) Finally, let us consider how Ryle's thesis fares with regard to statements about the past or the future. If we cannot refer to *any* (kind of) nonexistent thing, it follows that we cannot think or talk about either past or future occurences, or things that existed in the past or may exist in the future. For it is an essential part of the thesis itself that we cannot *restrict* it to the sort of nonexistent things that occur in works of fiction, such as Mr. Pickwick or Hamlet. Thus when we say: "World War I ended in 1918," we are not really talking about World War I; rather, we are talking about something present (for things exist only in the present[29]). But what could this possibly be, such that the statement would be, or remain, true? I see no way of accomplishing this along the lines of Ryle's "paraphrase" of, e.g., "Mr. Pickwick went to Rochester" in *SME*. Now suppose I say: "Napoleon Bonaparte had an ulcer" (N). On Ryle's positive account in *IO*, this would in part assert that there is some real person who has (all?) the properties of "Bonaparteness," and, moreover, had an ulcer (N'). But this too will not do. For first, N is true, whereas N' is clearly false. N' asserts in part that there is one (real) person, in whom are present all those *existent instances* of the properties of which Napoleon possessed *another set of instances*, but which are actually scattered among many different living persons. But this statement can be (and can only be) regarded as equivalent to N if we are able to refer to the now-nonexistent instances *a, b, c, d,* etc., of those properties (universals or determinables), which Napoleon himself had when he was alive, *x, y, z, w,* etc. The identification of the determinate properties *x, y, w*, etc. as of the same kind as *a, b, c, d,* etc., presupposes our ability to compare and so to think about (hence to refer to) *a, b, c, d,* etc., themselves—which are, at the time this is done, nonexistent. Thus in this case reference to something past is inescapable. The tense of statement N, the notion of pastness attached to it, is ineluctable. The same kind of situation arises with regard to attempts to paraphrase, *à la Ryle*, statements which we ordinarily say are about the future.

II. Turning to Moore's analysis of type A sentences, the following criticisms can be made in addition to the one I made in subsection (A), and which, if valid, shows that Moore is mistaken in holding that all such sentences are false. My general criticism is that Morre's analysis, though less inadequate than Ryle's, is not completely correct; even if we ignore Moore's mistake in thinking that type A sentences assert the existence of that which they are about. With regard to Moore's analysis, the following additional points can be made.

(1) Moore is mistaken in holding that a fictional sentence such as "Mr. Pickwick went to Rochester" states[30] "There was *only* one man of whom it's true *both that I'm going to tell you about him* and that he was called 'Pickwick' [and that, etc. etc.]." (a) It does not state "There was only one man ...." Rather, this is indicated by the sentence (and by the speaker in using the particular sentence) by virtue of the employment of certain linguistic devices, for example, in "Mr. Pickwick went to Rochester," by the use of "*Mr.* Pickwick" or "He." That the reference is to only one man can actually be said to be implied by the statement (or by the speaker in making the statement). If someone asked Dickens: "Are you implying that in your novel there is only one man who is called 'Mr. Pickwick,' and who ...?" he would reply: "Of course—it's obvious from the sentence." But he would not say: "The sentence states this." But Moore is right in holding that (b) the fictional sentence does not state or assert—hence does not mean[31]—that "he [the man referred to] was called 'Pickwick.'" This too is implied by Dickens' use of "Pickwick" as the subject of the sentence. In the sentence he *uses* the name "Pickwick" and does not *mention* it, does not talk about it. For "He was called 'Pickwick'" means: "His name was 'Pickwick.'" It may be objected that "Pickwick went to Rochester" does mean exactly the same as "The man or person called "Pickwick" went to Rochester." But this is not true—the sentence does not commit the speaker to the view that "Pickwick" refers to a man rather than a woman or even an animal. Even "*Mr.* Pickwick went to Rochester" does not do so. However, since this sentence is part of a long piece of writing and so occurs in the context of passages in which Dickens speaks a great deal about Pickwick, "Pickwick went to Rochester" has the meaning (the "force") of "The man called 'Pickwick' went to Rochester"; not because, as a sentence, it means this, but because in that context it grammatically refers to the same character who is throughout called "Pickwick," and who is described by Dickens as a man.

(c) Finally, our fictional sentence does not state or mean: "I'm going to tell you about him [Mr. Pickwick]." In the first place, this is not ture of the vast majority of fictional sentences about Pickwick, say. At best, only Dickens's very first sentence about Pickwick—or the opening sentence of the novel—would state that. In actual fact, like most other novelists, he does not do even that. Generally, it is superfluous. Had Dickens used such as sentence, we could say: "We *can infer from the context* in which Pickwick went to Rochester occurs that this is part of the story which Dickens stated he is telling about Pickwick."

(2) It can be readily seen that type A sentences-in-use do not (any more than sentences-in-use about existing things, which have, e.g., the form "So-and-so is Y," where "Y" does not stand for "exists" or any of its cognates) in part mean, or assert, the existence of their subject. For the question of whether a sentence is about a fictional thing, a contingently non-existent thing, or a real thing is independent of the meaning of the sentence. It is determined solely by what exists—which is a matter of extralinguistic fact—and by the speaker's intention. One and the same sentence can be used, in different contexts, to refer to the one or the other or the third.[32] Hence if as a sentence it does in part *mean* that what it is about exists, it will do so in every case. It cannot do so in some cases but not others. Thus, e.g., "John Smith is tall" can be about a real person or a fictional character, and, e.g., "I see a flying saucer" can be about something real, something only possible, or something fictional (the sentences could be part of the script of a science fiction TV program).

III. Let us now turn to what I believe is the fundamental reason why type A sentences cannot be either true or false. Let us start by noting that not all indicative sentences about nonexistent things, employed by people in everyday situations rather than written by a writer as part of a work of fiction, acted out on the stage or recited at a poetry reading, are ordinarily regarded as false. As I pointed out earlier, some are regarded as true, others as false. "A sea serpent is a nonexistent serpent that is imagined to live in the sea" is an example of the former, while "The Red Sea teems with sea serpents" is an example of the latter. Among the probably true statements about various nonexistent but empirically possible things are many scientific predictions about projected inventions.[33] The conclusion that can be drawn from this is that the fundamental reason why type A sentences cannot be either true or false is that they *refer to something that occurs in a work of fiction*, a work of imagination called a novel, a play, etc., e.g., that they refer to fictional characters, objects, etc. It is not simply the fact that they refer to something not found in the real world; and I have already attempted to show that they do not assert or imply the existence of that which they are about—and so are false by virtue of that assertion or implication. Their lack of truth value rests on the unique character of fictional characters, objects, episodes, settings, and so forth, on their *difference* from the kind of "fictitious," "nonexistent" or "unreal" things that can but as a matter of fact do not exist in the world. Stated otherwise, type A sentences, by their very nature, cannot possibly be about anything outside a work of fiction, anything that actually exists or may exist. As I maintained in my "About Imaginary Objects," there is a basic conceptual, categorial difference between the nonexistence of a fictional thing and the nonexistence of something that is contingently nonexistent. That is why—and this constitutes a further objection to Ryle's account of type A sentences, where the phrase "complex predicate" is understood as referring to *specific "instances"* of qualities that may be possessed by some real person[34]—the existence or nonexistence of anything in the universe that does or may possess the "complex predicate" Pickwickishness is completely irrelevant to what type A sentences are about. Moreover, this basic difference underlies and explains a fact which constitutes Miss Macdonald's positive reason for asserting that type A sentences are neither true nor false; namely that they are untestable by any facts about the real world.[35] For if what I said above is true, no facts respecting the actual world can be logically relevant to their putative truth or falsity; *since they are not about anything actual or possible*. And I have already attempted to show that the preceding, italicized sentence, is true. Further, I attempted to show in "About Imaginary Objects" that this is part and parcel of the ordinary way in which we talk about works of fiction as a whole, and the fictional characters and the like that occur in them.

In saying that a fictional statement (really sentence) cannot be verified (or disconfirmed) I mean (a) "It is impossible for a statement to be both fictional and verified," rather than (b)" If a statement is fictional, it is logically impossible for it to be verified"—which is the sense in which W.E. Kennick thinks Miss Macdonald claims that a fictional statement cannot be verified. I agree with Kennick that "(type A) fictional sentence" does not *mean* (b); and so, I may add, (b) would be a *non sequitur* if it is not expressly *shown* to be true by, e.g., some kind of argument. Yet (a) is to my mind true precisely because "(type A) fictional sentence" *refers* to a type of sentence which, by its nature, i.e., with reference to the type of context or circumstances in which it is made, precludes the meaningfulness of applying the concepts of truth and falsity.

There are various sorts of reasons why certain kinds of sentences are unconfirmable and undisconfirmable in principle. In "On Referring" Strawson gives us, in offect, one sort of reason in the case of one such class of sentences. But there are various other kinds of sentences which share this feature with them. And type A sentences are one further class. A fundamental error of the logical positivists is their supposition that lack of cognitive meaning is in every case the reason for the untestability of sentences that purport to express factual propositions but which are untestable. In point of fact, though sentences that lack cognitive meaning are untestable in principle in the required sense, the converse is false.[36] Type A sentences illustrate the latter point. (It is true, however, that these sentences do not, and are not intended to express, empirical statements.)

The next question is whether anything that forms part of a work of fiction can in principle either confirm or disconfirm a type A fictional sentence. The answer to my mind is again "No"; though for a different reason from the untestability of such sentences by facts respecting things outside the work itself. The reason is readily seen if we recall the nature of type A sentences. For instance, I cannot see what dialogue, episode, character, or the like given by Jane Austen by means of any of the other sentences in *Emma* could possibly make "Emma Woodhouse [was] rich" either true or false. The only—and very special—type of situation I can think of which might possibly make us say "Yes, there are some such possible facts," would be Austen's contradicting herself by, e.g., writing, after our sentence, either in the same sentence or separately: "but she was not rich," and the like. But this is, at best, an extremely rare occurrence, and could only happen if the writer is sloppy and forgets to keep track of what he was already said, as he goes along, or if he fails to go over the completed manuscript, and so on. Indeed, I know of no actual work in which such contradictions occur. Thus with regard to the vast majority of type A sentences, which are perfectly free of such contradictions, there is no possible way to *dis*confirm them and so to call them false. But do not at least some of the other type A sentences, or other sorts of sentences in Emma, which are *consistent* with "Emma Woodhouse was rich," serve to *confirm* it? For example, "[Emma Woodhouse] . . . with a comfortable home and happy disposition . . . had lived . . . in the world with very little to distress or vex her," is logically consistent with the reinforces "Emma Woodhouse [was] handsome, clever and rich." But does it have any tendency to confirm the latter sentence? It is clear that logical consistency, though a necessary condition for the joint truth of two or more statements, is not a sufficient condition of the truth of any. The essential question is whether we can say that *one* of two contradictory type A sentences "X" and "Y" is true and the other false: which is what we have to say if we suppose that type A sentences are either true of false. But then, which one would be true, which false? We could only arbitrarily decide to call or regard one of the two as true, and consequently the other as false; for on what possible grounds cound we determine the alleged truth or falsity of either? Clearly the *number* of A type sentences consistent with "X"—whether more or less than those consistent with "X" in the particular work—will not do.

It is noteworthy that in *ordinary* discourse we do not, as far as I know, speak of a self-contradictory sentence-in-use as false. We appear to raise the questions of truth or falsity only where a statement is self-consistent. Whether or not this is correct we have the option, when we encounter a self-contradictory A type sentence, either to refrain from calling it false—in line with what I believe is the fact that we ordinarily refrain from applying any truth values to self-consistent type A sentences—or to say that it is necessarily false. For obvious reasons I prefer the former. But this is a matter which each individual user of the language must decide for himself.

II

Fictional Sentences of Type B

The logical grammar of type B sentences is quite different from the logical grammar of type A sentences. This is seen, for one thing, from the difference of these two classes of sentences with regard to truthvalue. They are different in, e.g., their literary or aesthetic uses in a work of fiction, and, correspondingly, in the way in which they would be treated by the reader or spectator when he properly reads or watches a performance of the work in which they occur. I shall here concentrate on the question of whether they are true or false, and why, and will leave for the future the question of the aesthetically proper way of treating them, so far as spectators or readers are concerned. But before I do so we must sharpen the notion of a type B fictional sentence. We must distinguish (1) "descriptive" sentences which we imagine to have been made by some character in a work of fiction about himself or some other character, object, episode or situation described in the work; and (2) evaluative sentences or value judgments made by such a character about himself or some other character, etc. Now I believe that *in a certain sense* value judgements in the usual employment of "value judgement"—evaluative sentences made by actual persons in real-life situations—are true or false; hence I would argue that, analogously, value judgments falling under (2) above can be properly said to be either true or false. But this is not the place to attempt to show the former. To show it would require a whole essay, if not a whole book. Consequently I shall leave aside fictional sentences falling under (2), and will not refer to them in my subsequent use of "type B fictional sentence."

In addition to composing sentences of kinds (1) and (2) a writer frequently imagines characters in works of fiction to be making various utterances intended by him and are normally considered by the reader or spectator as obliquely or implicitly about something real or possible, e.g., some actual or possible aspect of human behavior or society—or some aspect of Nature. We ordinarily describe them as sentences which express or suggest ideas about the particular real or possible things. It is worth noting that in the vast majority of actual works of fiction the characters who express these ideas are not "supposed" to "know" or "think" that these ideas are obliquely or implicitly about what we call the real world. For in most actual works of fiction it is important that the characters they contain should "think" and "behave" as if the "world" in which they move and have their being is the one and only "world" there is, is the "real" world.[37] (At the same time it is essential for the aims of *any* work of fiction that the reader or spectator regard the type B sentences in question that occur in it, together with the ideas conveyed and the episodes and characters portrayed, as being and as intended by the author to be obliquely about what does or may exist. This is true, though clearly to a lesser extent, of fantasies, fairy tales and the like.) The distinction between reality and fiction is a distinction drawn between our world and the "world" or framework of a work of fiction, e.g., between what happens in our world and what "happens" in a novel or play, not a distinction drawn within the latter. It is possible to draw a distinction between "reality" and "fiction," as well as between "reality" and "appearance," within the "world" of a work of fiction. But it would be a different sort of distinction. For both "reality" and "fiction" (or more exactly, the realm of possibility) in the latter case would be forms of fiction. This notwithstanding, it is quite possible for an author to make some character in a novel "aware" that he is only a "figment of the imagination," created by some being belonging to a different kind of "world," a "more real" world (or "the real" world). Compare and contrast this with God's relationship to the universe, according to, say, theism.

Sentences of this type, in their pure form, are not fictional sentences in our usage. I only mention them in order to dismiss them. But because I do so let us note that there are sentences in works of literature which are, in a sense, a hybrid of fictional sentences and sentences of kind (1) or (2) above. Such are sentences uttered by a fictional character, which are obliquely about some real or possible thing.[38] Indeed, many "fictional sentences" in serious novels, plays and short stories are of this kind; and this fact is frequently a main source of the philosophical, social, religious or "existential" significance they (and through them, the work as a whole) may possess. This is a noteworthy feature of the best works of literature, and is one important facet of their great relevance to the world and to our lives. The following are a few passages which illustrate this type of sentence:

"It depends on God," said Aunt Styofa soothingly. "God sees everything. You should submit to him, Dyomusha."

"Well, if it's from God it's even worse. If he can see everything, why does he load it all on one person? I think he ought to try to spread it about a bit . . . ."[39]

"There was this philosopher Descartes. He said, 'Suspect everything.' "

"But that's nothing to do with our way of life," Rusanov reminded him, raising a finger in admonition.[40]

Insofar as such sentences are made by a fictional character directly or explicitly about some character, object or episode in the work, they are, if sufficiently precise, either true or false in the sense in which fictional sentences of type (B)(1) are, I claim, true or false. That is, in the sense in which such sentences are imagined to be asserted by a fictional character and are not actually asserted by some real person. Their hybrid character does not logically affect their nature as type B sentences. On the other hand insofar as they can be considered as indirectly about existing or empirically possible things, they are neither true nor false, though in another sense of "true" and "false", viz. in the commonest everyday sense in which we speak of, e.g., "The earth is round" as true or "The moon is made of green cheese" as false. They would be true or false only if or when they are asserted by a real person in a reallife situation, totally independently of the work in which they also occur and of the fact that they occur in it. I shall not defend this latter thesis but will concentrate on the former one.

Sentences of the present type, in contrast to type A sentences, are in a certain ordinary sense true or false. For (a) we do normally speak of a fictional character's "speaking the truth" or "lying," or of his "not being sure whether what he says is true," or "whether he sould believe what some other character says about a third one, or about some object, occurrence or situation in the work." And so on. Thus in *An American Tragedy,* for instance, we find the following passage:

> Jephson ... at once interposed with: "Clyde! You really loved Roberta Alden at first, didn't you?"
>
> "Yes, sir."
>
> "Well, then, you must have known, or at least you gathered from her actions, from the first, didn't you, that she was a perfectly good and innocent and religious girl."
>
> "Yes, sir, that's how I felt about her," replied Clyde, *repeating what he had been told to say.*

Thus we learn, from Dreiser's words at the end (italicized) that Clyde was "lying" about his true feelings toward Roberta Alden.

(b) Further, a character may be "right" or "wrong" about himself or other characters, situations, places, times, etc., described in the work. With respect to both (a) and (b) there is a clear parallel between the sentences uttered by characters in works of fiction and those spoken by human beings in real-life situations. And just as the latter are either true or false—unless they are extemely vague—relative to the real world, the former are either true or false—in the other sense I mentioned earlier—relative to the fictional framework of the particular work of literature.

The ways in which we attempt to find out whether a particular type B sentence is "true" or "false" parallel the ways in which we attempt to find out, in real life, whether a particular statement is true or false. The obvious differences are consequent upon the differences between the real world and the imaginary "world" of a work of fiction. We "test" the particular character's "statements," "remarks," or "observations" about himself or herself, or about some other character, etc., with what we "know" about the character from the author's discription of his or her behavior, character, feelings, thoughts and experiences, and so on, which constitute the "real facts" or the "reality" in his or her case. These form part of the total "facts" or the "reality as a whole" which constitutes the work (or as we commonly say, is depicted by the work). The author's direct descriptions, i.e., type A sentences, thus constitute the frame of reference, the ultimate "ground" of the "truth" or "falsity" of type B "statements"—certainly in the case of novels and short stories. The situation is, clearly, different with regard to the majority of plays. The characters in a work—also the objects that "occur" in it, and its physical setting—are what the author says they are or depicts them as being. It makes no sense to say that the author tells lies, or says what is false (correlatively, it makes not sense to say that he tells the truth, or what he says is true, in the sense of "true" and "false" in which these words are applied to real people in real-life situations[41]). It also makes no sense to say that the author does not know the truth about this or that character he creates[42]; though the reader may quite often not know whether a particular B type sentence is "true" or "false." Still, the author may unwittingly portray characters that behave inconsistently, or makes them say inconsistent things (hence make sentences all of which cannot be "true"). In such cases he would not know that some of the things these characters say must be "false."

It may be argued that all type B sentences must be false; for example, on the same grounds on which Moore argued that all type A sentences are false; i.e., because they are about some fictitious thing. Thus it may be argued that, e.g., "I'm so sorry about last night, really I am—terribly .... I love you so. You know I do"[43] is false because it means "There was a woman called Roberta Alden who wrote in a letter to a man called Clyde: 'I'm so sorry about last night, really I am—terribly .... I love you so. You know I do'," and the latter sentence is false since there is or there was no such person as Roberta Alden in the real world. But by the same token, the counterarguments I urged in Section I, in relation to type A sentences, apply *mutatis mutandis* to the present type of sentence. For example, we can say that the preceding view misconstrues the logical grammar of type B sentences, and so of "There was (is) a man (woman) called ...," or "Once upon a time there was a man (woman) called ...." Yet it can be argued with a greater show of reason that the fictional speaker of a type B sentence "intends" to assert, is imagined by the author to have the "intention" to assert, the "existence" of what he is talking about. (And if he uses the appropriate sentence he will succeed in referring to that thing, if it does occur in that or some other work of fiction. For example, the author can imagine the character to have read some real novel, and to be familiar with the characters in it.) However, all that this entails is that the fictional speaker cannot be consistently imagined to assert the *nonexistence* of that which he "talks" about, in the *usual, everyday sense of "nonexistence," as the negative of "existence" in the sense in which it is employed in real-life situations*, in sentences asserting the existence of lions, dogs or ICBMs. A character can assert the "existence" *or* "nonexistence" of that which he talks about in a different sense, the sense in which the distinction between existence and nonexistence is drawn within the imaginary (imagined) world of a work of fiction. For instance, a character can be made to "imagine" all sorts of things or happenings as "nonexistent" or "unreal" relative to the story. But they do not have an analogue in anything unreal that *we* can imagine to exist in our world.

In other words, just as a type A sentence does not in part mean, and so does not assert, that that which it is about exists (or does not exist), a type B sentence does not in part mean, and so does not "assert," that that which it is about "exists." In the case of the latter the "existence" of that which the sentence refers to *may be implied* by the fact that the sentence is about something that (like the speaker himself) forms part of the "reality" of the work of fiction. Where the latter is not the case, the context may indicate to the reader that the speaker is referring to something he or some other character in the work has imagined or is imagining.

In this paper I distinguished sentences in which the author imagines a character in a work of fiction as speaking about himself or some other character, etc., from sentences in which he describes or otherwise refers to or talks about some character, etc., in the work. I referred to them as two different types of fictional sentences. I think our analysis of them in Sections I and II—and what Macdonald says about the latter type of sentence in her paper—justifies their classification into two types. Although sentences of both types are about some fictional character, object, or occurrence, the speaker of a sentence of type B (who is sometimes the subject of the sentence) is explicitly or implicitly a fictional character created by the author, not the author himself. The novelist, playwright or story writer is the author of the sentence, but not the "speaker" (or, sometimes, the "writer"); the "speaker" (or "writer") is a character, not a real person. In type A sentences the speaker, *in a similar though not identical sense* of "speaker," is the author, a (particular) real person. Yet in different ways both types of sentences constitute part of the text of the work, part of the sentences which together make up the novel, play or short story. Further, a sentence of type B cannot be regarded as a logical constituent of a sentence of type A. Nor is a sentence of the former type a logical constituent of a sentence of the form "Jean Giraudoux wrote in *Electra*: 'AEGISTHUS. Electra, I promise that tomorrow,

. . . the guilty . . . shall disappear, . . .' " or "Brecht wrote in *The Threepenny Opera*: 'POLLY. Oh, Mac, I'm so unhappy. I do hope the clergyman won't come!' " For though "I'm so unhappy" is a type B sentence, the sentence "Brecht wrote . . ." as a whole is not a type A sentence. As for "Jean Giraudoux wrote . . .," it does not even contain a type B sentence. The foregoing two complex sentences, and other sentences of the same logical type, state that a particular author wrote a particular type B—or some other type of fictional—sentence. Type A sentences, like type B sentences, are written or uttered by an author himself.

The logical relationship of type A and type B sentences appears to me to be the following: both types of sentences can be considered as species of the same genus; namely *descriptions* by the author of fictional characters, etc.—including, sometimes, what they say to or about one another. Yet this way of looking at the matter should not blind us to the fundamental logical differences between the two species of description, which account for the difference in truth value. Sentences of type A are the author's description of a character; sentences of type B are the author's description of a character's statements about himself or his activities, thoughts, etc., or another character or that character's activities, thoughts, etc. But in novels and short stories sentences of the former type are, in a sense, logically more primary than sentences of the latter type. For only when (logically speaking) the author has created identifiable characters by means of sentences of type A can he "make" his characters talk about themselves or other things in the work. On the other hand, sentences of the latter type are one chief way in which an author endows a character with traits, with individuality, in novels and short stories as well as in plays and operas. But in plays and the librettos of operas this type of sentence plays a relatively greater role than it normally plays in novels and short stories.

The last piece in the group critically examines analogous attempts to provide a "real" essentialist definition of painting and of sculpture, respectively, but which in effect redefine them in terms of certain chosen criteria-features.

NOTE

1. Theodore Dreiser, *An American Tragedy*, *The New American Library*, New York, [1964], p. 677.
2. In *Art And Philosophy*, W.E. Kennick, ed. (St. Martin's Press, New York, 1964),

pp. 295–307.

3. *PAS*, Suppl. Vol. 12, 1933, pp. 18–43. (Johnson Reprint Corporation, New York, 1968) Hereafter referred to as *IO*.

4. *Ibid.*, p. 27 and *passim*. For the reasons he gives in "Systematically Misleading Expressions" (hereafter referred to as *SME*), in *Logic And Language*, First Series, A. Flew, ed. (Oxford, 1955), pp. 11–36 see subsection B.

5. *Op. cit.*, pp. 55–70. Reprinted in *Philosopical Papers* (Collier Books, New York, 1962) pp. 101–113.

6. See also my "About Imaginary Objects," in this volume, for further criticism of Ryle's negative and positive theses.

In his contribution, Moore attributes to Ryle the view that "there is *no* natural sense of the word 'about,' such that the words 'That proposition of Dickens was about Mr. Pickwick' expressed a true proposition." And to this Moore replies: "With this I simply cannot agree. It seems to me that these words are perfectly good natural English for something which *is* true." (*Ibid.*, p. 104) In *SME* Ryle states that "Mr. Pickwick" is the grammatical subject of, e.g., "Mr. Pickwick went to Rochester" but is not the real or logical subject. In terms of this, later statement of the matter, the issue does not revolve round ordinary *usage* but the correct *analysis* of fictional sentences of type A.

7. This is not always the same as S's success in referring to *something*—which may happen to be X or something else. Some sentences, e.g., "The highest mountain in the world is 29,000 feet high," succeed in referring to something whether or not the speaker intends to refer to it. Also, a sentence may succeed in referring to something real whereas the speaker may intend to refer, by it, to something he thinks is only possible.

8. Since he actually believes that he is referring to something existent.

9. I am thinking of "centaur" in those instances of its use in which it is employed to refer to a centaur in a novel, or some other work of imagination.

10. *Mind*, Vol, 73, No. 291 (July 1964), p. 367.

11. *Ibid.*

12–13. And if P.F. Strawson is correct in maintaining that it will then be neither true nor false, this would be so for a different reason from the reason why fictional sentences are neither true nor false.

14. *Ibid.*, pp. 15–16.

15. *Ibid.*, p. 18.

16. *Ibid.*, p. 20.

17. In the case of "Dickens wrote a fable" and "*Pickwick Papers* is a pack of lies," the speaker *implies* the existence of the subject in his real-life employment of them.

18. I have discussed the everyday distinction between "directly about" and "indirectly about," and related matters relevant to the present discussion, in "Acerca de" ("About"), *Diánoia*, Vol. XVII, No. 17, pp. 89–102.

19. *Op. cit.*, p. 104.

20. See *op. cit.*, p. 105.

21. *Ibid.*

22. See *Ibid.* for Moore's reasons. But see my "The Meaning Of Proper Names," in the *American University Centennial Publications* (Beirut, 1967), pp. 121–156, for certain qualifications that must be made respecting Moore's view.

23. Moore has his own, different reasons for the same view. See *op. cit.*, pp. 68–69.

24. Cf. Moore, *ibid.*, p. 68.

25. *Op. cit.*, p. 296. Note how Ryle is unaware of the essential point [which is in line with what I said under (A) about referring] that in the way we ordinarily talk, a sentence

such as "Mr. Pickwick went to Rochester" cannot possibly refer to or be about anything or anyone—not even "accidentally"—that its author did not have in mind or refer to in making the sentence. Nevertheless, a sentence that is not about something X is ordinarily said to be true *of* or not true of X when it is considered as being about X by the hearer or hearers.

26. *Op. cit.*, p. 64.

27. In *SME.*

28. "The Meaning Of Proper Names," pp. 121-156, *passim.*

29. I am ignoring here the (alleged) nontemporal existence of such things as God.

30. Moore speaks of "equivalence" rather than "stating" or "meaning"; but I doubt whether he wishes to assert that the analysans he gives is only logically equivalent to the proposition (the analysandum) expressed by the appropriate fictional sentence of the present type. Actually, I do not think that even the more modest claim is true. Note that on Moore's conception of analysis as set forth in, e.g., *Principia Ethica*, one condition of a correct analysis is the synonymity of the verbal expressions expressing the analysans and the analysandum, respectively. In analyzing type A sentences, Moore is really making explicit what is only implied by them or is implicit in the context in which they are employed (plus other things which are not even implied, but which he mistakenly thinks are expressed, or are in part meant, by them.)

31. What a sentence-in-use asserts is logically determined by what it means, as a sentence, in that context.

32. This is also the (or at least a) reason why, *pace* Russell, a sentence (in-use) does not *imply* the existence of the subject.

33. These statements, I believe, are true or false at the time they are made, not only at the future date to which they refer. We say: "What you say *isn't* true: people won't be able to travel to the moon by 1970." We predict the truth, at the time we make the prediction, of certain statements about the future. Predictions come true or are verified. But to come true is not to become true, in the sense in which something which was before untrue or neither true nor false may later become true. We do say: "All that gossip, which was mere lies and slander about so-and-so at the time, has come true." But we do not say: "It has become true." So this does not, I think, invalidate the foregoing.

34. This is the only sense in which "quality," "property" or "predicate" can be intended by Ryle without committing himself to the reality of qualities as unexemplified universals. And I do not think that he holds the view that qualities, properties or predicates exist as unexemplified universals.

35. I agree with W.E. Kennick's following remarks about Miss Macdonald's argument, in *op. cit.*: "Why ... can no factual discovery verify or disconfirm a fictional statement? (The premise is central to Miss Macdonald's argument.) Because it is false? That view is rejected. Because fictional statements are necessarily, by virtue of the fact that they are fictional, neither true nor false? But that begs the question." (*Ibid.*, pp. 378-379) In other words, I agree that Miss Macdonald does not show how or why "no factual discovery" can verify or disconfirm a fictional statement. To that extent she begs the question. In one sense, however, whatever she or anyone else (e.g., the present author) could say on the subject, short of giving at least an outline of the ordinary conception of a *work of fiction or even a work of art in general*, would beg the question. (For one attempt to do the latter, see *The Concept of Art*.) The setting forth of that conception is the really fundamental way of gaining an understanding of the nature of fictional sentences of type A (also sentences of type B and other types of sentences which occur in works of fiction). Nevertheless, there is a less stringent sense in

which it is possible to show how or why type A sentences are empirically untestable, as I am attempting to do in this essay.

36. See my "Vagueness, Verifiability And Metaphysics," *Foundations of Language*, Vol. 1 (1965), pp. 249–267.

37. In such works the author is successful in his treatment of the particular subjectmatter, in his characterization, plot, dialogue, etc., to the extent to which the work succeeds in giving us the "illusion of reality."

38. This is so by virtue of the reference of a work of fiction as a whole, and analogously, *mutatis mutandis*, of all other kinds of art; namely, the fact, essential to it as literature (as painting, music, etc.) and hence art, that it has a reference to what exists or is possible. This reference, this connection is always there, inseverable and secure; whether the particular work makes it explicit or leaves it unsaid. In this sense we can say that the indirect reference of all sentences of type B is to the real world or a logically possible world; though in the corresponding sense they are directly about a Lohengrin or a Lord Jim. (Compare and contrast the use of "directly" and "indirectly about" here and in relation to statements that are directly about the world.)

39. Alexander Solzhenitsyn, *Cancer Ward* (Dial Press, New York, 1968), pp. 121–122.

40. *Ibid.*, p. 132.

41. Except where the author is not writing fiction at all but, say, his autobiography.

42. We do (truly) say that, e.g., Dostoevsky does not take God's standpoint, the standpoint of the omniscient creator, toward the characters he creates. But by this we mean that he deliberately leaves certain facets of the experiences, motives, emotions and thoughts of his characters "in the dark," "unrevealed," to dramatize, for example, his conception of man as a being whose existence is shot through and through with ambiguity.

43. Dreiser, *op. cit.*, p. 298.

PART THREE

Chapter 5

Movement and Action in the Performing Arts

I

Dancing—performing a dance—consists of certain activities, generally indulged in by human beings. These activities consist of patterns of movement—either pure movement or movement representing certain imagined actions of imagined characters, imaginary situations, and so on—made by parts or the whole of the human body, the creation of dynamic visual, or visual and auditory, forms. Likewise a particular theatrical dance, as a work of art in the descriptive sense of "art" and "dance,"[1] consists of a certain temporal sequence of theoretically repeatable patterns of movement. There can be no dances without physical movement; consequently a completely motionless figure in some particular posture or pose on a stage cannot constitute the performance of a dance. Like music and its performance, dances and dancing are essentially temporal and dynamic in a straightforward sense: a scene in which paintings, sculptures and works of architecture are not temporal works of art.

The point of departure of this essay is, first, that a dance—and this applies as well to social or ballroom dances, which cannot be generally dignified with the name "art"[2]—and second, that dancing, *consist of actual movements and not, or not also, of actual actions* of some kind or other. Or more correctly, they consist in movements in the first place and include *imagined* actions (if and when they do so) only as represented or otherwise depicted or conveyed by means of movements. The same is true, though not necessarily in the same way or kind of way, of drama and opera; as can be seen from the way we talk about them. Although (instrumental) music, like the preceding, is a performing art, it is significantly different from them in that it does not partly (like drama and opera), or wholly (like the dance), consist in or include movement of any kind. Only the performance of music, in one sense of "performance," [3] partly involves movements of the performers' fingers, hands, arms, and so on, and partly consist in the vibration of strings and other kinds of sound producing physical movements of musical instruments, etc. Even then it is not even partly constituted by these movements. Here we must be careful to distinguish the temporal sequences of heard or audible sound patterns that constitute part or the whole of a work of music, and the sound waves or vibrations which are certain kinds of movements in air or other physical media and which are the physical causes of our hearing the notes that constitute elements of the work of music. The physical vibrations are not objects of hearing and do not constitute part of what we ordinarily call a work of music. The latter is, necessarily, partly or wholly an auditory phenomenon.

The relation between the movements and the represented action which constitute, say, a dance by Balanchine or Robbins and those that constitute or include the faithful performance of the dance, is extremely important. But it is not a question I shall concern myself with. Still, my remarks in "The Identity of a Work of Music," and in *The Concept of Art* (Chapter 1) regarding a work of music and its faithful performances, apply to it too, as well as to the corresponding question in the case of the other performing arts. What I shall be here concerned with is the philosophical *significance*, for an understanding of these arts and their performance, of the movement/action distinction, and the relation of movement and action in each case.

I said that a narrative dance is partly a series of usually connected movements, generally (at least in the case of good or sucessful dances) heightened and rhythmical in an appreciable degree; and a "pure" dance consists entirely of a series of usually connected movements, etc. But a dance consists of perceived or perceptible movements, and quite often, it also includes sequences of heard or audible sounds (the music as part of the dance). As a series of connected movements of human bodies, it is a sequence of dynamic, constantly changing spatiotemporal forms; and these are perceived as a series of dynamic three-dimensional gestalts or images, using "image" in an inclusive and metaphorical sense. This last description agrees with Susanna Langer's description of a dance as an appearance or "apparition of active powers, a *dynamic image*."[4] However, she appears to me to go too far in apparently thinking of a dance as consisting wholly and solely in an apparition or perceptual object, an image, rather than this in addition to (and necessarily) a series of physical movements made by physical forms we call human bodies. This is why she also, erroneously, contrasts the physical activities (movements) of the dancers with what she considers to be the real dance; though she significantly conceives of the latter as a "virtual entity," an image, like a rainbow or a mirror image, or any other object that exists only for perception,[5] rather than as a series of *actions*. For she says: "It—the dance—springs from what the dancers do, yet it is something else. In watching a dance, you do not see what is physically before you—people running around or twisting their bodies; what you see is a display of interacting forces—."[6] To my mind, the truth of the matter is that, in at least one ordinary sense of "see," we see both physical movements and "interaction of forces" in some sense. But in what immediately follows the foregoing quotation, Langer disabuses us of the notion that by "interaction of forces" she is talking about physical forces, and so, perhaps, of something partly or wholly sensible; hence that she is merely contrasting the interaction of physical forces and physical movements. For she says:

> But these powers, these forces that seem to oparate in the dance, are not the physical forces of the dancer's muscles, which actually cause the movements taking place. The forces we seem to perceive most directly and convincingly[7] are created for our perception; and they exist only for it.[8]

Langer's view that a dance is only a perceptual thing, a virtual image (leaving aside the ideal elements, the quality of expressiveness, which it also includes for her), an interaction of nonphysical forces or powers, is interestingly similar to the idealist conception of a work of art in general as something (wholly) ideal or imaginary: a view that has been much—and in my view convincingly—criticized especially in the form in which it was held by Croce and Collingwood,[9] for I do not see how such "virtual entities" can exist independently of a perceiver; though this does not necessarily entail (as many philosophers commonly suppose) that what is perceived is mental. What it *seems* to entail is that, in one common philosophical use of the word, it is a "subjective" and not an "objective" entity. (If Langer is unhappy with this imputation, as I think she would be, it is incumbent on her to show that what esists only in relation to perception (consciousness) can be nonetheless "objective" in some sense. Such a view is indeed held by a group of 20th century American philosophers, including Whitehead and Deway, and goes by the name of Objective Relativism.

Whether Langer would classify herself as an objective relativist I do not know.[10] On the other hand, her statements can also be interpreted to mean that a dance, like any other work of art according to her, is (partly) a perceptual entity in the sense of a complex of sense date, whether physical or mental (or physical but with mentally apprehended expressive qualities). But I do not know whether she would be happy with this account of her view either.

I should add that Langer makes clear that a dance "is more than a perceivable entity."[11] She holds that it is, like any other work of art, "a perceptible form that expresses the nature of human feeling"[12] (i.e., an "expressive form"); and "human feeling," which she uses synouymously with "psychic life," includes mental or "ideal" elements and relationships.

I said earlier that in one ordinary sense of "see," we see both physical movement and "intersection of forces" in some sense. The question of whether we sensibly perceive the *action* of an object or a physical force, or the interaction of physical forces, has been a crucial philosophical problem since David Hume maintained the negative, as part of his celebrated critique of the necessary-connection theory of causality. Fortunately, this problem does not concern us here. In any event, the view presented in this essay, which I believe is "the ordinary view," is that a dance—perhaps including a pure dance—is a physical-*cum*-ideal thing. The same, *mutatis mutandis*, is true of plays, pantomine, and operas.

It is, finally, worth mentioning that Langer's account appears to confuse the nature of a dance and its performance—which, she would agree, I think, consists of or includes a sequence of movements of a certain description. On the ordinary view, a dance as well as its performance consists of or includes a sequence of movements; though I would certainly agree that, from the fact that the performance consists in or includes movements of a certain kind, we cannot conclude that *a dance* must consist of or include movements of a certain description. Compare this with a work of music and its performance. Compare and contrast too the movements of the actors or singers on the stage and the play or the opera performed.

Again, I agree with Selma Jeanne Cohen's definition of a theatrical dance as rhythmical movement,[13] but only to the extent that for any sequence of movements to constitute a dance, good or bad, they must be rhythmic *in some degree*. However, there is no sharp line between "rhythmical" and "nonrhythmical" or "unrhythmical" movements; and so it is sometimes theorectically impossible to decide whether a sequence of movements is a—a very poor—dance or not a dance at all. Further, Langer is right that being rhythmical is not a sufficient condition of a dance: gymnastics, ice skating and other sports, military marches and parades, and so on, may be quite rhythmical but are not ordinarily called dance. The movements, she says, must be also charged with or expressive of feeling. This is true of *good* dance, not however of all that we call dance; i.e., not poor or mediocre dance as well. In other words, the putative differentia does not provide a sufficient condition of dance.

The preceding discussion of Langer's Views on the nature of dance ties in with an important related matter; namely, that in English "dance" ("ballet," etc.)—and similarly with "play," "pantomime," and "opera"—has only one descriptive sense, like "music" ("symphony," "concerto," "cantata," "opera," etc.) and "poem" "novel," "short story," etc., and unlike "painting," "sculpture," and "work of architecture."[14] That is, unlike the latter expressions, "dance" ("opera," "play," etc.) is not, depending on the context, sometimes used to refer to (1) some phycical object or set of objects, a physical activity or a set of activities, a sequence of sounds, and so on, sometimes to (2) "images" or perceptual (visual or auditory) forms or patterns created by physical materials: pigments on canvas, metal or wood, clay and so on. For the physical medium of a dance is physical (bodily) movements, not human bodies in motion; since human bodies, which are physical though living entities, are not part of the dance. This is in contrast to the fact that physical surfaces, objects and substances are the media of painting and sculpcure, respectively. "Dance" invariably refers to the perceptual (and ideal) forms or patterns made by the moving (generally heightened and rhythmic) bodies, corresponding to the two- or three-dimensional visual designs created by the pigments on a canvas or the engraved or sculpted stone, clay, and so on. I should add that even in the case of painting, sculpture and architecture, the artistically important sense of the word is (2). It is as a perceptual design, together with whatever perceptual and ideal content and meanings it has, that a painting, sculpture or work of architecture constitutes an "aesthetic object"; it is this that in the case of *good* works gives the spectater what is called aesthetic enjoyment. It is therefore also the qualities of this design or form-*cum*-content that spectators, particularly professional critics, evaluate in judging the work's artistic merit.

The same observations apply, *mutatis mutandis*, to "play," "opera," and "pantomime." But granted this important similarity, there are of course basic differences between a dance, an opera and a play, some of which serve or help to distinguish them from one another. For instance, a dance may consist of nothing but movement, representing and so including no action at all. A "pure" dance is just that. But a play without any action at all, though perhaps not impossible, is a limiting or possibly a borderline case of a play, even supposing that *good* or even great plays are possible with *very little* action. The discussion in this essay as a whole should make clear why this is so. An opera, just like a play, also needs some action. If any work of vocal music represents no action at all, it would be, I think, generally regarded as more properly classifiable as an oratorio, mass, cantata or song depending on its form and content. The movements of the characters have significance (meaning) almost wholly insofar as they depict character and represent action; and action without characters is impossible. Nevertheless, we must admit that we can conceivably have what we call plays and operas—works containing characters—without any action in the usual meaning of the word; where the characters do absolutely nothing but talk about themselves and other characters, and in that way exhibit their various character traits.[15] (This would undoubtedly be a poor substitute for characterization by action; but it would serve to some extent.) But to say that a play or an opera without action is almost impossible is not to say that such a work cannot exist without a *plot*; though I do not generally equate "action" with "plot" in this essay. For strictly speaking, action is "story"—or more precisely, intentional or unintentional activities initiated by characters as agents, and not these together with what happens to them—which may or may not qualify as a plot in the familiar Aristotelian use of the work. (See also later, for Elder Olson's definition.) Whether a play can be good theatre or whether opera can exist without any plot whatever, is another matter.

The basic reason why a play or an opera is well-nigh impossible in the absence of all action is that such a work *consists* of actions, among other things. It is also impossible in the absence of all movement. Actors and operatic singers, like dancers, move about and make any number of movements on the stage. But in a play or opera these movements mainly represent action, and derive their aesthetic interest chiefly from the significance of the action represented; whereas the movements of a dance may—and in a good dance do—have aesthetic interest in themselves as movements. In this respect (but clearly not in other respects) a play is not, while a dance often is, largely or wholly, a "sensuous" work of art.

II

It is neither necessary nor possible for us to go in any detail into the notions of movement and action, and the distinction between the two. I shall be satisfied with some pertinent observations about these matters, to make the ordinary notions of movement and action perhaps a little more explicit than we "intuitively" employ them in everyday discourse.

(1) We speak of the movements a person makes as movements of his body; whereas the actions he performs are never "of his body," though they may relate to the body, such as in shaving or cutting oneself. On the other hand, both movements and actions are initiated by persons (I am leaving aside the movements and actions of animals). In both cases the agent is necessarily a person as a whole; though a person moves his body or parts of it. But in order that a person may perform a physical action, he must move his body or parts of it. Yet movements are often necessary for action, not as a means to some distinct end (which is what the means/ends distinction implies), but as that which, either partly or wholly, constitutes the particular action. In other cases action involves relevant movements without being partly or wholly constituted by them. For instance President Nixon's political and military actions (also called decisions) relating to the Vietnam War go far beyond and are not constituted by any of the movements of the pen or any verbal declarations he made or now makes. Humanly the most important or significant actions, which are the stuff of morality and of dramatic art, are of this sort.

But though there can be physical action without bodily movement, the converse is false: since not all movement, not even all connected movements, necessarily constitute an action or a set of actions.

(2) It follows from (1) above that when we think: of bodily movement we think directly of nervous impulses, muscular contractions, and other physiological or other biological processes; while these are involved only indirectly in thinking of actions, i.e., insofar as they involve the appropriate movements.

The epithet "bodily" or "physical" in "bodily movement" and "physical movement," respectively, which I have so far used, can be generally dropped, since talking and mental activities are not actions in ordinary English.[16] (But we speak of talking as an act or activity, and of writing as an action or an act.) Some philosophers speak of "mental act"; but this, as well as "speech act," which is not confined to the act of uttering meaningful sounds, is a technical use of "act."

In any event, "act" is not always interchangeable with "action," even if the converse is true. However, in relation to dramatic and other performing arts, what we call the action (e.g., the plot) does of course include the characters' imagined mental activities, their "inner life" as a whole; though as far as I can see, not also the activity of talking as such, as opposed to the feelings, emotions, thoughts, images or moods thereby conveyed. But though a character's inner life is part of *the action* of a dramatic work, it does not, in contrast to such activities as fighting a duel, killing, making love, carousing, constitute *an action* or a set of *actions* in an ordinary sense. (I might add parenthetically that a person's talking, feeling angry, imagining a hydra, and the like are all instances of doing something; but clearly this notion is not exhausted by the notion of action.)

(3) In ordinary usage as opposed to the current philosophical employment of our terms in Anglo-Saxon philosophy, both movements and actions may or may not (a) be voluntary, and/or (b) intentional, hence (c) have reasons in addition to or instead of causes. A person may make a certain movement intentionally, for a certain reason; and he may perform some action unintentionally or involuntarily. Thus we say: "The burglar forced Henry to open the safe and hand over the money it contained" (involuntary action); and "He knocked over and broke a valuable Ming vase, when he absent-mindedly moved his arm" (unintentional action). These are familiar and important facts in relation to, e.g., moral action. However—and this appears to be a crucial difference—there can be wholly unconscious movements, but there cannot be wholly unconscious actions, in the relevant *ordinary* meaning of "unconscious." As Stuart Hampshire states the latter point, "No action is attributable to an unconscious man as its agent."[17] It follows, *a fortiori*, that a toy, puppet or automaton cannot be literally said to perform actions: it can only make certain movements and thus go through the motions of performing the appropriate actions. Only human beings and (possibly) higher animals can perform actions by, among other things, making appropriate movements. Consequently these contraptions can be (figuratively) said to perform certain actions only if they are imagined to be conscious beings. This is of some significance in relation to, e.g., puppet shows, or a play such as Jean-Claude Van Italie's *Motel* in which three dolls with oversize heads constitute the "characters."

The phrase "go through the motions" is very interesting in many ways. For instance, we speak of a mime or ballet dancer as going through the motions of opening a door, kissing, embracing, dying, etc. We also speak of human beings who, *fully consciously and deliberately*, "go through the motions" of expressing love, concern, compassion, solicitude, etc., for someone else. This is quite a different, usually metaphorical use of the term, and describes a different form or sense (a metaphorical sense) of make-believe, play-acting or illusion than that which is indulged in by the actor or actress, mime or operatic singer, and by the dancer performing a narrative dance. In the latter case, no intention—*a fortiori*, no appropriate intention—can be ascribed to the performer *qua* performer, and even less to him as a person, in making the movements required by the text. That is why these movements do not wholly or partly constitute, but only represent, actions in the full sense. (See Section III.) In the former case there is an intention, but not the appropriate one; i.e., the intention which normally goes with the movements, which provides their reason for being. I mean the intention in the case of sincere persons. The intention present is that of deceiving the observer into thinking that the subject has the feelings or emotions, attitudes, desires or beliefs whose presence these movements normally indicate.

Although all actions are conscious activities, not all actions are intentional actions. Only actions in the full sense[18]—in the sense in which "action" is most commonly used in current writings on the philosophy of action—where it is contrasted with movements, are so. This fact helps justify, e.g., Hampshire's close linking of consciousness and action, in such pronouncements as "A conscious mind is always and necessarily envisaging possibilities of action, of finding means towards ends . . . .",[19] and "To be a conscious human being, and therefore a thinking being, is to have intentions or plans, to be trying to bring about a certain effect."[20]

For the purposes of our discussion, the foregoing means that when we say that movements of the performers (may) represent actions,[21] we essentially mean that we think of or imagine these movements as those of (generally human) characters, i.e., of conscious agents who have certain intentions in making them. We do not (generally speaking, imaginatively) attribute them to (lower) animals, and least of all to inanimate things, such as objects or natural forces. When we imagine inanimate things to be characters and so conscious agents, we personify them.

My brief analysis of movement and action has assumed that we know what intention is; and indeed for our purposes we must leave this crucial notion unanalyzed, relying on the reader's preanalytical knowledge of the word's meaning and common uses. But I definitely think that Hampshire is mistaken in identifying intention with certain settled beliefs, as when he says: "My intention to do something is a settled belief about my future action, a belief that illuminates some part of the future . . . ."[22] Although an intention necessarily implies certain beliefs, including perhaps some settled beliefs, it is not identical with beliefs of any sort. Certain beliefs may help give rise to an intention to do certain things, by helping to provide a general or specific, vague or definite goal, or certain means (actions) for their attainment. But no beliefs are, I think, sufficient to give rise to a particular intention. Desire, want, inclination, tendency or disposition may also be necessary. An intention is not, entirely, an intellectual matter. Of course a belief necessarily involves some inclination or tendency, sometimes a disposition, to do certain kinds of things, including, generally, certain kinds of actions. But a belief is not just, or primarily, a tendency, inclination, and so on.

However, these are large and controversial matters and I cannot possibly do them justice without going too far afield. I shall therefore leave them to a future occasion.

III

A dance with a narrative line is a sequence of movements created by human forms, representing the imaginery actions or other activities of imagined characters. In some cases the actions and activities represented are part of the dance, just as the representing movements, and the representation (representing) itself are. The actions and activities represented are part of the work whenever they are imaginary or fictitious, not when they are historical happenings. Again, if the dance represents actual persons, the latter are clearly not part of the work. The actions, etc., represented, the "story" "told" by the dancers by means of movements, are conceptually distinct from any qualitatively similar actions that actual human beings, including the performers of the particular dance, may perform in real-life situations. This distinction also arises between the dancers as representing various characters, and as human beings (and between them as human beings and as dynamic or static forms). Similar distinctions arise with respect to plays and operas, as well as fiction in general.

The above are paralleled, *mutatis mutandis*, in drama and opera, indeed, all "dramatic art," including novels and short stories and narrative poetry. Again, what I said above about the objects represented in a narrative dance applies to the representation in representational paintings and sculptures. The woman called La Gioconda, who modeled for Leonardo da Vinci's "Mona Lisa," is clearly not part of the painting; whereas a painting of Hamlet the Prince of Denmark in Shakespeare's *Hamlet*, would include its subject, the *painted* Hamlet. However, just as La Gioconda is not literally part of the "Mona Lisa," the Prince of Denmark is not part of any paintings of Shakespeare's *Hamlet*. He "exists" in and only in the play *Hamlet*, and "nowhere" else.

I said earlier that a dance is a sequence of generally rhythmic movements with certain types of characteristics. But it can also be described —and from the perceiver's point of view this is aesthetically more significant—as a sequence of constantly changing three-dimensional forms. As a perceptual object it is a sequence of qualitatively related three-dimensional gestalts. Using "image" in the very inclusive, even metaphorical sense in which Langer uses it, we can agree with her that a dance is a visual or a visual and auditory image or succession of images. The dancers are not part of the dance as persons or even performers; hence the sensuous medium of the dance is strictly physical, bodily movement, not moving things. This is not inconsistent with the above statement that a dance is a sequence of dynamic three-dimensional forms. For a human being is not a physical form but something that has a form.

In talking of the action of a dance, opera or play (also fiction), we must note an important distinction made by Elder Olson in "The Elements of Drama: Plot,"[23] in relation to drama. Olson distinguishes the plot of a play and its scenario or dramatic representation. The latter is what is shown on the stage, whereas "parts of the plot, indeed crucial and central ones, may be omitted from the representation, that is, may occur off-stage .... Conversely, events may be shown on the stage which form no part of the plot."[24] Again: "The plot may begin before the representation, or after it, or simultaneously with it; similarly, the plot may end before or after or simultaneously with the ending of the representation."[25] Further, "the incidents of the plot are *time-bound*, that is, must occur in a given chronological order, and are consequently not convertible. The incidents of the representation are not time-bound, and conversions of chronological order are common. The commonest instance is the flashback ...."[26] In short, "the representation is *what represents*, whereas the plot is *what is represented*. They are thus, obviously, distinct."[27] Olson defines plot as "*a system of actions of a determinate moral quality*. I use the word 'actions' in a very general sense, to include the inner workings of the soul as well as external action. In this sense, any actualization of a capacity for thought, emotion, or action is to be considered an 'action.' "[28]

Utilizing this distinction, we can restate a little more precisely certain things I said earlier. The movements of the dancers, actors or operatic singers may represent action either in the sense of scenario or in the sense of plots and drama. Where language is utilized, only part of the plot need be presented by means of the scenario; though at least part of the plot must be presented: certainly if the play is to be good theater. The entire sequence of incidents constituting the action cannot be merely described, hinted at or implied by what the characters *say* on the stage. If no such action is shown on the stage, what action is presented cannot be part of the plot, and so, in the words of Olson, can have "no effect whatsoever upon the train of consequences which make up the action [plot]";[29] e.g., it would be merely expositery, such as Act I, Scene i of *Julius Caesar*, mentioned by Olson. On the other hand, a "play" which presents no action on the stage, i.e., lacks a scenario, would really be a novel or a short story, not a play. A scenario is absolutely indispensable to a play, and is crucial for distinguishing it from a novel or a short story. It follows that some action, in the form of a plot, is also essential to drama; though the question of the relative importance of plot and character(ization) in drama remains an open question.

The situation is somewhat different with the dance, if we suppose, as I think we must, that the synopsis of the "story" of a narrative dance, printed in a program, is not part of the dance. For since the dance does not (normally) utilize language, which could be used to describe, hint at or imply action not presented on the stage, the greater part of the plot or the plot as a whole must be presented by the scenario. I add "the greater part" because (as is partly the case with a play or an opera) the audience fills in the gaps between the different segments of the scenario by inference, establishing connections not shown on the stage; and these can be regarded as part of the plot whenever they are, first, consistent with the scenario as a whole and that part of the plot which is presented on the stage, and second, have a textual basis in what is said (e.g., is hinted at by a character in a play or opera, or is indicated by the playwright's or composer's description of the characters or action in the text or libretto). Yet this does not mean that in every narrative dance every single part of the scenario is essential for the plot, represents dramatic action. Examples to the contrary are mentioned by Selma Jeanne Cohen in "A Prolegomenon to an Aesthetics of Dance."[30] She points out that in the prologue to *The Sleeping Beauty* there are solo dances (or variations) "which have no dramatic structure in themselves .... As a group, they are all rather sweet, and this serves as a foil to what follows: the entry of the wicked Carabosse, who is to utter the fatal curse on Aurora. But their individuality does nothing for the plot. Dramatically, fewer than seven fairies would have served the purpose."[31] Yet, as Ms. Cohen rightly adds, "we do not, however, object to the superfluous quantity. The dances are varied and charming, and the story is not urgent. Why rush?"[32] In other words, as she emphasizes earlier in her essay, the movements, the dynamic patterns of the dance may be enjoyable for their sake and interest, for their sensuous beauty, apart from their interest of meaning, if any.

What, then, is the relation between the scenario and the movements of the performers in a dance, a play, an opera? From the definition of "scenario" given by Olson, it is clear that the scenario partly or wholly consists of these movements: wholly in the case of the dance but partly in the case of the drama and the opera, where other elements besides movement represent the action of the plot. If this is true, Olson is mistaken in stating that representation (scenario) is action; though it is obviously true (as he says) that plot is action, not movement, or not just movement.

In this section I have been continually speaking of the movements of a narrative dance and the movements of the actors and actresses, or the operatic singers, on the stage, as *representing* action (the plot). I also spoke of the action as something *presented* on the stage by means of the appropriate movements of actors and actresses, dancers or singers. We must now attempt to understand, as precisely as space permits, what these words mean here, or in exactly what way movement is related to action in these kinds of art.

Let us start by noting some senses of the word "represent" in which many or all bodily movements in a dramatic work of art *cannot* be correctly described as representing actions, but which are important ways in which movements or actions may function in such art. First, they do not represent them in the sense of serving as an "artificial," man-devised and in that sense conventional *sign* (or $sign_1$, to distinguish this type of sign from "natural" signs or $sign_2$[33]). If an actor lifts his hand to his head and makes the movements that are part of the action of scratching his head, these movements will not be a $sign_1$ of the action of scratching his head. But some of the movements of an actor or an operatic singer on the stage, instead of representing an action, may constitute a sign$_1$ of it. An example is making what we call "the sign$_1$ of the cross." The action of making that sign consists of the well-known conventional movements with the intention of signifying one's Christian beliefs, one's identification with a Christian (or some particular Christian) Church, and so on; hence this action also includes the religious meaning or significance of these movements as described. For the latter to be present, the person in question must go through the movements with the express purpose of making the sign of the cross, viz. performing the action with a particular religious significance. The action and the movements, as perceptual or phenomenological things, are therefore not in fact but only conceptually distinguishable. But second, movements do not necessarily represent actions in the sense of being *symbols* of them. In some works, certain gestures or other movements are obviously symbolic. They may symbolize certain actions or activities, or objects, experiences, occurrences, qualities of character, mental states, objective states of affairs, and so on. But only in allegorical dances, plays or operas are most or all of them symbolic. The existence of considerable stylization in classical or even modern dance is a distinct matter. With respect to stylization, dance and opera are generally more "artificial" or "contrived," less "realistic" than a good deal of drama—at least in the West. Stylizaton is not symbolism, though it can and frequently does conveniently serve a symbolic purpose. In many instances a stylized movement represents an action in a direct, straightforward way, rather than obliquely or symbolically. This happens whenever the movement is qualitatively, phenomenologically similar to—indeed, if we can use this term in this connection, if it is numerically identical with—the action it represents. A movement is symbolic when it represents a qualitatively, phenomenologically different action, generally by virtue of a convention established by the artist or a particular community; or if it represents something entirely different from an action, such as a feeling or emotion, a state of being, a particular relationship, and so on. It cannot symbolize an action which is phenomenologically identical with it. However, it can symbolize a complex action of which it is, phenomenologically speaking, a part, since a part can be used to symbolize the whole.

The upshot is that many of the movements in a dramatic work represent actions or other things in a more direct, more "literal" or straightforward way than the ways noted above: either alone or together with these other ways of representing them. But there are important differences in this respect between (1) drama, (2) mime, (3) dance, and (4) opera. Although the representation is more straightforward and direct than in the case of signifying—functioning as a $sign_1$ or symbolisation—it varies appreciably in degree, in (1)-(4) as a whole. Thus pantomime usually represents actions more by suggestion than explicitly or literally, by leaving more to the audience's imagination, then, generally, drama and opera. A mime creates the illusion of a well, a prison cell, a pane of glass, a mirror or any other object, by means of highly suggestive movements; whereas the actor (but much leas the operatic singer) usually utilizes such objects or furnishings, and so generally makes the movements that constitute the action he wishes to portray, rather than merely suggesting them. He carries objects, moves chairs or tables around, smashes vases, pours drinks, and so on. Dancers, generally like the singers in classical operas, do both; e.g., they do the former when they suggest, either by stylized or natural movements, the art of lovemaking; the latter, when they actually kiss or at least touch lips, embrace, and the like-even though they often do so in some stylized way. Of course, actors too pretend to punch one another in the nose, knock one another down, stab their adversaries, get drunk, and the like; and the same goes for operatic singers, who also mingle pretence and realistic or stylized movement in different proportions, in different classical and modern operas.

Dance movements are generally more suggestive, less explicit than those of actors and actresses on the stage, with opera perhaps usually occupying an intermediate position between the two. Certainly realistic and especially naturalistic drama avoids stylization as much as possble and relies most heavily on direct, explicit movements that are more or less culture-neutral. In this respect they are unlike all stylization (cf. Cohen), and some everyday movements relating to such simple actions as eating, drinking, yawning, etc., which are culturebound. Meaningful gestures, in the sense of gestures that are either $signs_1$ or symbols, are generally culture-bound; though some gestures that have meaning insofar as they possess a general human significance, not as a $sign_1$ or symbol but as a $sign_2$—i.e., a natural expression of particular mental or emotional states or traits of character—are universal in character. Examples are gestures that people make involuntarily and spontaneously with the hands, the head or the body, to ward off sudden danger, e.g., in the case of bodily assault. Such gestures or movements are also made on the stage.

To understand the present sense of "representation," let us go back to the notion of meaning we mentioned a little earlier.

I said that some movements in a dance may signify$_1$ or symbolize the actions they represent, if any, while the latter themselves may in turn function as symbols of various imagined or conceived of states of affairs, states of being, ideas, and the like. Another way of stating this is that some movements may have meaning either in the sense of being signs$_1$ of certain actions, or in the sense of being symbols of them or of other things; and that some represented actions may have symbolic meaning. The question then is whether there is another sense or "meaning" or "meaningful" in which many or all the movements of a dancer, actor or operatic singer *means* some action or set of actions; a sense in which "X is a meaningful movement or set of movements insofar as it means action A" would mean "X represents action A" in the desired sense. The answer appears to be that in ordinary discourse we would describe as a meaningful movement, a movement on the stage which represents an action; but I am not sure whether we also say that it consequently has a (certain, or a certain kind of) meaning. Do we speak of the mime's movements, which certainly represent certain actions, as meaning these action? I do not think so. Yet they are like many movements and gestures we involuntarily make in actual life, which we would describe as devoid of any meaning, e.g., as merely reflexive gestures of gestures totally irrelevant to what the person does or feels at the time (if such a thing is possible). But even such "meaningless" movements may have a meaning in a *different* sense, say to a psychoanalyst or psychiatrist, in the sense that they may tell something about the subject's emotional hangups. The hunch that representation in the present sense in not a form of meaning is somewhat reinforced by considering the way we talk about the representation in a portrait, landscape, seascape or still-life painting. For I think we do not say that a bowl of apples or a mandolin in a painting means "a bowl of apples" or "a mandolin"; nor, by the way, do we say that they *refer* to these things, though we would deny that the forms and colors that *depict* or *stand* for the apples or the mandolin are simply "meaningless" colors and lines. Again, when a spectator asks the painter what certain forms in his paintings mean (or what he means by them), what I think he wants to know is their putative *symbolic* meaning. The questioner would not be inquiring about what they represent, if anything. But we must guard against ignoring differences between the way (or sense) in which representational paintings represent their subjects or objects, and the way (or sense) in which the movements in a dance, a play, an opera, and so on may represent actions or situations. For it is obvious that the relation between a picture of a cluster of grapes in a bowl on a table and what is represented—a cluster of grapes, etc.—is a different sort of relation from the relation between, say, the movements made by Laurence Olivier on the stage representing Hamlet's stabbing of Polonius behind the arras (in Act III, Scene iv of *Hamlet*) and the action of stabbing represented. In both cases there is—indeed, must be—some resemblance between that which represents and that which is represented. But in painting and sculpture, formal or structural resemblance can be sufficient, in contrast to movements representing actions. What is more, movement appears to offer no precise analogue to the extremely stylized or formal, semi-abstract representations, of, say, cubist paintings. Only in pantomime and highly stylized classical or semi-abstract modern dances does movement appear to come close to offering such an analogue.

We must not forget to add, in our discussion of the possible meaning of movements on the stage, that they have meaning in a sence we touched on but have not yet discussed; namely that they may be indications or "natural signs" ($signs_2$) of the mental state or the personality of the characters imagined to be making the movements; in the same way that the observer may take some of the movements of people in actual life as telltale signs of their immediate mental state or their personality, and so on. In the case of the performing arts the work's creator or performer may intend the audience to interpret certain movements in that way; and it provides both creator and performer with an important way of suggesting the workings of a character's mind or emotional state, as well as with useful though not primary way of helping delineate character. This applies to all the performing arts. (But Hamlet's advice to the performers of the play within the play in Act III, Scene ii reminds us that "sawing the air too much" with the hands and other exaggerated movements or gestures can easily obstruct or prevent this.

We must now note a basic difference between the relation between (a) movement and action in a dramatic work of art, on stage, and (b) movement and action off-stage. This difference is reflected in the way we describe the relation in each case. As we saw, we speak of the relation in (a) as one of representation in some sense, whereas this is not the way movements and actions are related in actual life, i.e., when the actions and not just the movements are real rather than fictive. In real life, movements do not represent actions. Whenever they are "related" to some action—i.e., when they are intentional or purposive movements, initiated by the particular person in a sense in which he does not initiate more movements.[34] If it does not confuse matters, we can say that in ordinary life, hence in the primary sense of "action," an action is a movement or a series of connected movements together with its or their meaning, if we can speak of the agent's purpose or aim in making the movements as their meaning (or at least, as one sort of meaning they may have). In the case of (a), it is clear that the movements cannot constitute an action since the former is real and the latter imaginary. The former are objects of sensuous perception, the latter only objects of the intellect, emotion or imagination.

The foregoing constitutes an important difference between (a) the performance of a dramatic work and everyday activities; and (b) between the work performed, as a work of art, and real-life actions and activities. Connected with these differences is the fact that the actions represented by the performers are actions "of" the imaginary characters which the performers impersonate. The latter, *qua* performers, cannot be ordinarily said to perform any actions on the stage. On the other hand, characters in dramatic works of art are imagined to make movements as well as to perform actions; indeed, "their" actions are imagined to be *constituted* by the intentional and purposive movements they "make." In the performing arts the latter are made by the performers impersonating the characters. In a novel or short story, the movements of the characters as well as their actions are imaginary. Because of the fact that in the latter case both movements and actions are of a kind, just as they are (only in the opposite way) in real life, but especially because it is the characters and they alone that are imagined to make various movements and to perform certain actions, gives rise to the presumption that we would not speak of a Kirilov's or a Portnoy's movements as *representing* certain actions. And this is, indeed, the case. For we think of their deliberate movements as constituting the appropriate actions.

Although we speak of the movements of the performer as (sometimes) representing certain actions of the particular character portrayed, we significantly speak of the latter as *presented* on the stage; that is why we speak of it as "the action on the stage." For this means, I think, that in an ordinary use of "see" or "perceive" we see or perceive the action, enacted or unfolding before us on the stage, not merely the movements which we somehow interpret as representing (standing for) certain actions. In other words, no process of inference from something present (or presented) on the stage to something not presented but merely apprehended by the mind, appears to be involved. At least nothing appears to be involved beyond the unconscious inference that may be involved in, e.g., *recognizing* that a certain painted shape represents, say, an apple. But since an action in the most common real-life sense consists of intentional or purposive movements, it must be an object of both sense-perception (i.e., movements) and the intellect (i.e., intention or purpose). In the performing arts, the recognition that a given movement (merely) represents some particular action is obviously an intellectual matter, and is an important part of understanding or knowing what "make believe," "artifice," "pretense" or "illusion"—hence art—is. What is wrong with the proverbial country bumpkin who jumps on the stage to wrest the beleagured heroine away from the clutches of the murderous villain is not the alleged lack of paychical or aesthetic "distance" but ignorance of the convention which states that the movements of the actors and actresses are not actions but only movements representing imaginary actions. His plight is similar to what Edward Bullough calls "underdistancing,"[35] in that the bumpkin fails to distinguish art and life in the aforementioned respect. His failure does not consist in inability to "put out of gear," or his interdisposing of, his practical, personal concerns or preoccupations. His practical motive of saving the lady from a tragic fate is misplaced, simply because he had not been taught the difference between movement and action on the stage and off-stage. It is therefore quite unlike the case of Bullough's allegedly cuckolded husband who foolishly attends a performance of *Othello*, and whose personal hurt prevents him from enjoying the work properly, as a work of art.

IV

I stated in Section I that a narrative dance consists of a sequence of generally rhythmic bodily movements, etc., representing certain actions (a plot); while a "pure" dance consists of sequences of such movements, which include or represent no action whatever. In the former case the movements, *que* representing actions, have the complex purpose of (a) representing action, (b) creating various "aesthetic qualities," including emotional qualities, conveying certain conceptions or ideas, delineating qualities of character, and so on[36]; and (c) especially in the case of good dances, creating perceptually pleasing forms or designs (sensuous grace, beauty, delicacy of line, etc.). In the latter case, (a) is lacking, but (b) and (c) are or may be present. But this purpose, which is (1) the purpose of the dancers' movements, should be clearly distinguished from (2) the ends which the characters portrayed are imagined as striving to realize in different scenes or sections of the dance, and which form part of the plot, as well as from (3) the various episodes in the plot, including, especially, their culmination in the dance's denouement, if any. Finally, if should be distinguished from (4)(a) the goals—effects, message, etc.—which the choreographer may intend to get across, achieve, etc., by means of the work, and more important, (b) the work's actual aims as concretely embodied or realized in and work, to the extent that it has some general aim, drift or direction and is not totally aimless. The same distinctions arise, *mutatis mutandis*, in relation to pantomime, drama and opera.

The distinction between (1) and (2) is easy to perceive, since the ends which the various characters strive to achieve are part of what is represented by the movements in the dance, hence by the performers of the play, pantomime or opera. The distinction between (2) and (3) helps us perceive, among other things, the distinction between (1) and (3). The distinction between the former is also, I think, quite obvious; since what the characters strive for and what they succeed in realising, as well as what befalls them, are logically and often in fact quite different things. As the old saying goes, there's many a slip between the cup and the lip; and this divergence between intention and execution is, of course, the stuff of which drama, narrative dance, and opera—as well as fiction and films—are made. Indeed, we are here reminded of a whole constellation of familiar Aristotelian notions, such as "complication," "denouèment," "turning point" and "reversal."

The distinction between (1) and (4a) should also be readily seen. The character of the work's plot, as the (or an) end of the movements representing them, hence the particular movements themselves, is itself just one of the devices he harnesses to achieve his overall purpose in creating the particular work. The characters' attempt to achieve their particular goals, and these goals themselves [2], as well as their success or failure to realize them [3], are further means for the realization of his intended overall goals. These consist of the emotional, imaginative and intellectual impact he wishes to have on his audience, as well as specifically the ideas or insights he may wish to convey to them. In this connection we must note that we speak of the artist's creation of the particular work as an activity (or act?), not as an action, even if or when it is goal-directed. Least of all do we speak of it as a series of movements. However, various physical movements are a necessary part of the creation of paintings and sculptures, such as the movements of painting a canvas, sculpting stone, welding, constructing, etc., though not the particular arts we are concerned with. The action of writing the score or libretto of an opera, or the text of a play, is not, hence the movements that phenomenologically comprise it are not a necessary part of the creation of an opera or a play, since it is conceivable for the artist to compose them in his head. (This does not mean, however, that they would be ideal or "imaginary" objects.) Yet these actions, hence the physical movements, are normally part of the entire process vaguely called composing an opera, play, etc. Whenever the choreographer goes through the paces of the dance for the benefit of the dancers, he performs the movements of the dance mainly for the sake of instructing them in the movements of the dance, not only for the sake of representing action. Where the choreographer creates the dance in and by dancing it (somewhat like the composer who composes, say, at the piano) he would be doing something else: performing the physical activities which are a normal part of creating a dance, since there is as yet no viable device to set down a dance on paper the way a composer or a poet can write down a symphony or a lyric.

Finally, the actions represented by the movements of a dance or the movements of the actors and actresses, mimes, etc. must be distinguished from the aims of the finished work as a whole; though both are internal to, are part of, the work, in contrast to (4a), which lies outside the completed work. the work's aim[37] is its general "drift," the "direction" it takes, the "movement" of thought, imagination or feeling in a certain "direction," toward some imaginable or conceivable end; consequently its presence implies a certain degree of coherence or unity, hence the work's possession of an appreciable degree of meaning. The former may include or wholly consist in extra-aesthetic ends; but the latter is, by definition, necessarily aesthetic. It may or may not coincide with (4a), depending on all sorts of known and possibly unknown factors, such as the artist's technical skill and overall artistic ability, his relevant insights or knowledge, and his serious application to the task at hand. The action in the work, as the end of the performer's movements, is logically distinct from the work's aim itself; but the nature of the episodes comprising the action, and its general line of development and unfolding, constitute one of the chief ways in which the work's overall aim is determined or defined. This parallels the relation(s) between (1) and (4a), since the (good) artist strives to construct a plot he feels would best realize his overall goals in and by his creation of the particular work.

To sum up: the movements of the performers (and in the case of a narrative dance, of the dance itself) are, among other things, a means to the depiction of action (the plot), which, in turn, serves the artist's overall aesthetic aims, yet helps determine or constitute the created work's own aims or goals.

NOTES

1. Throughout this essay, unless indicated otherwise, these words will be used in the present way.

2. In "A Prolegomenon to the Aesthetics of the Dance," in Lee A. Jacobus, ed., *Aesthetics and the Arts* ([n.p] , 1968), Selma Jeanne Cohen states that "Aesthetics is not equally concerned with all kinds of dancing. The ritual, which is designed to ask a favor of the gods, and the social dance, which provides enjoyment for its participants, may—accidentally—give aesthetic pleasure. But this is not their purpose, nor is it the test of their success. The rain dance succeeds when the rain falls. The square dance goes well when the performers have a good time. Only thestrical dancing is designed to provide the observer with an aesthetic experience." (*Ibid.*, p. 82). This is true. But it is also true that some social dances do give aesthetic enjoyment to the observer and so qualify as art; irrespective of the purpose for which they were designed. Many folk dances are among the most outstanding examples of nontheatrical dances that rise to the level of—some to the level of great—art.

3. In another sense a performance is, roughly, the production of sequences of expressive or meaningful musical tones or other sounds, and does not include the motions or movements that performers and instruments go though in the production of these sounds.

4. "The Dynamic Image: Some Philosophical Reflections on Dance," in Lee Jacobus, *op. cit.*, p. 78. Italics in original.

5. *Ibid.*

6. *Ibid.*

7. Note how she shifts here from her earlier categorical statement that you do not see "what is physical before you," to the more defensible—or less indefensible—view that "what we see *most directly and convincingly*" are "forces created for our perception." Note, however, that she has inadvertently shifted one (the physical) term of the contrast she has been making from the physical movements of the dancers ("people running around or twisting their bodies") to "the physical forces of the dancer's muscles," which is a different thing. (See also *Ibid.*, p. 78.) A dance on the ordinary view is not, even partly, the physical forces of the dancer's muscles, or even the flexing and unflexing or these muscles as the dancers run around, twist, leap, etc., which can be sometimes perceived by an attentive spectator sitting near the footlights, but the movements resulting from these muscular contractions and the forces they generate.

8. *Op. cit.*, p. 78.

9. For my own general critique of the idealist position, and especially for an explication of the ordinary conception of a work of art, see *The Concept of Art*, Chapter 1. See also "The Identity of a Work of Music" I and II, in this volume, for a specific discussion of the nature of music and the plastic arts, respectively.

10. See my "On Professor Lafferty's 'The Metaphysical Status of Qualities'," *The*

Journal of Philosophy. Vol. LV, No. 10 (May 8, 1958), pp. 397–412, for an attempt to show that the objective relativist cannot withstand the objections of epistemological dualism and is logically forced to embrace the latter position.

11. *Op. cit.*, p. 79.

12. *Ibid.*

13. Lee Jacobus, *op. cit.*, p. 83. Actually, she defines a dance as movement that is both rhythmic and expressive. But expressiveness—possession of *positive* aesthetic qualities—is a quality of good as opposed to poor dances. It is not a quality of all dances, irrespective of their aesthetic quality or worth.

14. See *The Concept of Art* (New York University Press, New York, 1971), Chapter 1.

15. In this sense alone there can be tragedy without character, in the sense of "characterization by action," in the usual meaning of "action." But this is emphatically not what Aristotle had in mind in maintaining that there can be tragedy without character, since he also held that there cannot be tragedy without action.

16. But in such sentences as "President Nixon acted hastily (or illegally) in sending troops into Cambodia" or "President Nixon's decisions regarding the Viatnam War and other actions were justified," "action" is used to refer to something nonphysical, though (1) only in an extended use of "action," and (2) not meaning any mental activity and/or the physical activity of talking as opposed to what he said.

17. *Thought and Action* (Chatto and Windus Ltd, London, 1969), p. 94.

18. Cf. Hampshire, *op. cit.*, p. 119. Cf. also the central position which P.F. Strawson assigns to the concept of action, in his delineation of the concept of a person. (*Individuals*, p. 111 f.)

19. Hampshire, *op. cit.*, p. 119.

20. *Ibid.*

21. For an analysis of the sense of "represent" involved, see Section III.

22. *Ibid.* Cf. "an action is an attempt, ... a trying, to achieve some result...." (*Ibid.*, p. 131)

23. *Perspectives on Drama*, J.L. Calderwood and H.E. Toliver, eds. (Oxford University Press, New York, 1968), pp. 284–297.

24. *Ibid.*, p. 285.

25. *Ibid.*

26. *Ibid.*

27. *Ibid.*, p. 286. What is represented here is clearly used in the way I used it earlier; where 'what is represented by the movements in, say, a narrative dance' referred precisely to the plot. However, "the representation" too may also mean what is represented; though it is better to limit it to what Olson means by it.

28. *Ibid.*, p. 286.

29. *Ibid.*, p. 285.

30. *Ibid.*, P. 89.

31. *Ibid.*

32. *Ibid.*

33. I have discussed these two types of signs in "Words, Signs, Signals, and Symbols," *The Philosophical Forum*, Vol. 1, No. 4 (New Series), (Summer 1969), pp. 493–508.

34. The latter are movements that have only causes, not reasons.

35. I ignore the confusions in his account, which I have touched on in *The Concept of Art*, Chapter 8.

36. (a) and (b) together constitute what we call the meaning of the dance.

37. See also *The Concept of Art*, Chapter 3, for an explication of this notion.

Chapter 6

Film As Art

I

Introductory Remarks

This essay is a first venture into the aesthetic of the film. It proposes to explore briefly the nature of film as an artform, as opposed to film as the product of a technic or craft aiming at a variety of practical goals: e.g., imparting information to the viewer by presenting slices of social or personal life, nature, and the like; moral and religious instruction or edification; political and military propaganda; education of the general public or a particular segment of it, such as the young; and last but not least—that most ubiquitous of all the aims of the film making industry—affording relaxation, pastime and entertainment to the populace. Films share these and like goals with television programs in general. Of course, an increasing segment of television programs in this country and elsewhere consist of short of feature films, as well as prefilmed and prerecorded soap operas, variety shows, spectaculars, and so on.

In view of the aim of this essay, it is essential for us (A) to attempt to clarify in the following sections the distinction between the concept of film as art and the concept of film as mere craft or technic, hence between films that are examples of cinematographic art and films that serve nonaesthetic goals alone. This involves (B) ascertaining whether the generic concept of film (or *G-film*) is an open textured concept, and whether the concept *art-film* (*A-film*) is (1) an open textured, and (2) a family resemblance concept. Comparing film and architecture, another major art form that frequently caters to various practical human concerns, which is also functional, the concept *G-film* obviously corresponds to *architecture*$_1$, while concept *A-film* corresponds to *architecture*$_2$ in my notation in "Architecture As Art." It should be noted that films which do not merit the honorific name "art film" are not members of a *second species* or *subclass* of G-film, film-as-sheer-entertainment, etc., logically on par with "A-film." Films of that sort are simply members of the class of G-films which are, as a matter of fact and not logically, excluded from the subclass of A-films, because they contingently lack certain features or because they possess certain other features. (Diagram 1.) The same is true, *mutatis mutandis*, of architecture.

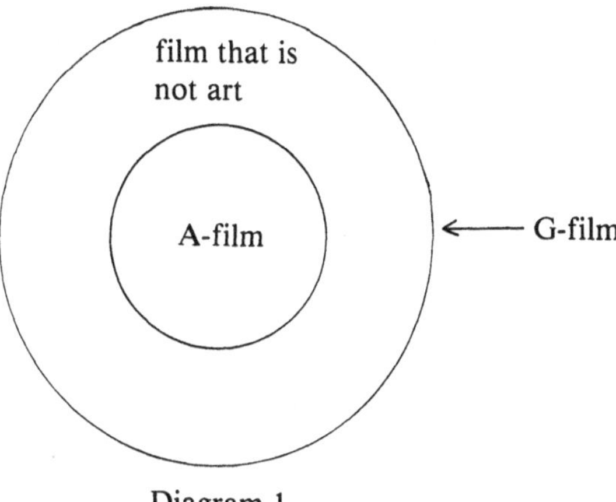

Diagram 1

Leaving aside certain qualifications or controversial matters,[1] a film may generally satisfy one or more of the usual practical functions of a G-film—even satisfy them in a high degree—and be a work of art as well, or vice versa. For instance, a fair number of the documentaries, horror films, comedies and cartoons that are on the market are also cinematographic art; or many (i.e., narrative as opposed to non-objective) art-films have considerable social, political, moral or religious, or other kinds of "human" significance. Indeed, it is difficult for narrative art-films to be otherwise.

(C) In addition to (A) and (B), and essentially connected with them, we must endeavor to ascertain the conditions and criteria of film art; consequently the conditions and criteria of artistic excellence in film. (Cf. "Architecture As Art.")

Finally, I shall analyse in general terms (D) the basic components of G-films and especially A-films as multimedia products. I shall also touch on the related question of the most desirable or optimum relation between film as art and the other visual or auditory arts that often contribute to the visual or the complex visual and auditory product we call a film. But in the main, I shall do so negatively, by considering some actual or possible misconceptions of film art, including misconceptions regarding its proper relation to other arts.

II

G-Films and A-Films

A little reflection shows, I think, that the concept of a G-film is a closed concept. The phrase "motion pictures," which well describes or defines "(G-) film," shows this, since it states the necessary and sufficient conditions of a G-film. Anything which is a motion picture is a (G-) film by the conventional meaning of "(G-) film," and anything which is not a moving picture—including a group of still photographs connected by a common theme or subject matter—cannot be so. In order to include nonobjective film, and so to be completely general, the word "picture" must be understood in the sense of "(visual) image," not necessarily in the sense of a visual form that represents, even if only remotely, some objective reality. This is not a strained use of "picture." For example, we refer to nonobjective paintings as pictures. (Cf. the locutions "the pictures of Jackson Pollock" or "the pictures of Arshile Gorky (Klee, Mondrian, Kandinsky, etc.).") We can describe a G-film more directly and completely by saying that it is a succession of images taken by a movie camera and projected on a screen or some other surface at certain definite speeds (normally, 24 frames per second).

The fact that a film is (a) *a series of pictures or images projected on a screen*, distinguishes it from all the other arts and technics in existence, with the exception of slide projection. On the other hand, (b) the fact that a film is a succession of *moving* pictures or images distinguishes it from slide projection as well. By "a succession of *moving* pictures . . ." I mean, more precisely, a succession of qualitatively similar or different images, perceived by the viewer as a motion or a series of motions of parts or the whole of the visual forms constitution these images. In the case of narrative or "representational" films, where the visual patterns are understood as representations of sensible things, we perceive the qualitative changes (though a simple unconscious mental "interpretation" that eventually becomes part and parcel of what we see) as the spatial movement of these represented objects, persons, and the like.

Thus two different generic features distinguish film from different arts, or from other groups of art. Neither of these features is sufficient to distinguish it from all the other arts and arts/crafts.

The conjunction of visual imagery and motion provides the necessary basis for a film's actual properties. Consequently A-film, as a species of G-film, has at its disposal these very same resources, hence the kinds of qualities they make possible. The *visual* medium gives an A-film certain nonsensuous or ideal potentialities and ranges of possible nonsensuous qualities. Some of these are in common with the ideal potentialities and ranges of qualities possessed by the other visual arts, in particular, photography and painting, which are the closest members of the immediate family of art-forms to which film belongs. But as an auditory as well as a dynamic visual art form, film also belongs to the family of art forms of which literature, theater and music are the chief members. As with these other arts, the auditory media of film provide it with further "expressive" resources and possible ranges of N- and A-qualities, both sensuous and ideal.

Although art-films theoretically share with all other films the technical, sensuous and ideal resources of the film medium in general, a film must clearly utilize these resources more fully or completely, hence more skillfully and with greater sensitivity, and use them for the specifically aesthetic purposes of film as art, in order to rise to the level of film art. The qualities which distinguish art-films from other films are the specifically aesthetic features of A-film, those qualities which make it a work of art. (The same applies, though to a lesser extent, to an *artistic* film; i.e., a film that possesses some but not enough aesthetic merit to deserve full-fledged membership in the class of A-films.)

The general view underlying the preceding is that a film, albeit a multimedia art, "is" primarily a visual art; that auditory qualities (dialogue, music and sound effects) "are" ancillary to the visual qualities. This view will be discussed in the next section. I should, however, point out one thing it entails and something else that it does not entail. It entails that films that exploit in a high degree the visual resources of the camera and the arts of the actor, the film director and the film editor, would be what I shall call *cinematographic art*. And the greatest cinematiographic art would be those films that stretch to the limit or almost to the limit the visual resources of a film. But it does not entail that no film can be art *on other grounds*; i.e., by exploiting the *nonvisual* resources of film, e.g., if it is highly expressive and humanly significant because of its "literary" or "theatrical" qualities.[2] Some films based on or adapted from good or great fiction, such as *Dr. Zhivago*, *One Day in the Life of Ivan Denisovitch*, and *Look Back in Anger*, are, I think, good examples of this. Many of the artistically satisfying films we have are of this type: indeed, it is perhaps not an exaggeration to say that they constitute the bulk of aesthetically satisfying films. But they are not, I think, the films we usually call "artistic." The phrase "artistic film" appears to be more or less confined to works that are visually—or both visually and aurally,[3] but especially visually—satisfying in high degree; likewise with the terms "art-film" and "film as art." (The word "artistic" in the latter, relatively narrow sense is cognate with the word "art" as it is commonly used to refer to the visual arts of painting and sculpture, particularly the former, as opposed to its general use to refer to *all* the art-forms and their products.) In other words, there is an important difference between a film's being *a work of art in general* and its being *cinematographic, especially great cinematiographic, art.* The terms "art-film" ("A-film") and "film art," as I use them in this essay, are intended to cover *both* types of artistically successful films.

The same basic distinction obtains in the case of all the other art forms, both "functional" and "nonfunctional." Later in this volume I shall mark this distinction in relation to sculpture, a propos of Herbert Read's claim regarding the primacy of the tactile qualities of sculpture, hence the tactile sensations it can arouse.[4]

If Read is right, the greatest sculpture, *qua* sculpture (or as "sculptural art") consists of those artifacts that chiefly exploit, in the highest degree and in the most skillful and effective manner, the tactile resources of its three-dimensional medium; and a "painterly" sculpture cannot be great sculptural art. Even so, Read is confused insofar as he appears to infer from this that painterly sculpture cannot be great art, *simpliciter*. (Similarly, Rudolf Arnheim's failure to appreciate the artistic potentialities of sound film is at least partly due to his failure to draw or perceive the parallel distinction in the case of film. See Section IV.) A sculpture can be great art without being a great sculpture, in the sense of great sculptural art; similarly with a poem, a novel, a symphony or a film.

The perfectly literal "temporal" or "dynamic" character of film allies G-film with the arts of literature, music and dance, and separates it from the "non temporal" or "static" arts of painting, sculpture and architecture, among others. There are, of course, other senses in which paintings, sculptures and works of architecture, in common with such things as poems, symphonies and films, may be dynamic or have temporal characteristics. With regard to these particular characteristics, the differences between the so-called temporal and non temporal arts are immaterial. For example, Degas' celebrated ballet dancers, Giacometti's "Falling Man" or Brancusi's "Bird in Space" are as highly dynamic or convey as strong a sense of physical movement as some frames in films by a Bergman, a Truffaut, a Godard or a Fellini. And the sense of *temporal flow* can be conveyed by still photographs, paintings and other kinds of visual art no less than works of literature of music. The opposite is also true. Parts of Wordsworth's "Lines Written Above Tintern Abbey" or Wagner's "Siegfried Idyll" give me, and probably others too, a profound sense of timelessness, of time's cessation and in that sense, of eternity and immutability, together with a feeling of perfect stillness and tranquillity, just as much as, say, an Egyptian statue of the third millenium B.C., The Great Sphinx, or the Pyramids at Giza. It is one of the main failings of Lessing's *Laocöon* that it has no adequate room for these facts, as a result of its author's simplistic supposition that what a work of literature (or music) on the one hand, and a painting or sculpture on the other hand, allegedly can or cannot "express" (hence also, what it does or does not merely "suggest"), simply depends on the fact that sounds and words exist in time while colors, forms and masses occupy space. If Lessing were right, film could "express" action *only* by virtue of the *succession* of its images on the screen; while it could represent (as opposed to merely "suggesting") visible objects only by virtue of its utilization of (spatial) images.

In contrast to the concept of a G-film in general, the concept of an A-film is open textured. For as we shall presently see, the line between (a) the concept of film as art and (b) the concept of a G-film, and even the line between (c) an art-film and (d) a merely artistic film, is far from sharp. In addition, and intimately connected with its "open" character, the concept of film as art is a "family resemblance" concept, in the sense that there are no logically necessary and sufficient conditions for its correct application. This will be seen in Section III, after we consider the conditions of an art-film.

Before we turn our attention to these conditions of art-film, we should note that there is only *one* ordinary use of "film," hence of "(A-) film," in contrast to the uses of the other visual art-names; e.g., "photograph," "painting," "sculpture" and "architecture."[5] That is, the term is used to refer exclusively to the images or visual patterns projected on a screen, the words, musical tones and sound effects of sound-films, and the expressive and symbolic qualities of, hence the ideas and meanings conveyed by, the visual and auditory elements in question. In this sense a film *is* an "apparition," "appearance" or "virtual image," in Susanne Langer's use of these words; i.e., a purely perceptual phenomenon. In the case of photographs, paintings and sculpture, this corresponds to the use of these words to refer to the visual forms and designs, colors, visual and tactile textures and other sensuous features and relationships perceived, under normal perceptual conditions, on a painted surface; likewise, *mutatis mutandis*, with architecture and the dance.[6] The reason for this difference between the uses of "film" on the one hand and "photography," "painting," "sculpture," etc. on the other, is that there is no palpable medium utilized by a film. For example, the screen on which the images are projected is not part of the film itself, or its medium. Nor is the celluloid film strip the medium of a film as a *perceptual phenomenon*; though it is indispensable for the existence of what we call ordinarily the film, and though the film editor works with it in editing the strip for viewing. I italicize "perceptual phenomenon" because, in the ordinary uses of "art," a work of art must be at least partly sensible. *Consequently*, a film must be at least partly sensible. The succession of images projected on a screen is obviously different from the surface, e.g., the photographic paper, on which a still photograph is printed, or the canvas on which the colors and forms of a painting are painted. Hence in *another* common use of "photograph." a photograph is a printed picture (taken by a camera), and a painting is a painted canvas (wall, wood, or some other surface). In either case we have a tangible object or artifact possessing weight and size, something which can be moved around, hung on walls, and even mutilated or destroyed. Likewise with a sculpture and, with certain differences, a building, a bridge or an arch.

I now turn to the conditions for a film's being an art film, an A-film. Thus (1) one condition of an A-film is formal beauty, satisfying formal composition and design of the images in the individual frames, and, especially, in the successive frames in each scene—ideally, in the entire film. In the case of narrative films the organization of the action, dialogue, music and sound effects, and other structural elements, constitutes a further part of the formal condition. A second main condition is (2) the "expressiveness" of the individual shots, the sequence of shots in each scene, and the entire set or sequence of scenes which constitutes the film as a putative unified whole. (3) The aesthetic and the human significance of the action and the characters depicted, the dialogue, the ideas stated or implied, and the situations portrayed, constitutes a further condition of film art; paralleling the analogous conditions in the case of architecture$_2$.[7] Further, (3) the notion of human purposes, including the notion of practical use or function, applies, *mutatis mutandis*, to film as art. Consequently, I tend to believe that (4) the fitness or appropriateness of a film's form and content, including its "expressive" qualities and its human significance, if any, to its actual or intended human purposes, constitutes an additional condition of A-film.

I shall now say a few words about these four conditions, mostly about (1) and (4), as they apply specifically to A-films. This is intended merely to supplement the general remarks I made about them in "Architecture As Art."

In the case of film, the sensuous *formal* qualities are generally both visual and auditory: they pertain to the sensuous components of the spoken words in a sound-film as well as to the music and sound effects in the soundtrack. In the cases of a silent film, the subtitles, since they consist of words, possess mental "auditory" associations by virtue of the sounds conventionally associated with them: we mentally "hear" the words in addition to seeing them as certain visual shapes, and understanding their meaning, if we do. Although this is not true of the silent films I am familiar with, such as the celebrated silent films of Chaplin, Griffith, Eisenstein, Dreyer, and others, the visual shapes that constitute the subtitles, and their spatial deployment on the screen—if imaginatively done—can also add a pleasing and meaningful visual dimension to the visual qualities of the pictures themselves and their cinematographic treatment. This can also be done in dubbed sound-films. The imaginative visual use of words—with all the resources of different types of lettering and calligraphy available at present—has of course become commonplace on commercial television in the United States and elsewhere, as well as in print journalism. In concrete poetry and in such prose works as James Joyce's *Ulysses*, we find the most notable counterparts, in literature, of the visual exploitation of language.

The verbal element is normally absent from nonobjective films; though there is nothing to prevent the addition of a verbal element, say spoken poetry, to the completely abstract visual patterns on the screen. An important auditory element, in the form of synchronized music, is a common feature of such films. To the extent that both auditory and visual elements are employed in a film, the harmony of the two types of elements is essential to the artistic quality of the film's "form" or structure. It is clear that I am using "form" in an inclusive sense here and elsewhere in this essay. Form encompasses a veriety of auditory-*cum*-visual qualities (as well as the ideal organization of the work's nonsenuous aspects, whenever present) not merely the visual organization or the visual and auditory organization separately.

The organization of the action of a narrative film, together with the organization of the ideas and imagery contained in it and the emotional states portrayed and/or evoked in the viewers, need no special discussion here. Suffice it to note that the multi media character of film both gives it a greater possible range of N- and A-features than single-medium arts, and makes it more difficult to organize its diverse aspects or components into harmonious wholes. Later, We shall have to say something about the dynamic tension between film as visual image and the aural—particularly the speech—components of film. Whenever the feat of perfect or near-perfect fusion of all media and materials is achieved, the impact is proportionately greater than in single-medium arts, other things being equal. For it must be added that the latter—and also a silent film—at its best, can possess a degree of concentration that makes its impact quite comparable to that of a very powerful sound film, an opera, a play or a work of choral music. But as we all know, concentration and unity can be easily bought at the expense of variety and interest; and so the Greek ideal of unity in variety is an indispensable canon of film art.

Turning to condition (4), it may be noted that the basis of this condition is the fact that a G-film is a useful or practical device; that it is intended to serve various human purposes, though different from those that architecture and the other "functional" arts are normally intended to serve. The former are the purposes of G-film I noted at the beginning of this chapter: instruction, moral and religious guidance, entertainment, etc. These are not, as such, the *aesthetic* aims of film as art, or A-films. Nevertheless, I am inclined to believe that a G-film that has one or more of these purposes can go some way toward becoming film art if its formal—and I may add, material—qualities reflect, manifest or embody these purposes. For example, if a documentary film intended for the instruction of children presents its material in an imaginative or original, hence interesting and pleasing way, conducive to its instructional goal. However, the aesthetic aims and the extra-aesthetic human purposes of a film sometimes actually clash as they not infrequently do in the case of architecture and the other functional arts. When they do, either art or utility suffers.

One the other hand, a G-film can be an A-film without having any human purposes in the sense described;[8] such that no question of its form (or content) "following" its human purposes arises. Nonobjective films in general are the clearest though not the only examples; though some such films may be intended to instruct and/or entertain.

My earlier remarks about the complex formal qualities of an A-film also apply to its expressive qualities and human significance, hence also to the mutual fitness of its formal and contentual qualities. This reflects the logical harmony of conditions (1)–(3) on the one hand and the condition that, in order to be *film* art, a film should satisfy the human purposes for which it is intended.

I stated that a film is commonly a complex product consisting of sensuous and ideal elements—ideas, mental images and associations, and psychological experiences or states forming part of the film. It is important to remember that this is true of A-films, not just of films that lack the good-making qualities of an A-film. For it does *not* follow from the fact that a G-film may be a complex of visual, auditory and ideal components that an *art film* is or can be so. It is logically conceivable that an A-film is only—can only be—, say, a visual-*cum*-ideal phenomenon. In other words, it is conceivable that, by the way in which we apply the terms "art"and "work of art" (or even perhaps, the word "artistic") to certain G-films, all but visual, or visual-*cum*-ideal components or aspects of a film are necessarily "nonaesthetic" features; that auditory qualities cannot, strictly, form part of it as a work of art, as an "aesthetic object." (Compare and contrast the formalist thesis regarding the representational or descriptive components of representational visual art, or the Croce Collingwood thesis regarding all the sensuous qualities of paintings, sculptures, music, literature, etc.) This is why Rudolf Arnheim's theses that film is primarily a visual art[9] is perfectly consistent with a G-film's being an auditory-*cum*-ideal as well as a visual medium. Indeed, since by "primarily visual art" Arnheim means "primarily visual-*cum*-ideal art,"[10] I am in full agreement with his view, as will be seen in Section III.

A-Film: A "Family Resemblance" Concept

If I am right in my contention that an A-film is a G-film that satisfies, especially in a high degree one or more (ideally, all) of the four conditions of film art, it follows that the concept of an A-film is a "family resemblance" or cluster concept. For in the first place, none of these conditions by itself appears to be logically *necessary* for a film's being an A-film. A film can be an A-film even if it fails to satisfy any one, perhaps even any two of them; provided that it does satisfy some or all of the other conditions. Consequently, although the satisfaction of all four conditions (especially their satisfaction in a high degree) is more than sufficient to make a G-film an A-film, the satisfaction of even two—nay, perhaps even one—of them in a very prominent way may suffice for this. For example, a film may be an A-film on the strength of its formal grounds alone.[11] For example, *Elvira Madigan* can be classed as an A-film solely on the strength of its strikingly visual beauty; apart fıom, e.g., its nonsensuous A-features and its human significance as a tragic-romantic love story. On the other hand, *Wild Strawberries* would qualify as an A-film of very high quality on the strength of its expressiveness and human significance, quite apart from its cinematographic qualities. The same is true of another Bergman masterpiece, *The Seventh Seal*, which is also cinematographic art of very high quality. The moral is that there is *no absolutely fixed number or subset* of conditions which are jointly *sufficient* for the application of the concept *A-film* to a G-film. Different G-films may be A-films by virtue of satisfying different, or different combinations of some or all of the four conditions. Further, there is no fixed degree or range of degrees in which any one of the four conditions must be satisfied so that the concept *A-film* may properly apply to a G-film.

In order to see better how the absence of logically necessary conditions and the absence of a fixed set (or set of sets) of sufficient conditions positively means that the concept of an A-film is a cluster concept, we must see what the foregoing means in terms of an A-film's N- and A-features. What it does mean, it seems to me, is that an indefinite number of different (including overlapping) sets of N- and hence A-features constitute actual sufficient criteria-features of an A-film, that a film's satisfaction of any one or more of these disjunctive sets may be sufficient for the application of the concept *A-film* to a G-film. The N- and A-features in question may be formal or material, visual or auditory or both (in the latter two cases, they may be verbal or nonverbal, e.g., "pure" music), intellectual, imaginative or emotional, and so on. Indeed, the situation here exactly parallels the scheme Helen Knight provides for the use of "good X" in such sentences as "This is a good tennis match," "This is a good painting," and so on.[12] For example, she says à propos of tennis matches, which she takes as one of her paradigms in analysing the present type of use of "good": "We sometimes get one set of criteria, sometimes another; and the sets overlap, providing a number of different combinations."[13] Again: "On different occasions, . . . we judge by different criteria . . . ."[14]

The essential similarity between the use of "good X" and "A-film" is not surprising, in the light of the evaluative (honorific) use of "A-film." For the counterpart of, say, (1) "Fellini's *8½* is an A-film," in the case of the "nonfunctional" arts of painting, music, sculpture, etc., is not, e.g., (2) "Da Vinci's "The Virgin of the Rocks" (Louvre) is a painting" or "John Updike's *Centaur* is a novel," and so on, where "painting" and "novel" are used in the descriptive sense, but (3) "Da Vinci's 'The Virgin of the Rocks' (Louvre) is a good (excellent, great, etc.) painting" or "join Updike's *Centaur* is a fine novel." Thus "A-film" corresponds to "painting," "novel," "music," etc. in the evaluative (honorific) use of these words.

If this is true, it follows that what I have said about the use of "good X" in my writings elsewhere,[15] as well as what Helen Knight says about it, applies, *mutatis mutandis*, to the concept of A-film. (By the same token, these things also apply to "architecture" and to "ceramics," "rug," "tapestry," "jewelry," etc.—or the concepts these words convey—whenever they are used to praise buildings, vases, rugs, rings, and so on as fine art and not merely classify them as certain kinds of artifacts.)

But what about the concept *cinematographic art*, it may be inquired. Is it not an "essentially" defined, and so, a closed concept? My reply is that it is also an open concept, though considerably less so than the concept of an A-film *qua* art *simpliciter*. The reason is quite obvious, since, by definition, cinematographic art is film that excels primarily or even wholly in cinematographic qualities. (The latter usually happens in the case of mute nonobjective A-films.) In either case the concept is open; since borderline cases of cinematographic art are always in principle possible—basically for the same reasons noted with regard to the concept of A-films that are art *simpliciter*. The concept is also a cluster concept: and for the same reason(s), *mutatis mutandis*, as in the latter case.

III

Film As Primarily a Visual Art

Earlier, I indicated my agreement with Arnheim's view in *Film As Art* that film is primarily a visual art; or more precisely, I hold that in order to be art, film *should become*, as completely as possible, a technic that exploits for artistic purposes the visual properties or potentialities of its medium. Another way of putting the matter is that the best art films, *qua film art* (as opposed to simply excellent art, *simpliciter*) are those that excel most in their visual qualities. This conception animates the more specific views expressed in this essay as a whole; and the various actual or possible practices I shall label misconceptions of the nature of film art, to be discussed in the next section, are negative corollaries of it. The present view, together with some of its implications to be discussed a little later, is clearly expressed by Paul Rotha. He says:

> It is essential, in the first place, to assert that film is an independent form of expression, drawing inspiration with reservation from the other arts. Furthermore . . . the attributes of the film are derived from the nature of the medium itself, and not from other matters of subject, story-interest, and propaganda. It should be remembered that the film is essentially *visual* in its appeal; and that light and movement are the two elements employed in the creation of these visual images. As I shall demonstrate later, the abstraction of the 'absolute' film is the nearest approach to the purest form of cinema' . . . .[16]

Again, the Czechoslovak film director Jan Nẽmec writes:

> I regard most of the films made up to now merely as reproduction art. Stories and fact are captured, and the film shows them in a way which would be just as successful in the theater or in literature. But a pure film—which I should like to achieve—should be interpretable in itself: it should have its own esthetics and poetry.[17]

Although Arnheim and Rotha (but not Nẽmec) talk in the "descriptive mode" instead of the "evaluative mode" about the nature of film as art, just as I myself sometimes do in this essay, we must constantly bear in mind that what they (and I) propose is an *evaluative concept or conception* of film art. If my earlier analysis of the concept of A-film *vis-à-vis* G-film is correct, this is in the nature of the case, and is clearly reflected in the normative character of the four conditions of A-film outlined in Section II. (Indeed, the same is true of the concepts of architecture, ceramics, rugs and tapestry, jewelry, metal work and leather work, etc., as art, as distinguished from mere crafts or technics.) Consequently the preceding concept(ion) of film art is "essentially contested" in W.B. Gallie's sense of the phrase, i.e., is contestable in principle.[19] The same is true of all rival concept(ion)s of film art that have been or may be proposed, in lieu of the present concept(ion), by filmmakers, critics or aestheticians. The multimedia character of a film encourages (though it is not a logically necessary condition of the existence of) a multiplicity of alternative concept(ion)s. A relatively small number of rival conceptions is also possible in the case of architecture, ceramics, rug weaving, jewelry making and other arts/crafts. The theoretical disagreement is particularly evident in the case of architecture). But some rival concept(ion)s are more worthy of serious consideration than others. Such is the view that an A-film is a multimedia art in which *all* the different media involved—literary and theatrical, photographic, musical, etc.—ought to play as equal a role as possible, with no one medium or type of medium dominating the others. On the other hand, one can easily rule out the hypothetical claim that the projected images are ancillary to the sound track. An appropriate sequence of visual images accompanying a serious work of music can be, of course, good multimedia art. But I do not think that we would normally call it a film or film art, unless the visual images have substance and wholeness in their own right, especially aesthetically speaking.

The essential contestedness of any concept(ion) of film art may be exemplified on two main levels: (1) one may contest the four putative *conditions* of film art I proposed in Section II, as demarcating the concept of A-film *vis-à-vis* a G-film: consequently, the putative *criteria* for the application of the concept *A-film* to (some) films. On a still more fundamental level, (2) one may contest a particular ranking of the possible visual N- and A-features—and the ideal N- and the ideal N- and A-features—of a film *vis-à-vis* its possible nonvisual sensuous qualities—and the ideal N- and A-features made possible by the nonvisual sensuous qualities—with regard to importance as potential good- or poor-making qualities of an A-film. It is clear that contesting (1) logically effects (2); for one may contest (1) in either of three ways. One may either (a) reject one or more of the four putative conditions, or (b) contest their proposed ranking, or (c) propose additional conditions. For example, a Formalist would do the first—and so the second, as a consequence. The elimination, promotion or demotion of one or more of these conditions clearly affects, logically speaking, the ranking of the N- and A-features of the particular kind. Thus the elimination of all but the formal and (formal) expressive conditions of film would eliminate all but formal sensuous and ideal N- and A-features from the ranks of criteria features of film art and consequently raise these formal features to a position of unchallenged preeminence.

On the other hand, one can consistently contest (2) without also contesting (1) above.

The essential contestedness of the concept of an A-film, in any of the aforementioned ways, or in other possible ways, is not necessarily a bad thing—quite the contrary. The challenging of any given concept(ion) of film art—such as the one Arnheim and Rotha propose—by creative film makers, film critics and the discriminating lay viewers, can be quite salutary. For one thing, it can stimulate experimentation by good film makers in their constant quest to find, in each of their films and in A-film as a whole, what they think are the happiest, aesthetically optimum interrelations of the different media, and of the film's various facets. Since the optimum interrelations are a holistic, "contextual" matter, determined by the individual film as a whole, and so never exactly the same in any two films, this makes the film makers' task more difficult, but also more interesting and creative. The competing concept(ion)s may also have the salutary effect of constantly testing the limits of the film as an artistic medium, and of constantly probing and redefining its artistic relations to the other arts. In these and like ways they can nurture the creative spark in the art of film.

In its possible salutary effects, the contesting of any given concept(ion) of A-film is similar to the contesting of any current concept(ion) of art as a whole, such as Expressionism, Organicism or Formalism.[20] In this respect the alternative concept(ion)s of A-film are analogous to the various "honorific redefinitions" of the concept of art, which Morris Weitz describes in "The Role of Theory in Aesthetics." Compare what he says about the latter:

> But what makes them—these honorific definitions—so supremely valuable . . . is the *debates* over the reasons for changing the criteria [and we should add, the conditions] of the concept of art which are built into the definitions. In each of the great theories of art, . . . what is of the utmost importance are the reasons proffered in the argument for the respective theory, that is, the reasons given for the chosen or preferred criteria of excellence and evaluation. . . . The value of each of the theories resides in its attempt to

> state and to justify certain criteria which are either neglected or distorted by previous theories. Look at the Bell-Fry theory. . . . Of course, "Art is significant form" cannot be accepted as a true, real definition of art; and most certainly it actually functions in their esthetics as a redefinition of art in terms of the chosen condition of significant form. But what gives it its esthetic importance is what lies behind the formula: In an age in which literary and representational elements have become paramount in painting, *return* to the plastic ones since these are indigenous to painting. Thus, the role of the theory is . . . to pin-point a crucial recommendation to turn our attention once again to the plastic elements in painting.[21]

Although everything or practically everything in this passage applies, *mutatis mutandis*, to A-film, part of the penultimate sentence in it (by the substitution of "film" for "painting") sums up especially well the fundamental recommendation of this essay; viz. "In an age in which literary and representational elements have become paramount in film, *return* to the plastic ones since those are indigenous to film."

IV

Film and the Other Arts

Writers on film, including Arnheim, have frequently cautioned against the mechanical, unimaginative reproduction or attempts at reproduction of objective reality in films purporting to be art. Since the principles underlying this sound injunction are the same with respect to all the arts, I shall not concern myself with it. But I shall consider a logically unrelated though equally sound prescription; namely, that a film aiming to be art should not imitate any other art or arts. I mean that a film should not attempt to reproduce (with the absolutely minimum inevitable changes required by the nature of the new medium) either the forms or the contents of works of fiction, operas, ballets, plays, and so on *without regard to whether the extremely close reproduction of the "original" makes good cinematographic sense.* In other words, any film that purports to be art must not slavishly reproduce another work of art, simply for the sake of reproducing it: taking fidelity of reproduction as a desirable aesthetic goal. For in actual fact, film makers are constantly tempted, and often succumb to the temptation, to imitate other arts: not just in sensory, imaginative and emotional effects, which is unobjectionable as far as it goes,[22] but also in technical devices, in the media and the forms utilized, and in the content or "message" conveyed. The latter are full of pitfalls, and sometimes seriously damaging to film art. A well-nigh endless stream of commercial Hollywood and Hollywood-type European films, going back to the beginnings of moving pictures, illustrates this. The art form which the film maker must be most careful not to imitate is, in my opinion, literature, and specifically fiction. It must also carefully avoid imitating theatrical productions. The imitation can take a number of distinguishable forms, all amply illustrated by many films that fail to be art as well as by some that succeed in being art in spite of these failings.

(1) One such form concerns the widespread adaptation of literature for the cinema, or the basing of film on a literary work. The imitation involved here goes logically hand in hand with a type of implicit or explicit *evaluation* of films *vis-à-vis* literature. That is, adapted films or, to a lesser extent, films based on a literary work, are quite frequently evaluated by the general public and even by some writers whose works have been adapted for the cinema,[23] on the strength of their "faithfulness" to the "original," with respect to plot and characterization if not also dialogue, without particular regard to whether the film medium (a) readily permits such "fidelity," or the extreme fidelity required, or even whether such fidelity is (b) desirable in a film in general or in the films in question. Correlative with the ignoring of (a), people tend to ignore the question of whether the films in question (c) do or do not exploit the peculiar, or even characteristic, resources of the film medium. Fidelity to the original is apparently widely regarded by the general public as an essential condition of an "adapted" film's aesthetic worth. The disconcerting presupposition of this view is that a film is (or rather, ought to be) mainly a means of recording and widely disseminating or "communicating" (in a pleasing way) subjects or themes that can be depicted just as effectively and as pleasurably as any other art form. The idea is therefore that "the medium is not—even part of—the message." Like the present writer, the reader may have frequently heard people disparaging such films as *Crime and Punishment*, *The Brothers Karamazov* or *One Day in the Life of Ivan Denisovitch*, to mention just a few examples, not for their genuine shortcomings as putative cinematographic art but for the spurious reason that they "fall short" of the novels on which they are based; meaning that they are criticized for not producing the *same* or a *very similar* effect on the viewer as the novels have, or are supposed to have, on the reader; for changes in the story and the characterization if not also the dialogue; or for leaving out or adding certain passages, scenes, characters, dialogue, and the like. In the case of films based on Dostoevsky's or other highly philosophical novels or

plays, another common criticism is that they completely leave out or are unable to handle as effectively as in the novels the philosophical and religious ideas or the existential agonies and conflicts of the major characters. In this last case, they wrongly attribute to the particular films what may well be limitations inherent in the visual medium of film itself, especially *vis-à-vis* the medium of language and the native forms of the novel, the play and the short story. Since the visual medium of film in its *pure form* can present the "inner life," including thoughts, only through their usual or unusual visual manifestations or correlatives, such as the expression on human faces, bodily gestures and movements, and the like, as well as by the use of physical surroundings that in the particular film maker's world or in the particular culture possess the appropriate meanings and connotations, a film is, paradoxically, the more limited in the present respect the "purer" it is as film. However, even so-called nonobjective films can convey personal and communal meanings, by virtue of the color schemes (including black and white) and the visual forms or designs it employs; since these are normal vehicles of ideas and meanings, outside of art as well as in it. For example, colors can function both as signs and as symbols in a work of art. The same is true of visual forms or designs. Both colors and forms can also function as signals in real life; but this is a rather unusual use of them in most art. Moreover, on those rare occasions on which they may be used in a painting, a sculpture or a work of architecture, they would generally function as cues to action for the viewer, not aesthetically. The chief exceptions occur in dramatic art, where a color or a form can function, as a signal, as part of the play's, opera's or film's imagined action, hence as "aesthetically" as any other part of the work.

We are all familiar with those pictures that are little more than recordings of celebrated operas, ballets or plays on celluloid. In some cases, the film is—and is frankly intended as—mostly a record of a stage presentation of the work. Little attempt is made to adapt the work to the film medium, to exploit its native resources. To different extents, the film *La Traviata*, *Hamlet* (Olivier's), *Sleeping Beauty* and *Swan Lake*, among others, illustrate this. To a lesser extent this is also true of Olivier's *Richard III* and the recent *Trojan Women*. In many cases what is recorded is a great work of art in its own right; but these films are for the most part convenient records of masterly performances of these works by some of the outstanding performers of the time. They make these performances available to millions of viewers, present and future, who would be otherwise deprived of the opportunity to see them. The benefits of the recording from a practical point of view as well as from the standpoint of aesthetic education, are undeniable. But these services do not amount to the creation of a new work of art.

The moral of the preceding is that the film director must make the decision as to whether the adaptation—which should be a creative act in its own right—would result in a film that is comparable in aesthetic worth to the "original." If the evidence indicates that the adaptation would probably result in an inferior film, doing so would be artistically unjustified. This is similar to the decision that a painter, poet or other artist must make—whenever a decision of this kind is involved—as to whether a particular projected work should be executed with a particular technique, use of a particular form, materials, style, and so on.

The error outlined above can be regarded as one form of a kind of conceptual error which I shall call the *genetic evaluative fallacy* (or *GEF*). The latter should be distinguished from, say, the genetic fallacy of attempting to describe or define the nature of art in general simply in terms of the way in which it is believed to have been created. I define the genetic evaluative fallacy thus. Consider a work of art WA, consisting of certain elements A, B, C, D in certain relations. The fallacy consists in evaluating WA in terms of the putative value(s) of A, B, C, D, and evaluating A, B, C, D, in turn, in terms of (i.e., as directly proportional to) their *resemblance* to or *difference* from elements A_1, B_1, C_1, D_1[24] (usually forming part of another work of art, WA_1, or other works of art, WA_2, WA_3, etc.); hence in terms of the value(s) assigned to A_1, A_2, $C_{,1}$, D_1 themselves. A variant of this error occurs when WA_1, WA_2, WA_3, etc. are works of art of a different kind from WA.

GEF is in some ways similar to, if not a special case of, a still more general error; namely, what Alfred North Whitehead calls the "fallacy of misplaced concreteness." The latter fallacy essentially consists in one's mistaking an abstraction for something concrete; hence in ascribing to it qualities of concrete existents.

The preceding shows that there is a subtle connection between imitation—and the prizing of imitation—of the two sorts outlined so far; more correctly, that there is a common erroneous assumption underlying the two. In its more moderate form, the assumption is that film is an adjunct and so ought to be subservient to the older and more established art forms. In its more extreme form, the assumption is that film cannot be an art form in its own right, possessing an individual, even unique character as an art; that the "composite" character of a film makes such individuality, and especially autonomy and uniqueness, impossible. On this latter view film is thought of as chiefly, or at best, an extremely powerful and versatile technic for the recording and transmitting of art works belonging essentially to one or another of the bona fide arts: painting, music, dance, literature and so on. Neither assumption is really surprising in view of the attitudes that have often prevailed in Europe and the United States toward photography and, later, the motion picture, since their fairly recent invention.[25]

I think it is safe to say that (a) historically, the processes or products of a medium or technic considered artistically inferior to a particular art form or group of art forms, A, B, C, tend to be regarded as artistically successful in proportion as they emulate, even imitate, the processes and products of A, B, C. Similarly, (b) history appears to show that when a particular medium or technic is regarded as inherently nonartistic—and especially if it is considered *in*artistic—people tend to suppose that, in order to put it to any artistic use, one must "fortify" or supplement it with the media or techniques or subjects of the appropriate bona fide arts; in particular the most prestigious among them. In that way, what would otherwise be a mere technical accomplishment would rise to the heights of art. Conversely, I think history shows that a medium or technic that (usually for complicated moral or religious, metaphysical, social or other extra-artistic reasons) is widely judged as inherently artistic—particularly one that is generally ranked high on the scale of "fine art"—tends to be granted considerable autonomy early in its life history. In fact, it tends to become a model or paradigm and thus a legislator for the would-be arts or the less prestigious arts. Its techniques or methods, even subjects are widely borrowed, adopted or adapted. An aspiring art/craft is supposed to become artistic or to become more artistic in proportion as it utilizes the resources or effects of such prestigious arts. But if Herbert Read is right in claiming that most pre-19th century sculpture in the West (as well as in Ancient Egypt) is not "sculptural" but "painterly,"[26] and if we agree with him that sculpture is—or rather, ought to be—primarily a tactile art, we see how such misconceptions even of the nature of a *major art form* can lead to its tutelage to some other art-form or group of art-forms.[27] Of course, the phenomenon Read describes is partly a result of the fact that, until very recently, painting overshadowed and somtimes eclipsed sculpture in the West, in putative importance as an art form.

Like (a), (b) above is amply illustrated by the history of film. It takes the form of (i) overextensive reliance on dialogue, with relatively few interludes of silence, (ii) overemphasis on physical action, and (iii) excessive use of background music or sound effects. I think the New Wave Cinema has shown Arnheim to be dead wrong with respect to his claim that "The complete visual action accompanied by occasional dialogue represents a partial parallelism, not a fusion"[28]; consequently that in the talking film, speech should accompany the film throughout its length, more or less without gaps (i.e., should be "complete"), and in that way fulfill "one of the elementary conditions for the compounding of media, namely parallelism."[29] One need only think of *L'Avventura*, *8½*, *Hiroshima Mon Amour*, *Lost Weekend*, *High Noon*, and especially *Last Year at Marienbad* and *Rashomon*, to see how effective films using speech so sparingly, in a "nonparallel" way, can be; similarly with many of Bergman's films, particularly *Wild Strawberries*, *The Silence* and *Persona*." In this last work, the silence of the emotionally disturbed actress is particularly expressive and laden with psychological and symbolic meaning. Here—as in different ways, in *Rashoman* and *Last Year at Marienbad*—the excruciatingly long silences are of the essence of the film's plot and the character of the emotionally disturbed actress. Continuous or almost continuous speech here (also in *Rashomon* and *Last Year at Marienbad*—if not also the other films I mentioned) would not be just superfluous but would almost destroy the work. The dogmatic, *a priori* reasons which Arnheim gives for his "completeness" or "parallelism" thesis, is worth noting here. He says: "A medium of expression that is capable of producing complete works by its own resources will forever keep up its resistance against any combination with another medium".[30] The reason, according to him, is that "One of the most basic artistic impulses derives from man's yearning to escape the disturbing multiplicity of nature and seeks, therefore, to depict this bewildering reality with the simplest means."[31] Again, although (iv) color (*pace* Arnheim) is an important part of the visual equipment of film as art, it is largely misused in the majority of color films with which I am familiar. At the very least, it has been often neglected as a potent source of positive aesthetic features, as an "expressive" device, both sensuous and ideal. In commercial films, especially in Hollywood, it has been mainly used to enhance the illusion of reality, though the garishness and artificality of much of the color used—particularly in Hollywood and Italian superspectacles—have the exactly opposite effect! Its worse offense, however, is that it is in such bad taste. The same is true of (v) the use of the wide screen and cinemascope, giving it considerably greater illusion of lifelikeness than in more conventional films. This is most true of the breathtakingly naturalistic cinerama. The same applies to the almost uncanny effect of so-called circlarama,[32] which involves a circular screen completely surrounding the viewer. This gives the viewer the very real sense of being an actual part of the action, moving right along with it. The sense of seeing something out there, distinct from oneself and one's immediate spatio-temporal environment (or "lived" space and time in the phenomenologist's sense), which one has even with wide screen films, is completely obliterated. Yet as Arnheim rightly notes in "A Personal Note" (1957) in *Film As Art*, with regard to the wide screen and the recent substitutes for stereoscopic film, the artistic potentialities of cinerama and circlarama remain, as far as I know, almost completely unexploited

The general presupposition underlying the preceding moves is the mistaken supposition that the specific, not just the general effects that a kind of art is capable of producing, is actually independent of or separable from the nature of the media utilized by that art from, hence by individual works of the particular kind. The same applies, *mutatis mutandis*, to the materials utilized by particular works of art, in this case particular films. Hence it is supposed that films can produce aesthetic effects only when the techniques or methods they utilize, including the techniques and methods of formal (and color?) composition, are derived from some other art—painting, fiction, music, and so on. The adoption of these methods, techniques or devices is not thought of as straining or, in extreme cases, destroying the art they are intended to serve.

The use of techniques, subjects or themes, and the like, borrowed from other arts, can be perfectly legitimate, even salutary, provided that they are properly modified and adapted—hence to begin with, are adaptable—to the *different* medium of the film or whatever the art or technic in question is, and provided that, in particular cases, only those techniques, etc., are used which harmonize with and increase the effectiveness of the work's own aesthetic qualities. Finally, this would be true provided these techniques, etc., are used to create not a melange but a unified whole. In other words, the aesthetic principle of unity, especially of organic unity, must be even more carefully observed, because of the greater difficulty of so doing, in the case of the multimedia arts of film, opera, dance and theater. Noteworthy exceptions are works in which the juxtaposition of incongruous elements or techniques, subjects, and so on is calculated to produce, say, a comic or some other special effect, or to convey a special philosophical, existential or some other idea or conception.

In the preceding discussion, I outlined some common misconceptions of film in general and A-film in particular. They are all fairly obvious errors; also, the best Western and Eastern film directors, both those on the current scene and the early pioneers of film art, have generally avoided them. But it is instructive to point them out, for a number of reasons. The most obvious and important for our purposes is that, by implication, they bring out the positive nature of film art. An important practical reason is that, unfortunately, the foregoing and similar misconceptions *are* quite common; they are reflected in much of what the film industry grinds out around the globe. This explains why the vast majority of films made since the invention of the medium are not art. The sad thing is that this is not always or perhaps mainly due to the lack of a true appreciation of the potentialities of film as art, or even to a lack of directorial, cinematographic, acting or editing talent or skill. It is partly due—exactly how much cannot be ascertained—to the industry's catering to popular tastes, as reflected in the box office. In other words, the majority of film makers are giving the public precisely what it demands; and since what it demands is not film art but "exciting adventure," "action," especially sex and violence, portrayed as naturalistically as possible, the result is quite predictable. Small wonder that the popular misconceptions of film find their way into most of the films on the market. Thus these errors, although elementary from a theoretical point of view, are more detrimental to film making than any popular misconception of the nature of any other art, not excepting architecture or even fiction, for the simple reason that the great cost involved in producing even the least expensive film makes financial considerations more compelling than in practically any other artcraft. The auto making and the building industries are possibly the only exceptions. It also brings home the overwhelming odds that good script writers, directors and producers have to contend with.

Does the preceding discussion in this section, and in the present essay as a whole, render illegitimate (1) the *evaluation* of the film of a novel or play *vis-à-vis* the latter itself? For example, does it render illicit the judgment that the film *Ulysses* is better, worse or just as good art as Joyce's novel of that name? I think the answer is "No." This activity, as well as the *comparison* of the two works with respect to their phenomenological and affective features, is perfectly legitimate; and what I have said does not entail the opposite. As indicated earlier, what it does preclude, and is indeed illegitimate, is (2) the evaluation of a film of this type by reference to the novel or play on which it is based, taking its literal "faithfulness" or "approximation" to the "original" as a or the standard of its aesthetic value, (a) as cinematographic art, or even (b) as putative art in general. The same mistake would be patently committed if, say, Mussorgsky's *Pictures at an Exhibition* is evaluated by reference to the paintings that inspired it; or even if the operas *Manon Lescaut, Othello, Macbeth* or *Carmen* are evaluated by reference to the literary works on which their librettos are based.

It is important to distinguish clearly (1) the constellation of questions pertaining to the logical, causal and aesthetic relations between a multimedia work of art MW and its various (kinds of) "sources" or "raw materials," which, by the meaning of "a work of art" or "a film," "an opera," "a ballet," etc., logically lie outside it, which are complete individual works of art or other kinds of compositions in their own right, and (2) the constellation of questions pertaining to the relation of MW as a whole to its component aspects or parts. It is clear that the discussion in this section as a whole pertains to (1) alone. I distinguish (1) and (2) particularly because it is perfectly legitimate to evaluate the various components, A, B, C, etc., of a work MW in terms of their appropriateness to or coherence with one another and with MW as a whole. For example, it is legitimate to evaluate the music of a song by its appropriateness to the poem for which it is the music, and vice versa.[33] Indeed, this is essentially no different from the evaluation of the various N- and A-*features* of a single-medium work in relation to one another. However, if the music is set to a preexistent poem, we think it legitimate to raise the question of the former's appropriateness to the latter, not the opposite. Similarly if a lyric is composed to a preexistent piece of music. But this is legitimate, it seems to me, because, unlike Joyce's *Ulysses vis-à-vis* the film *Ulysses* or Jean Genet's play *The Balcony vis-à-vis* the film *The Balcony*, a poem by Goethe, say "Der Erlkönig," in addition to being an independent work, is *part* of what we call the song of the same name, consisting of the poem and the music together. The situation is quite otherwise with the novel *Ulysses vis-à-vis* the film *Ulysses*. What exists of the novel in the film is not the novel as a whole but certain elements or parts of it—various characters, such as Mr. and Mrs. Bloom, and Stephen Dedalus, portions of the plot and the dialogue, and so on.[34] Equally important, what the film presents is *a* putative cinematiographic "correlative" or "equivalent" of the literary, linguistic portrayal of the characters and the action in the novel.[35] This kind of relation is absent in the case of the poem "Der Erlkönig," say, and the song of the same name. Indeed, the former is not even a linguistic correlative to or equivalent of the music which Schubert wrote for it, and is part of the song as a whole.

The foregoing, especially the distinction between (1) and (2) above, is useful in evaluating the view, recently advanced by Rudolph von Abele in the essay noted a little earlier, that the film of a novel (or a play) can be considered an "interpretation" of the latter in some sense. Taking the film *Ulysses* as a case study, he holds that "In one sense, the film functions as a speciously continuous illustration of the novel. . . . In another sense, the film functions as the acting-out of what the novel describes. . . . Put these two analogies together, and we may say that the film of a novel is a kind of illustration-by-acting-out, or of acting-out-as-illustration."[36] Again, "Relative to the novel," a film of this type "is indeed an interpretation, a critical commentary, a judgment as to what is centrally significant in the novel. But it is *an* intrepretation, one among many that may be offered; and yet it must be experienced as if it were exclusive."[37]

Now it *may* be useful (a) to think *metaphorically* of the film of a work of fiction as "interpretation" of the latter; for example, it may help us perceive certain similarities or relations, in addition to certain differences, between the two which may otherwise escape us. It may even be useful (b) to think of a film "made from" an original film script "cinematographically conceived from start to finish,"[38] as an "interpretation" of the script, in *another metaphorical* use of the word. If so, any film can be usefully spoken of as an interpretation in sense (a) or sense (b) of this word. But in order to preserve whatever usefulness this term may have here, the following points must be carefully borne in mind.

First, we must distinguish our two metaphorical senses from either of the two common literal uses of this word in aesthetic contexts, viz. (c) "executant's interpretation," i.e., a performance of a work of music, play, dance, or other "instance" of a "performing art" (where the performance consists in playing the music, acting out the play, dancing the dance, and so on); and (d) "critical interpretation." Senses (a) and (b) of "interpretation" are different from senses (c) and (d) of the word; though they bear certain analogies to sense (c). That is, the acting out of the film script is a performance in the literal sense, and this performance is part of the process of shooting or making a film. But clearly the resultant film as a whole includes considerably more than the acting. It is even more than the *action* or *plot* of the film as a whole, which includes "natural" events that, e.g., befall the characters in the film as well as what the characters (impersonated by the actors and actresses) themselves *do*. As a finished product, a film is not an interpretation in sense (c).[39]

Again, although the director and his team have to make a tacit or explicit (or conscious) critical interpretation of the work of fiction (or the original film script) from which the film is made, in the process of making it—in the sense of a "Judgment on its meaning"—neither the making of the film nor, in particular, the resulting film, can be said to *an interpretation* in that sense [sense (d)]. At best, we can say that making it *implies* a critical judgment on the part of its makers. Consequently, insofar as von Abele talks of the film of a novel as an interpretation in sense (d),[40] he is confused. It is interesting that, despite his statement that a film functions as the acting-out or illustration of what the novel describes, he apparently fails to perceive (e.g., in the passage on page 499 I quoted earlier) that "interpretation" in sense (a) is in some ways closer to sense (c) than to sense (d).

Second, *if* a precise meaning can be given to "interpretation" in the putative senses (a) and (b), they can be regarded as additional stipulated (*literal*) rather than as merely metaphorical senses of this word. Whether this can be done cannot be ascertained here, especially as von Abele himself does not really do so. The analogies with pictorial illustrations of a novel and with acting-out of "what a novel describes" is only a first step in this. One important thing in relation to this that he does do is to show how *Ulysses* "constitutes an interpretation of the novel, by describing the most important ways in which the film makers exercised their powers of choice."[41]

Finally, an important danger must be pointed out. Speaking of a film as an interpretation in sense (a) or sense (b) carries with it the danger of thinking of the film of a novel as somehow ancillary or subservient to the "original" in meaning or aesthetic value. That is, we must guard against the misconceptions noted earlier in this section, especially the GEF fallacy itself. Von Abele raises the question of how well *Ulysses* "stands up as an interpretation—leaving aside the question of how successful the film is in its own right?"[42] He thus seems to distinguish two legitimate ways of judging the film of a novel, thereby apparently avoiding the GEF fallacy. In pursuing the seemingly legitimate former question, he shows that the film markedly diverges in at least ten respects from the novel. The trouble begins when he *takes* the "transformation" or "transmutation" *to task* insofar as "the grand effects of the novel are either silently passed over, or lightly handled, or mishandled in the film."[43] That is, he does not merely note the respects in which the film is not a "faithful" "illustration" or "interpretation" but a transmutation of the novel: he judges it to be aesthetically unsatisfactory precisely insofar as it is so. Thus he in fact mixes the two questions he purports to distinguish, and in a way which lands him in the GEF fallacy. For he says: "such effects cannot be transformed from novel to film. . . ."[44] But if so, it is unfair to criticize this particular film *as an "interpretation"* of a particular novel, if the source of the limitation in question is the *kind* of film it is: namely a film with a novelistic parentage. Indeed, it would be to the film's (or at least the film makers') credit that these effects *are* silently passed over or lightly handled (though not insofar as they are mishandled) in the film! What one should perhaps criticize is the film makers, for deciding to make a—any—film "out of" the novel to begin with. But this can be construed as a criticism not just of *Ulysses* as a putative "interpretation" of the novel but of something logically prior: the desirability, from an aesthetic point of view, of making films from preexistent works of fiction. And indeed, he says this in concluding his essay: "in view of these difficulties, filmmakers might do well to liberate themselves from bondage to narrative fiction, and make films that are cinematically conceived from start to finish. [With this I heartily agree.] All genuinely imaginative film makers have long since recognized this necessity anyhow."[46] But this kind of judgment is justified only insofar as A-films *in general* are judged in terms of general standards applicable to them as art— "in their own right," in von Abele's phrase, for example, if they are judged in terms of the kind of impact a work of art of any sort is expected to have on sensitive and discriminating perceivers, under optimum environmental conditions.

NOTES

1. Perhaps the most controversial issue here is whether a film can be art if it excites sexual desire, or primarily sexual desire, in the viewer: something that is clearly possible in the case of some G-films, such as so-called pornographic films.

A much less thorny issue is whether an art-film can be (said to be) entertaining; or whether "aesthetic pleasure" is qualitatively different from, as well as "higher" than, "mere entertainment."

2. For reasons that are quite important from the standpoint of its autonomy as an art

form, this is not true to the same extent with respect to the possible "musical" elements in a film, either in the form of a sound track or as part of the content of a film.

3. In the case of the dialogue used, if any, it refers to the beauty of the language.

4. *The Art of Aculpture*, 2nd. Edition, Bollinger Foundation, New York, 1961.

5. See *The Concept of Art*, Chapter 1.

6. One difference between architecture and the aforementioned visual arts, including film, is that there is no restriction to so-called normal perceptual conditions. A building, say, has to be and is normally intended to be seen at night as well as in the daytime, under a great variety of natural and man-created atmospheric and lighting conditions. The changing play of light and shadow on its surfaces and volumes, and inside its spaces, is an integral part of the architecture as form or design in the present sense. In this sense, light and shadow are one of the media of architecture. It is true, nevertheless, that few works of architecture, especially as both interiors and exteriors, are equally satisfying in this respect under all actual or possible lighting conditions.

7. I have discussed the notions of aesthetic and human significance in *The Concept of Art*, Chapter 11.

8. Compare and contrast architecture.

9. *Film As Art* (Berkeley & Los Angeles, University of Califormia Press 1971). Foreword (1968), and *passim*.

10. *Ibid.*, *passim*. However, we shall see that "art film is primarily a visual (visual-*cum*-ideal) art" really expresses an *evaluative* judgment rather than merely describing (as its grammatical form leads one to suppose) the "nature" of art film. But more of this later.

11. In the case of nonobjective film, formal beauty would be a *necessary* condition *if and when* a work of this kind is purely visual, contains no ideal "expressive" qualities (assuming that this is possible). It is also a necessary condition of *cinematographic art*, in the case of both nonobjective and narrative film.

12. The Use of 'Good' in Aesthetic Judgments," in *Aesthetics And Language* William Elton, ed. (Basil Blackwell, Oxford, 1954), pp, 147–160.

13. *Ibid.*, p. 151.

14. *Ibid.*

15. For example, in "Art Names and Aesthetic Judgments," *Philosophy*, Vol. XXXVI, No. 136 (January 1961), pp. 30–48, and *The Concept of Art*, Part I, Chapters 5 and 6, and Part III as a whole.

16. *The Film Till Now* (Funk and Wagnalls, New York, 1949), p. 88. Italics in original.

17. Program notes of the Lincoln Center, New York, for 19 April 1967.

19. "Essentially Contested Concepts," *Proceedings of the Aristotelian Society*, N.S., Vol. LVI (March 1956), pp, 180 ff. There Gallie shows that all evaluative or appraisive concepts are, in principle, open to question or even rejection. He gives seven conditions which, in his view, a concept must satisfy in order to be essentially contested. For a discussion of these conditions, see my "Vagueness," *The Philosophical Quarterly*, Vol. 12, No. 47 (April 1962), pp, 138–152. In that essay I also distinguish the present notion from a concept's being open textured, or a family resemblance concept.

20. It would be instructive to ascertain whether the essential contestedness of the various possible concept(ion)s of A-film is of the same kind, logically speaking, as the essential contestedness of, say, the current Western concepts of art as a whole. Suffice it to say here that in terms of the kind(s) of *grounds* on which the two concepts or sets of concepts can be contested, there appear to be important differences between the two

cases. [Respecting the essential contestedness of the concept of art, see W. B. Gallie, "Art as an Essentially Contested Concept," *The Philosophical Quarterly*, Vol. 6, No. 23 (April 1956), pp. 97–114.]

21. In Melvin Rader, *A Modern Book of Esthetics* (Holt, Reinhart And Winston New York, 1961), p. 207. Italics in original.

22. But see later.

23. An example is Anthony Burgess' strictures on the changes made by Stanley Kubrick in creating the "film version" of *A Clockwork Orange*, at a reading of selections from some of his novels given at the University of Wisconsin-Milwaukee, during the 1972–73 academic year.

24. If WA is an *organic* whole, and its value is simply equated with the value(s) of the elements A, B, C, D ignoring the value(s) of their interrelations, we get a further error. But this error is not part of the GEF as I define it.

25. See, for example, Vladimir Nilsen, trans. Stephen Garry, *The Cinema As a Graphic Art* (Hill And Wang, New York, 1959), Chapter III, pp. 137–152.

26. "The Art of Sculpture," Kennick, *op.* cit., pp. 228ff.

27. In a sense, Lessing's *Laocöon*, though essentially mistaken in its general conclusions and in the way they are reached, is a major attempt by an aesthetician to prevent the subservience of one art to another or the confusion of their realms, through the mapping out of their respective natures and "limits."

28. *Op. cit.*, p. 210.

29. *Ibid.*, p. 211.

30. *Ibid.*, p. 202.

31. *Ibid.*, pp. 201–202.

32. Demonstrated in the U. S. Pavillion at the 1958 Brussels World Fair.

33. But see below.

34. See Rudolph von Abele, "Film as Interpretation: A Case Study of Ulysses," *The Journal of Aesthetics and Art Criticism* (Summer 1973), pp. 487–500.

35. Cf. "An animated pictorial representation (illustration-cum-acting out) of an event is not and cannot be the simple equivalent of a linguistic description of the "same" event. It might even be asked whether we can meaningfully speak of the "same" event in such a context; maybe at least we should confine ourselves to speaking of "related" or "analogous" events." (von Abele, *op. cit.*, pp. 487–488.)

36. *Ibid.*, p. 487.

37. *Ibid.*, p. 499. Italics in original.

38. *Ibid.*

39. Compare and contrast a play and its performance. In film, the "corresponding" distinction between the film and the shooting or making of the film is a different sort of distinction.

40. Cf. for example, *ibid.*, p. 488 as well as the passage on p. 499 quoted earlier.

41. *Ibid.*, p. 488.

42. *Ibid.*

43. *Ibid.*, p. 498.

44. *Ibid.*, p. 488.

46. *Ibid.*, p. 499.

Chapter 7

Remarks on the "Cinematic/Uncinematic" Distinction in Film Art

One of the most elementary but exceedingly important facts about cinema is that it is a multimedia art form. Consequently there are numerous varieties of film with respect to the possible relationships among the different possible visual and aural media involved. One such type of relationship concerns the character of a film utilizing two or more media; I mean the dominance or lack of dominance of the visuals vis-à-vis the dialogue, music, and so on. Films in which the visual images convey the film's entire meaning or so-called message—i.e., in nonobjective films with no sound track—and those in which visual images convey the bulk of the film's meaning—e.g., silent narrative films—are commonly called "cinematic,"while those that are predominantly nonvisual in this respect would be correspondingly called "noncinematic." (In fact, they are commonly called "uncinematic.") Some or all films in which there is a (rough) "balance" or "equilibrium" between visual image and sound are sometimes classed with cinematic, sometimes with noncinematic (or uncinematic) film. The many so-called novelistic and theatrical films constitute two brands of what are commonly considered to be noncinematic films.

Two major questions that confront us here with respect to film art are, first, which possible varieties of film in the sense distinguished can be, and which (if any) cannot be, *in principle*, film art; and second, which varieties provide the *best* examples of film art.

Although the terms "cinematic" and "noncinematic" are here intended in a purely descriptive, nonevaluative sense, they—hence the fore going classification—have tended to become evaluative in film theory and criticism, as we shall see. But even as a purely descriptive distinction, I now feel, this particular dichotomy is better discarded.[1]

To see why we must first note the basic reasons for the distinction, hence its alleged point.

The reasons for the distinction, it seems to me, ultimately lie in the simple fact that a film, in the sense of a movie or cinema, by the meaning of the word, is *necessarily* a sequence of visual images that create the illusion of movement, whatever else it may also happen to be; and no nonvisual elements (also) *necessarily* constitute part of it—not even the titles and subtitles or the musical accompaniment of extant silent films. These and other elements, such as natural sounds and dialogue, are optional elements in a film as conventionally understood or defined. A nonobjective film without a sound track is a paradigm of a completely visual film. This elementary fact is not contradicted by the further fact that, as André Bazin notes, it was merely a historical and technological accident that the silent film preceded the sound film. Indeed, I tend to believe that this "accident" is largely responsible for the character of the conventional concept of film just described. From this concept it follows that films that emphasize visual imagery for aesthetic or other purposes exploit the one essential component of the film medium, using "essential" in a descriptive sense.

From this point on, however, the road is fraught with conceptual pitfalls; and major and vastly influential theories of film have fallen into them. A main pitfall is that what is essential to film in the descriptive sense of "essential", i.e., the sequences of visual images, is wittingly or unwittingly deemed essential in an evaluative sense of the word: a relatively easy leap, semantically speaking. For it is significant that the word "essential" itself is often indiscriminately used in both senses, in scholarly and everyday discourse. This association of the two concepts or uses—"essential" as differentia (descriptive) and "essential" as that which is the most important, valuable, or best (evaluative[2])—in Western thought in general, can be traced all the way back to Plato and Aristotle. For these thinkers, the essence of any entity or phenomenon is its form, in both its Platonic and Aristotelian meanings, while form is identified with its final cause or purpose, conceived of as its perfection. Consequently, for anything to realize its essential nature, including what allegedly distinguishes it from everything else, is to attain its telos and perfection as that particular kind of thing. Moreover, this final cause is its *peculiar* good or excellence ("virtue" or *areté*) *qua* that kind of thing. Utilizing this pattern of thought with regard to cinema the fact that visual images are essential to a film in the descriptive sense of "essential" is *illicitly* used to infer that the best films (qua film) are those that are primarily or solely visual; i.e., that are cinematic in the descriptive sense. Or, in order that the desired conclusion may follow, one must add the false, or at least ungrounded, supposition that those N-features that are necessary or essential for something's being a film *in general*, (a) necessarily, or (b) uniformly as a matter of empirical fact, generate its most valuable positive aesthetic features (A-features), such as formal beauty, unity, etc.[3]

Returning to the philosophical sources of the descriptive-evaluative shift of meaning noted above, a further stage in the process should now be noted. I pointed out earlier that (1) in Plato's and Aristotle's essentialist view the common properties which characterize all the members of a particular class include one or more peculiar features, which distinguish them from the members of all other classes. These differentiae make them unique. But in the *Poetics*, Aristotle maintains further that (2) the different art forms are essentially distinguished by their distinct media. Since the medium of cinema is essentially "visual" in the sense described earlier, it seems natural for anyone who accepts proposition (2) to suppose that those visual nonaesthetic features (N-features) of a film which are peculiar to it are responsible for those of its A-features that are allegedly peculiar to it as an art form. The final stage in this reasoning is reached by the adoption of a premise implicit in Lessing's *Laocöon*; viz. (3) that *only* when a work utilizes the peculiar resources of its medium as a painting, sculpture, work of literature, etc., will it be best able to realize its maximum aesthetic potential. In the case of film, this leads to the view that art films that utilize the medium's unique *visual* potentialities will be the aesthetically *best* kind of film art. Thus cinematic art film in the descriptive sense of "cinematic" becomes equated with cinematic art film in the evaluative sense of "cinematic."

Now it is perfectly understandable for artists working with a particular art form, such as film, to do their best to assert their art's independence of the other arts. Sooner or later every art (especially a youthful art like cinema) tends to go through this process of rebelling against related arts: particularly older, more established and hence, in general estimation, more prestigious arts.[4] This is all the more natural in the case of cinema which is a little more than three-quarters of a century old, and which has had to struggle (and even now the struggle is far from over) to win itself a place among the major arts. This struggle has been compounded by its need to distinguish the artistic employment of the film medium from its vastly more powerful, popular, and publicized commercial uses, the so-called film industry. The multimedia character of cinema has also augmented these difficulties, hence the psychological need for independence, for the stressing of that which is putatively characteristic of or even unique to film art. For not only must film as an art stand up against its "competitors" from without, but must also attempt to settle the rivalries and tensions within its own confines: the competing claims of its various visual and aural materials. Compare in this respect the vagaries of the other multimedia arts in the West, e.g., the opera, dance, and theater.

But when all has been said, it must be added that this psychological need or stance must be philosophically and aesthetically balanced by the need for cooperation between the arts, not least between a multimedia art such as cinema and the arts that "contribute" voices or instruments to its complex choruses or ensembles. Indeed, if I may hazard a prophecy, the latter attitude is, I think, likely to dominate the scene with the passage of time, if film art becomes more generally accepted and more secure as a member of the family of major arts.[5] In my view, that would not be a bad thing either.[6]

The desire to "emancipate" film art from the "domination" or "encroachment" of the other arts, especially literature and theater, and to assert its individuality or "specificity" by concentrating on what is "truly" or "peculiarly" "cinematic," may be motivated by the laudable desire not to ape or duplicate in one art—here film—what other arts have done or are doing well.[7] It may also stem from the belief that each art has its own strengths as well as limitations. This view is perfectly true; though I see no *a priori* reason to suppose—on the strength of the everyday concepts of the various arts—that every art *necessarily* has *peculiar* strengths (and peculiar limitations?). Whether the latter proposition is true with regard to a particular art form can only be empirically ascertained by careful examination of as many instances and varieties of that art as possible. Cinema is no exception to this.

But theorists anxious to safeguard the "purity" of cinema—basing themselves first, on the fact that each art form has its own strengths and limitations, and second, on the supposition (really, the prescription) that each art ought to concentrate on cultivating its own strengths—forget one important thing. I mean that no art form can *literally duplicate another art form*; since what each can do and does is determined to a considerable extent by the nature of the materials, techniques, methods, styles, etc., utilized in actual works.[8]

Consequently, the purist[9] who inweighs against e.g., cinema's "trespassing the boundaries" of painting, theater, or the novel (or vice versa), is suffering from an unfounded fear. So-called theatrical, novelistic, or painterly films that utilize adaptations of novels or plays are not some kind of "film theater," "film novel" or "film painting," as we might say, except in a metaphorical or a loose literal sense. Strictly, there can be no such thing. There is only good, bad, and indifferent film: and *some* bad films result from an aesthetically inadequate treatment of a subject or theme derived from a novel or a play, or inadequate utilization of cinema styles, methods, and techniques reminiscent of or resembling some of the styles, methods, or techniques employed in novels, plays or paintings, etc. The same is even true, *mutatis mutandis*, of "filmed" or "canned" plays; for there is no such thing as "*simply* the filming" of a theatrical performance. And we must not forget that there are films which effectively utilize quasinovelistic, quasitheatrical, or quasipainterly techniques, subjects, or forms, creating (sometimes, even first-rate) art film. Examples are not hard to come by. (Of course, many mediocre or poor films result in part from the adaptation of mediocre or poor novels or plays. But that is a different matter.)

In summing up this discussion, we can say that, in a fundamental sense, the problems concerning the adaptation of plays or novels in films, and the failure of many attempts to do so (especially many attempts to adapt plays) in aesthetically satisfying ways, arise precisely because, not in spite of, the *impossibility* of merely transposing, and in that sense, duplicating, in cinema what a play or a novel has accomplished. And that is due precisely to the difference between these arts, with respect to media, techniques, and methods, and the like. In a sense, the problems of adapting novels or plays to cinema boil down to whether the latter's common and/or peculiar resources are or are not effectively utilized in the process; or more precisely, as Bazin puts it, whether or not their "cinematic equivalents" are found. Bazin defines this as the film's capturing the essence of the novel or play, which he variously characterizes as its tone, meaning, or effects.

In ending this paper I should like to return to the terms "cinematic" and "uncinematic." Earlier, it will be recalled, I argued against the cinematic/noncinematic distinction, using these words in a purely descriptive sense. I also argued against the honorific distinction between "cinematic" and "uncinematic" film, where "uncinematic film"(or aesthetically poor film) is equated with "predominantly nonvisual film." Now I wish to point out that a legitimate distinction can be drawn between a "cinematic film" and a "noncinematic film," but in a different way from either of the foregoing. In that use, the terms *are* honorific; but to say that *Five Easy Pieces* or *One Flew Over the Cuckoo's Nest is* "cinematic" is simply to say that it effectively exploits, for aesthetic purposes, the resources of the cinematic media and extant or possible cinematic techniques, *whatever these media and these techniques may be*, for example, whether or not it is wholly or predominantly visual and whether or not the techniques or methods employed are or are not similar to, influenced by, or even borrowed from some other art or arts. Clearly, then, "cinematic film" here is simply identical with "aesthetically good film, or *art film*," as a concept devoid of all *a priori* notions as to what is or is not proper to film art, what it can or cannot well accomplish, and so on.

In the same way, an "uncinematic film" in this sense is simply a film that fails to be film art by failing to exploit aesthetically, or to exploit in a sufficient degree, the resources of the film media and its actual or possible methods, techniques, and styles.

NOTES

1. My present view diverges significantly from the view I expressed in "Film as Art," *The Journal of Aesthetics and Art Criticism, Vol.33, No.3, pp., 1975*. 271—284, where I used the terms "cinematic" and "uncinematic" evaluatively.

2. Compare "the essential Shakespeare," "the essence of life," "the essence of happiness," as these locutions are now commonly used, where both sorts of meaning are ambiguously intertwined.

3. I use the terms "aesthetic feature" and "nonaesthetic feature" in Frank Sibley's well-known sense in "Aesthetic Concepts," *Art and Philosophy*, W. E. Kennick, ed. (St. Martin's Press, New York, 1964), pp. 351—373.

4. Cf. André Bazin, "In Defense of Mixed Cinema," *What Is Cinema*? Vol. 1, University of California Press, Berkeley, Los Angeles, and London, 1967, pp. 53–75.

5. In "Defense of Mixed Cinema," Bazin holds the opposite view. He says:" it is true that the history of art goes on developing in the direction of autonomy and specificity." (Ibid., p. 60) Apart from the continued existence of such multimedia arts as the dance and the musical in this century and the creation of new multimedia art forms, such as the musical and the cinema itself, the rise of, for example, collages and concrete poetry, tends to prove the contrary. Similarly with "happenings" that combine music, dance, poetry reading, etc.

6. Bazin's carefully qualified defense of the adaptation of novels and plays for cinema, in the special sense of "adaptation" he distinguishes, is an excellent example of a balanced view which well exemplifies the general stand I am advocating here.

7. The interested reader is referred to Bazin's telling reply to this in "In Defense of Mixed Cinema."

8. This is why, for example, Kracauer's distinction between the alleged "basic properties" and the "technical properties" of film (or, correspondingly, any other art form) is not only simplistic and artificial but logically untenable; as if "basic properties," as some kind of "essential, intrinsic or inherent" properties of photography and of film can exist apart from some *technique or other* for producing a photographic image or a sequence of cinematographic images.

9. Who, like Kracauer, follows in Lessing's footsteps.

Chapter 8

Movement and Action in Film

We speak of a film as a "moving picture" or a "movie," and writers on film art speak of film as the dynamic art. Just as there can be no dance without physical movement on the stage, there can be no film without perceptual motion, movement or change on the screen. Perceptual motion, movement and change (hereafter, unless otherwise indicated, referred to as "movement") are of the essence of film; indeed they help distinguish film from the plastic arts, and from still photography, as well as from literature and music. And as we shall see, there are certain differences between the role of movement in film and in theatre and opera which help distinguish them. The central question I wish to explore here is exactly what the preceding statements mean; or more specifically, the significance of the distinction between movement and action, for an understanding of film and film art. Part of our question is the relation of movement to the story or the plot, the "action" of a narrative film. In the course of answering these questions significant similarities and differences between film and the other mediums or art forms, with respect to movement and action, will be noted.

I shall advance two main propositions: (1) that the relation of movement and action in film resembles in varying degrees, hence also differs in varying degrees from, their relation in (a) dance and panto mime, (b) theatre and opera. It is more similar to (b) than to (a). Indeed, the role of movement in film is generally more different from than similar to its role in dance and panto mime. The same is true—only with additional differences—with respect to (c) painting and sculpture. And (2) that the reasons for the similarities and differences lie in the nature of the mediums and in the manner in which they are presented to our senses and our minds.

In "Movement and Action in the Performing Arts"[1] I maintained that dance and panto mime consist of, while drama and opera include, "movements in the first place and ... imagined actions (if and when they do so) ... as represented or otherwise depicted or conveyed by means of movements".[2] I should immediately add that in the latter two a variable number of movements of the performers also constitute actions rather than merely representing them. However, these actions by the performers themselves in some sense represent the characters' imagined actions or other things in the play or opera, such as ideas or states of affairs. Further, in that paper I also distinguished three ways in which movement in these arts or genres may *represent actions*; viz. (1) serve as a conventional sign (or $sign_1$), or $signify_1$, or (2) symbolize, serve as a symbol of, the represented actions. The latter may in turn function as "symbols of various ... states of affairs, states of being, ideas, and the like."[3] This is one way in which *action may represent* things in a work. Or (3) they may represent actions in a different, third sense; though as in (1) and (2) we would normally describe them as meaningful movements. But I am not sure that we would say that they have a meaning or mean the actions they represent. (3) is the most general and, for our purposes, the most important way in which movement in the performing arts may represent actions. It is illustrated by, for example, an actor's making the movements that represent—that we imagine "to be"—the action of stabbing someone with a dagger: e.g., in a performance of Shakespeare's *Julius Caesar* when the conspirators stab Caesar in the Capitol. On the other hand, an actor's hugging and kissing some other actor or actress on the stage are actions (consisting of various bodily movements) which represent the impersonated character's "hugging" and "kissing" the "corresponding" character in the play.

It is clear that the act of hugging and kissing described represents the impersonated character's imagined action in a different sense from "symbolize." Consequently there are at least *two senses* in which an *action in* a play or an opera may represent something or other in it; viz. (4) symbolically and (5) nonsymbolically. It is the latter sense (or "*a*-represent-2" for short), like the corresponding third sense of "represent" in the case of movement (or "*m*-represent-3" for short) that will primarily concern us in relation to film.

The foregoing senses of "represent" pertain to the movements or the actions of mimes, actors, singers and dancers on the stage, as distinguished from certain other senses of the word, as well as from a certain sense of "suggest." The latter pertain to the plastic arts of painting, sculpture and architecture. Thus René Magritte's *Hunters at the Night's Edge* (1928), currently in a major retrospective exhibition of the artist's work at the Pompidou Centre in Paris,[4] depicts hunters "at the night's edge" with nervously uplifted arms and bent heads suggestive of panic. (*Time's* caption is "Panic on the Horizon.") The hunters' posture and the position of their arms and hands *suggest movements* which in turn suggest or express panic.

Other senses of "represent" in relation to art, but which will not concern us in this paper, are: (6) the sense in which colors, lines, forms and textures in a so-called representational painting represent certain actual or imaginary things; (7) the sense in which two or three trees on a stage may represent a wood or forest; and (8) the sense in which historical characters in historical novels and plays, and their imagined actions, represent actual persons, living or dead, and their actions. A little reflection shows that senses (6) to (8) are different from senses (1) to (3) and from (4) and (5); though various criss-crossing "family resemblances" very likely obtain with regard to all eight of them.

Turning to the distinction between movement and action itself, this can perhaps be briefly explained as follows. Action, in what I shall call its primary sense, or action$_1$, is usually ascribed to—as something initiated by—living things, at least animals and, especially, humans[5]; though we also speak, perhaps by extension, of the causal action of, or effects of, natural phenomena, such as wind, snow or rain, on people and the physical world. Action in this secondary sense, or action$_2$, consists of physical events or occurrences that cause change, including the motion of bodies; and events consist in the movement of bodies in space or in qualitative-quantitative change. Events do not represent action$_2$ in any sense.

Movement is of two main kinds: "pure" movement, and movement that either constitutes or represents action$_1$, in any one or more of the senses of "*m*-represent" distinguished. Pure movement in my sense may be a natural expression or manifestation of the subject's feelings, emotions or attitudes, hence may serve as a *natural sign* (or sign$_2$) or *indication* of these states, etc.

With regard to movements that represent actions$_1$, we should note the following. First, that only movements that are existentially distinct from some action$_1$ or other, either wholly or in part, can represent it. Second, that movement that represents action$_1$ does so by means of some convention. This is obvious where movement signifies$_1$ or symbolizes an action$_1$; but it appears to be also true in the third sense of "*m*-represent." This may be more readily admitted, I think, with regard to the stylized movements of classical dance which represent actions than those of actors and singers in theatre and opera—or even those of a mime, representing various actions. Even in these cases, however, a convention appears to be involved: indeed, it appears to be both necessary and sufficient. The resemblance between a given set of movements and the action they represent, which is frequently present in pantomime and in action, appears to be neither sufficient nor necessary for that purpose. (Cf. Nelson Goodman concerning pictorial representation in *Languages of Art*.)

Finally, in ordinary usage "both movements and actions may or may not be (a) voluntary, and/or (b) intentional, hence (c) have reasons in addition to or instead of causes."[6] Yet "there can be wholly unconscious movements, but there cannot be wholly unconscious actions in the relevant *ordinary* meaning of 'unconscious.' "[7]

I shall now consider briefly the movement/action distinction in (1) cinematographic film, and (2) animation. Under (1) I shall consider (a) non-objective film and (b) narrative film.

(1a) In MAPA I stated that "a dance may consist of nothing but movement, representing and so including no action at all. A 'pure' [or nonobjective] dance is just that."[8] With obvious modifications this fits nonobjective film; which consists of nothing but colour patterns, lines, visual textures and nonobjective (or "abstract") forms, at rest or in motion, and/or in process of transformation or change. (Lumias phenomenologically fit this description too; but there the continually changing visual patterns are produced in quite a different way from the visual patterns in a nonobjective cinematographic film.) The change, motion or movement we see on the screen is "pure" motion, movement, change. It represents no actions (either actions_1 or actions_2), in either sense (1), (2) or (3) of "*m*-represent." To be sure, colors and forms, etc., can have or are sometimes given symbolic meaning; or they may signify_1 certain things. But when they do so, we do not have what I call nonobjective film, strictly speaking.

(1b) In contrast to nonobjective cinematographic film, (a) narrative cinematographic film, unless it happens to be nothing but a filmed pantomime (e.g., a film of a Marcel Marceau performance), will inescapably include considerable action_1 and action_2; though it may also include "pure" movement and movement representing actions in sense (1), (2) or (3). I am here excluding films in which the characters do nothing but talk. For talking is not ordinarily called an action_1; though it is called an activity. It is a form of doing something; but doing is a broader notion than performing an action. Even a filmed version of Beckett's *Waiting for Godot* or of Pinter's plays would include some action$_1$ or action$_2$. The actions$_1$ or actions$_2$ in a film, related to one another causally or in other ways, constitute the narrative film's "action." For a story or a plot necessarily consists of actions—or even of one action—not movements; whether "pure" movements or movements representing actions. This is true of drama, opera, dance, pantomime and fiction as well. Again, in narrative art the movements of the characters have significance (meaning) *largely* in so far as they depict character and represent or constitute actions; and "action without characters is impossible."[9]

Can a narrative film exist in the total absence of action? Since talking is not a form of action and a narrative can be verbally conveyed to an audience, a narrative film—just like a play—is possible in the absence of all action. That is not to say, however, that such a static film or play would not bore the audience to death (or to tears). Interestingly, opera cannot exist in the total absence of action; apart from the fact that there can be no opera (or even operetta) without any singing. For though singing is a form of action, the singing of the operatic actors and actresses is normally not part of the opera's action; rather, it is a major medium or means whereby the action of the opera is advanced. Contrast talking in a play.

Film in general, narrative or not, is impossible in the total absence of movement, change or emotion on the screen. This constitutes a basic difference between a film and stills projected on a screen; though the latter may form part of a film.

Turning to narrative film *vis-à-vis painting, drawing and sculpture,* we may note, first, the commonplace but important fact that the latter arts merely *suggest* rather than directly, perceptually, depict movement or action; except in the case of kinetic art. A painting may suggest pure movement—e.g., natural, nonconventional bodily gestures—or movements representing actions$_1$—e.g., the pantomime of a clown—or actions$_1$ themselves; depending on the subject matter it represents. It does not necessarily represent actions$_1$ merely by suggesting movement. A painting by Degas representing ballet dancers depicts movements; since a dance consists of movements. But it will also represent actions$_1$ if some of the movements depicted represent actions$_1$. Again, the painting by Millet representing the harvesting of wheat represents action and not movement representing action: the harvesters' action of mowing the wheat.

A comparison with kinetic art is instructive. A kinetic work of art (e.g., a mobile) has moving parts or moves as a whole. If it is nonobjective art, as many such works are, its movements will not constitute $actions_{1,2}$, or even represent them. They will be pure, "abstract" movements. They are presented to the viewer's eye and mind simply for their own expressive, aesthetic qualities or values, such as their grace and flowing quality. Now imagine a work of kinetic art consisting of a robot: we can imagine it to have aesthetically pleasing lines, textures, and colors. As a robot, it is designed to do certain things similar to the things humans do; e.g., move its "body," "walk," perhaps "sit down," or lift objects. These things are $actions_1$; so this imagined kinetic work would perform certain $actions_1$. But are these actions merely represented by its movements and motion, or do the latter constitute them? Without going into the intricacies of this question, especially concerning the relation of computers or machines in general to humans, it may be said—quite plausibly in my view—that *qua* nonobjective kinetic art our robot would only represent human-like $actions_1$ by means of its movements; and that we think of its movements as constituting certain $actions_1$ only because it resembles human beings in its form and behavior. That is, we treat it as a quasi-living thing. It is only by virtue of the latter that, by extension, we apply the concept of $action_1$ to it. Otherwise, we would at best speak of its movements as constituting, or as representing, $action_2$, as the case may be.

Whatever the correct position regarding this case may be, it is clear that our imagined robot-art is an unusual and very special case; and that where a work of kinetic art represents something inanimate, say a machine, we would normally imagine and speak of its movements as representing the $action_2$ of the machine it represents: provided it "goes through the motions" of doing these things rather than actually doing them, actually bringing about the states of affairs that the operations of the machine bring about.

(2) We can now deal quickly with animated narrative film. As a kind of film, the perceptual motion its projected images involve may either represent $actions_{1,2}$ or may constitute them. The difference between it and narrative cinematographic film is that these actions do not represent the imagined actions of the characters in the film but are these actions themselves. For what we see on the screen are the images of the characters themselves, not, as in cinematographic film, the images of the actors and actresses playing the roles of the different characters. This difference can be easily extended, *mutatis mutandis*, to theatre, narrative dance and opera, *vis-à-vis* animation.

We now turn to our final question; namely, to the basic reason or reasons for the differences—and the similarities—we have noted in the relation of movement and action. For it appears that the answer lies in the nature of the medium or mediums and so in the nature of the particular art or genre involved in each case.

It may be thought that in theatre and opera movements do generally constitute actions$_1$; that they do not do so only in those instances—quite infrequent in realistic drama and opera—where the actors, as we say, merely go through the motions of performing certain actions. This being the case—and I agree that it is the case—it *may* be concluded that *onologically speaking* there is no basic difference between the mediums of these art-forms and the photographic/cinematographic mediums of still photography/film, as far as movement/action is concerned. Consequently the only difference (it might be said) in this respect between theatre, opera and film on the one hand and dance on the other is that in the former art forms we have actors and actresses or singers *acting out, performing* the actions$_1$ that the characters in the text of the play, the libretto of the opera and the script of the film, respectively, are described (imagined) as performing. Acting is normally *not* going through the motions of doing something: these are indulged in only when the actions in question are: (a) impossible on the stage or require special or elaborate equipment to bring off; (b) are social taboos (e.g., sexual behaviour going beyond kissing and hugging); or (c) against the law or morality (e.g., acts of violence, especially acts of killing).

It will be added that in the case of film, there is relatively little need for "going through the motions." Because of the vastly greater technical resources of film than theatrical and operatic or dance performance, film is rarely hampered by the difficulty noted in (a) above. Only such extraordinary feats as flying (e.g., in *Superman*, or in the television programs *"The Flying Nun"* and *"Wonder Woman"*), or acts of superhuman strength (as in *"The Six Million Dollar Man* or *The Incredible Hulk"*) require special "trick" devices to look like the real thing and hence convincing. Only in this type of case would the actors have to go through the motions that approximate as closely as possible to the real thing. As for (b) and (c) above, these too pose no serious problems for the film maker or the actors. For the actors "kill" with retractable rubber knives or daggers, shoot with blank cartridges, and so on. Only such things as punches and (in nonpornographic films) the most explicit and realistic depiction of sexual intercourse (as in *Last Tango in Paris* and especially *I Am Curious Yellow*) must be "make-believe." In consequence, the vast majority of movements on the screen constitute actions$_{1,2}$, not movements representing actions$_{1,2}$.

All this is true; but two comments are in order. First, the foregoing does not and cannot account for the situation in the case of drawing, painting and sculpture. With regard to them, as their analysis suggested, the answer appears to lie in the character of the subjects represented. It is that which appears to tell us whether we should think of the suggested movements as constituting some imagined action$_{1,2}$ or merely representing it. Note that where some "objective" thing is depicted, the fact that what we have on the canvas, etc., is only a *representation* of people, animals or things is irrelevant to the issue in hand. Real people too sometimes go through the motions of doing something; they do not always perform actions. Likewise the real actors, actresses and singers on the stage sometimes go through the motions, sometimes perform actions. Of course, these people only "impersonate" this or that character, play-act a role. Thus their "actions" are imagined and not "real" actions; which are things done in real-life situations. This *is* somewhat analogous to the *representation* of people, animals, and other things by (means of) colors, lines, forms, etc., in painting and sculpture. Yet this too does not provide even part of the answer to our question. For consider film. What we see on the screen too is "make-believe," "imaginary" in an obvious sense.

This brings me to my second and final comment. The nature of the different art mediums, far from being irrelevant to the roles played by movement and action, and their relation, in each art form or genre, is essentially involved. The foregoing discussion clearly demonstrates it.

NOTES

1. *The Journal of Aesthetics and Art Criticism* (Fall 1978), pp. 25–36. Hereafter referred to as MAPA.
2. *Ibid.*, p. 25.
3. *Ibid.*, p. 34.
4. *Time (5 March 1979), p. 62.*
5. The word "activity" appears to be commonly used to describe what animals do; whereas "action" and "activity" equally appear to apply to humans. Here I shall use the two words interchangeably, ignoring their differences.
6. MAPA, p. 29.
7. *Ibid.* Italics in original.
8. *Ibid.*, p. 27.
9. *Ibid.*, p. 28.

Chapter 9

On the Nature of Painting and Sculpture

I

In "Family Resemblances and the Classification of Works of Art,"[1] I attempted to show in general terms that many art names in common employment, including "painting" and "sculpture," and many of the more specific art names in each case, express "family resemblance" concepts and so are open textured.[2] In this essay I shall attempt to show, among other things, some of the important consequences of the attempt, by some aestheticians, to provide an essentialist account of these concepts, and so, in effect, to convert them into closed concepts. For the purposes of this essay I shall concentrate on painting and sculpture, and will take as the main object of my discussion F.A. Trapp's[3] and Sir Herbert Read's[4] attempts to define (the first, in effect, to redefine) the concepts of painting and sculpture, respectively. I say "in effect to redefine" because Trapp actually claims that his efforts provide the putative necessary and sufficient conditions of all paintings.[5] Thus I describe Trapp's endeavor as an attempt to *re*define *painting* only because I believe, contrary to his belief, that painting lacks an essence in the traditional sense.

The fact that Trapp and Read themselves believe that they are describing the nature of their particular art form rather than proposing or stipulating, *inter alia*, a reclassification of some of the objects hitherto called paintings, or sculptures, explains the fact that they make no effort to show the alleged desirability, e.g., the utility, of thinking and talking in the way they in effect do.

In the second place, I shall attempt to show, both directly and by drawing some of its more important implications, the undesirability of the proposed redefinition of painting and the desirability of retaining the present open and nonessentialist character of the concept.[6] In the course of the proposed examination the nature of the two artforms, as artists, critics and laymen generally conceive of them, should become clearer. This constitutes the positive and, indeed, the more important aim of this essay.

For convenience and clarity I shall consider Trapp's and Read's views in separate sections. But the fact that both attempts exhibit certain common logical features or certain basic similarities, and so have some of the same implications, will necessitate considerable cross references.

The claim that certain features or types of features constitute necessary and sufficient conditions of painting, or sculpture, can mean one of two things. It may be, first (1) a semantic or conceptual (truth-) claim, a claim about the nature of the concept *painting*, or the concept *sculpture*. That is, it may consist in the claim that people conventionally employ these concepts on the strength of these putative necessary and sufficient conditions: moreover, that these concepts are correctly applicable only to things that possess these features.[7] But (2) the above may be a different, empirical (truth-) claim; viz. that all things (hitherto) conventionally called paintings, or sculptures *actually* possess certain common and peculiar features, and that nothing else does,[8] whether or not these features are conventional "defining features" of paintings, or sculptures.

In the light of the foregoing two theses, my general negative thesis (which my criticism of Trapp and Read is intended to support) becomes this: that, first, it is false that the features singled out by them are actually possessed by *all* things conventionally called paintings, or sculptures, and/or are possessed by them alone; which shows that, second, these features cannot be necessary and/or sufficient conditions for the current application of "painting," or "sculpture."

With this we turn to our two arts in order to see, among other things, whether our negative theses are true.

II

The Nature of Painting

Trapp's central claim, proclaimed at the outset of his essay, is that "In contrast to other visual arts, such as sculpture and architecture, painting has solely and specifically visual meaning. It serves no utilitarian function, as architecture usually does, nor does it actually occupy three dimensional space, as both the other forms do.''[9] The alleged differentiae of painting *vis-à-vis* sculpture and architecture, Trapp therefore claims, is (a) ''having solely visual meaning, ''(b) ''lacking a utilitarian function,'' and (c) ''not occupying three-dimensional space'' (or positively, ''occupying two-dimensional space''). (a) and (c) are supposed to differentiate painting from sculpture and architecture, while (a) and (b) are supposed to distinguish it from architecture. Moreover, (a) and (c) seem to be linked by virtue of the (generally) two-dimensional nature of the physical media employed by painting. Whether or not this is true, it is clear that (b) is logically unconnected with either (a) or (c), unless (a) is interpreted in a way which excludes the property ''having a utilitarian function.'' But this can only be done by defining ''meaning'' in a very inclusive and quite unusual sense, such that having a utilitarian function counts as a sort of ''meaning.'' But there is no indication that Trapp thinks of meaning in this way.

Trapp does not tell us whether he regards any of the foregoing three features as logically sufficient, though it appears that he thinks of each of them as logically necessary, for anything to count as a painting. The special attention he gives to (a) suggests that he thinks of it as the most important of the three putative differentiae—and perhaps it is, for him, a sufficient as well as a necessary condition of painting. In any event, I shall attempt to show in this section that neither it nor (c) is a logically necessary condition of painting, and that the three do not jointly constitute a sufficient condition of painting. Although (b) is a necessary condition of painting *as art*, the same is true of sculpture—and even architecture—as art. In the case of the latter, it is part of the concept insofar as architecture is a fine art and not a technic. (See Section III.)

A. In order to ascertain whether (a) constitutes a necessary or sufficient condition of painting we must ferret out the intended meaning of ''having visual meaning.'' Trapp does not explicitly tell us what he understands by the term so I shall give my own definition, but I think it does justice to what he appears to have in mind. Thus ''An artifact or some other perceptual object X, whether 'natural' or man-devised, has visual meaning'' = df. ''X exhibits evaluative or none-valuative visual aesthetic features (A-features).'' In the former case the A-features are ''positive'' or ''negative'', good-making or poor-making, in terms of some standard or standards of evaluation. Given this definition, Trapp's first suggested differentia would be

"Paintings (unlike sculptures and works of architecture) have (can have?) solely visual A-features: they cannot have e.g. tactile A-features." This implies that in the case of paintings as opposed to sculptures and works of architecture, *there are in fact no tactile A-features* (perhaps no such features can ever exist) for which tactile nonaesthetic features (N-features), such as tactile texuture and form, are responsible. If so, it is analytically true that running one's hand over the *Mona Lisa* does not (cannot?) give "aesthetic pleasure"; whereas we can get a great deal of "aesthetic pleasure"—pleasure caused by our perception of good-making A-features—from looking at it. For the purely visual N-features of the painting, such as its color scheme and composition, as well as the visual texture of the painted surface, give rise to a large number of good-making A-features (allegedly) perceived with the eye,[10] such as dynamism, graceful and harmonious flow of lines, repose, a high degree of visual unity, and the like.

My view is (a) that some paintings do exhibit tactile A-features to a limited extent. What is more important here, such qualities are sometimes good-making features of paintings. Consequently, that a thing's possession of tactile as well as visual A-features does not automatically disqualify it from being what we normally call a painting. In other words, "having solely visual meaning" is not a *necessary* condition of painting. Collages and "relief" paintings—paintings that create contoured, three-dimensional surfaces by heavy application of paint, are obvious examples. One would therefore expect Trapp to exclude collages from the domain of painting; and indeed, it can be argued with some plausibility that some collages, at least, are best regarded as borderline cases of paintings *vis-à-vis* constructions. Trapp characteristically refuses to acknowledge the openness of the concept of painting *vis-à-vis* sculpture (and vice versa), and unhesitatingly classifes collages as paintings.[11] He also states:

> Whether or not a *collage*, for example, has much actual three-dimensionality . . ., its appeal is *mostly* to the sense of sight within the established reference of its anframement. Even the textural elements, such as cloth, metal, or wood *ultimately* function in much the same way as paint, which may also have a variety of textures, with all that may imply of a direct sensuous appeal. That some of these efforts tempt also the sense of touch and seem at times more intended to invade the world of the spectator than to remain apart from actuality recalls historical attempts at *trompe l'oeil*.[12]

The word "mostly," which I have italicized, betrays Trapp. (Also, what is "ultimately" supposed to mean?) He also states that "a van Gogh painting may sometimes have more 'relief' than an Egyptian bas-relief sculpture."[13] He gives the following reason for his view that the former lacks "tactile meaning": "in all these examples a van Gogh 'relief' painting, trompe l'oeil, Baroque ceiling paintings, etc., the artist has had to relate his elements to each other within the two-dimensional limits of the enframement. These factors of two-dimensional structure of 'design' are common to all paintings, if not exclusive only to painting."[14] This is the wrong reason, since the question of whether a perceptual object possesses or lacks tactile A-features (meaning) is logically distinct from its two- or three-dimensional character and as we shall see, there is no relation of entailment, either way, between a thing's possession or nonpossession of tactile A-features and its being two- or three-dimensional. Moreover, it is false that in a "relief" paintng (unlike a *trompe l'oeil*) the pictorial structure or "design" is only two dimensional or involves only two-dimensional factors. Finally, Trapp admits that non-paintings (sculptures) may also be more or less two-dimensional, i.e., that his *third* alleged differentia does not constitute a sufficient condition of painting. I should add that the three-dimensional character of collages and relief paintings also prevents it from being a necessary condition of painting. But more of this later.

(2) A related point is that, with respect to much of the above, paintings are in the same boat with mosaics, stained glass, films, slides and photographs, whenever these things qualify as art in the word's descriptive sense; yet they are not either sculptures or works of architecture, and admittedly not paintings either. For if paintings lack tactile meaning, as Trapp maintains, so do they. Thus (a) would not suffice to distinguish paintings from these latter productions. Actually, the textured surface of a mosaic can give rise to tactile A-features, and in a good mosaic constructed with a view to tactile as well as visual appeal, these features may enhance the visual A-features, and vice versa. To a lesser extent, the same is true of photographs; but conventional stained glass his little or no tactile appeal, while films and color transparencies projected on a screen completely lack such appeal. They are better described than most paintings as possessing, at best, visual meaning only. (Cf. also purely visual phenomena, such as a sunrise, a rainbow or a mirror image; but the former two are natural phenomena, and can be readily distinguished from pre-20th century visual art, if not from all contemporary visual art as well.) Yet even here borderline cases are possible; e.g., we

can imagine someone producing "artificial" rainbows or making mirror images and calling them art.

(3) Can Trapp rightly maintain that *all* things called paintings have (better, *need* have) *visual* meaning? The answer is I think "yes," in the *descriptive* use of "meaning" in which I earlier defined "visual meaning." There is, however, another evaluative use of "meaning" in which only good or fairly good paintings (or any other kind of art) has some kind of (e.g., visual) meaning. In this sense to say that a painting X is a meaningless jumble of colors and lines (or shapes)[15] is to condemn it as, e.g., incoherent, and so, lacking in aesthetic value. In general, it is to condemn it as lacking a significant number of, or any, *positive* A-features. For if incoherent, it cannot properly represent, symbolize or otherwise mean anything, certainly not anything comprehensible, unless its aim is precisely to create an effect of disorganization, incoherence or chaos. In that case, it would be meaningful: its aesthetic significance would consist precisely in or include the absence of phenomenological and affective coherence.

The fact that in the evaluative sense only good paintings can have visual or any other kind of meaning does not affect Trapp's thesis. What matters for it is the descriptive sense of the word we discussed earlier. Consequently his claim that all paintings have visual meaning does not really restrict the class of paintings to *good* paintings, and so is not an honorific redefinition of "painting" in terms of a chosen criterion of artistic (or painterly) excellence (Morris Weitz).

B. Let us turn to Trapp's alleged third differentia, (c): namely, that unlike sculpture and architecture, painting does not "actually occupy three-dimensional space." I pointed out in (A) above that, in talking about visual meaning, Trapp at one point shifts from "having visual interest or appeal" to "appeal to the sense of sight" to "occupying two-dimensional space." But as I claimed there, there is at best only a one-way logical relation between the two concepts. For even regular two-dimensional paintings can have some tactile appeal as art; even though, perhaps, all sculptures and works of architecture also have some tactile meaning in the descriptive sense. In order words, "X has solely visual meaning" does, perhaps, entail "X occupies only two-dimensional space"; though "X occupies only two-dimensional space" does not entail "X necessarily has solely visual meaning." Trapp can consistently accept the thesis that regular two-dimensional paintings can have some tactile appeal *as art*, only if he argues that they cannot have such appeal *as paintings*. But this would not be a very happy position, since it immediately raises the question: "*Qua* what other kind of art, then, does (or can) it have this kind of meaning?" And this appears not to have an acceptable answer except "*Qua* no other kind of art, but only *qua* painting," for no painting as a whole can also be a sculpture or a work of architecture. And *strictly speaking*, no painting can be part of a sculpture or a work of architecture: though there are painted sculptures, and the walls and ceiling of a building may be covered with murals. In the latter case we distinguish the architecture and the painting, logically and in fact; in the former case we speak of the work as a whole as a (painted) sculpture and do not think of the painted surface as a painting. Thus painted surfaces may be part of a sculpture, but only because they are not then called paintings; while if they are (called) paintings, they are not part of anything except larger paintings, in diptychs, triptychs, and so on.

The situation is different in certain respects with the decor of a theatrical presentation, in an opera or a dance. Paintings are part of the total work called the presented opera, play or dance; but then theatre, dance and opera are normally considered composite arts, in contrast to painting, sculpture and architecture. Moreover there is a stricter, narrower use of "play," "dance" and "opera" in which the decor and other aspects of a play's, a dance's or an opera's performance are not ordinarily considered part of the work but of its performance in a sense in which the work and its performance are logically distinguished.[16]

The question now is whether painting can be sharply delimited from sculpture and architecture partly or wholly on the basis of the spatial media employed in each case. The answer is clearly "No"; rather, we find that there are various resemblances as well as difference here between painting and other kinds of visual art—not only sculpture and architecture, but (as we should expect if painting is a family resemblance concept) collages, stained glass, drawings and pastels, which in some respects form a loose family with painting at its head or center. It also has certain other similarities, respecting the media employed, to films and photographs, which (when they rise to the level of art in the descriptive sense) constitute another "family" of visual arts more or less distinct from the "family" of sculptures, works of architecture, bas-reliefs, mosaics and engravings. Further, the line between painting and drawing is not sharp, since pastels fall somewhere between the two. Likewise, in another logical direction, with lithographs, woodcuts, engravings and etchings.

The upshot is that no single quality or kind of quality distinguishes all members of a given family of visual arts from all members of another family of visual arts or genres; further, no single set of qualities distinguishes all paintings, say, from all sculptures, or all sculptures from all works of architecture. One main consequence of this is that the demarcation lines between them are nonsharp, always admitting of actual or possible exceptions or doubtful cases.

Trapp is aware of this last fact, as well as other facts mentioned above; but he fails to see that the former is due to the nonessentialist character of the concepts of paintings and other visual arts. For instance, he says:

> Distinctions even between sculpture and painting are not always simple. Although it may be agreed that sculpture has a three-dimensional surface, the margins of such a distinction are often blurred by exceptions. Many low reliefs appeal so minimally to our realization of actual three-dimensionality as to find much of their meaning within the contexts normally reserved for painting. This is especially true in considering polychromed sculptured reliefs which are in large measure the products of painters, as well as of sculptors.[17]

He continues: "One must realize too that our present separation of the two arts [painting and sculpture] is abnormal within the range of historical practice. Much, if not most of world's sculpture was once polychrome, and often combined with painting without sense of distinction."[18] But this involves a conceptual confusion, since these empirical facts have no tendency to establish the logical fact that the concepts of painting and sculpture are open with respect to each other. His reasoning is of the same order as arguing that the concepts *play*, *opera* and *dance* are open because these arts (or their enactment) involve the collaboration of several art forms, such as *decor* and music.

III

On the Nature of Sculpture

Read characterizes sculpture as follows: "The peculiarity of sculpture as art is that it creates a three-dimensional object *in space*. Painting may strive to give, on a two-dimensional plane, the illusion of space, but it is space itself as a perceived quantity that becomes the particular concern of the sculptor."[19] Connected with this is the thesis that sculpture is primarily an art of "touch-space," whereas painting is primarily an art of "sight-space."[20] He says: "For the sculptor, tactile values are not illusions to be created on a two-dimensional plane: they constitute a reality to be conveyed directly, as existent mass. Sculpture is an art of *palpation*—an art that gives satisfaction in the touching and handling of objects. That, indeed, is the only way in which we can have direct sensation of the three-dimensional shape of an object."[21] Thus there are certain (aesthetic) qualities that "can be conveyed *only* by the art of sculpture, but by an art of sculpture completely emancipated from painterly prejudices."[22] In the third place, "painterly sculpture"—bas-reliefs and other sculpture which are primarily or wholly visual—can only give "a limited pleasure"[23]; it has limited "expressive power."[24] To this category he consigns ancient Egyptian and, with qualification, Greek sculpture, as well as the typical Renaissance reliefs: "indeed the whole tradition of sculpture—until . . . Rodin began to reconsider the aesthetics of sculpture—was to create a pictorial illusion in which the ponderability of the material was etherealized. . . . The sculptor worked with and for the eye and never conceived his work as possessing any other unity than that of a visual image."[25]

This brief summary of Read's basic thesis shows, first, that like Trapp he attempts to provide an essentialist account of sculpture (and painting). He also claims that the creation of a three-dimensional object in space is the differentia of sculpture, which at first sight seems to constitute a partial agreement and a partial disagreement with Trapp: agreement insofar as for Trapp, "the creation of a three-dimensional object in space" (D_1) is a differentia of sculpture *vis-à-vis* painting; disagreement insofar as Trapp regards this as one of two differentiae of sculpture *vis-à-vis* painting, not the only differentia as Read seems to hold. I say "seems to hold" since he gives us, not indeed other differentiae but two alleged near-differentae of sculpture, in addition to differentia D_1[26], for in his definition of sculpture Read insensibly passes from D_1 to "Space itself *as a perceived quantity* is the particular concern of the sculptor" (D_2), and then to "Sculpture is primarily an art of "touch-space" (D_3). That D_2 and D_3 are distinct from D_1 and from each other is seen from the fact that a structure's being a three-dimensional object actually enables it to be seen as a three-dimensional object in space, makes three-dimensional space a perceptual phenomenon. The latter is an empirical consequence of the former and (by that very fact alone) is not identical with it.[27] (It would be interesting to inquire whether the fact that a painting creates a two-dimensional "object" has the empirical consequence that it can only succeed in giving the illusion of space, rather than present three-dimensional space as a perceived quantity.) Again, the distinctness of D_3 from D_1 and D_2 is not difficult to see. To see its distinctness from D_2, it suffices to note that perceiving (three-dimensional) space, as a sensible quantity, may be a visual or a tactile experience. D_2 may be visual or tactile, or both while D_3 is primarily the former. This means that as it stands, without qualification, the proposition expressed by the sentence "In sculpture we primarily perceive three-dimensional space" does not entail the proposition expressed by "The perceived space of sculpture is primarily a touch-space rather than a sight-space." The distinctness of D_1 and D_3 can be seen essentially along the same lines.

It is noteworthy that D_3 coincides remarkably well with Trapp's second putative differentia of painting *vis-à-vis* sculpture; viz. differentia (c), especially as I explicated "meaning" in "visual meaning." One difference, though, is that Trapp nowhere claims that sculpture (in contrast to painting) is *primarily* a tactile art. Also, Trapp does not state that the term "tactile meaning" means "tactile sensations (perceptions)"; though "providing tactile perceptions" may be part of what he means by "having tactile meaning," by analogy with "having visual meaning." For by the latter he appears to mean, in part, "providing visual perceptions." Significantly, Read does not deny to painting *all* tactile values[28]; he does not—and cannot—make as categorical a distinction between the two arts as Trapp does. Consonant with this he makes the controversial claim that "an art owes its particularity to the emphasis or preference given to any organ of sensation",[29] though this is obviously closer to the view that the concepts of the various art forms are "family resemblance" concepts than to strict essentialism.

It remains for us to evaluate Read's major claims, particularly D_2 and D_3; since we have, in effect, dealt with D_1 in relation to Trapp's view.

(1) "*Space as a perceived quantity is the particular concern of the sculptor*" (D_2)

In the first place, Read does not appear to mean, or mean primarily, space (a) "as a relationship between groups of objects."[30] (Cf. what he says about ancient Egyptian and Greek sculpture.) And though he says that "The idea of space as such, existing even if it is not filled by something, was unknown to the Greeks—with the exception of the atomistic school,"[31] the creation of (b) empty, or (c) inner or enclosed space cannot be the primary concern of the sculptor as he conceives it. For first, limited empty spaces, though not space as a whole, can be created by a group of objects; and that is not what D_2 is about. As for "inner space" *as a perceived quantity*, this has been rarely exemplified in Western sculpture until recently, with such sculptors as Henry Moore except in the modest degree in which, e.g., the arms and legs of human or animal statues create some "inner" sculptural space. It has not been the concern of most sculptors, most of the time: Rodin, whom Read regards as a leader of the new aesthetic of sculpture, being no exception. Finally, the creation of inner spaces *in the usual sense of* "inner" or "interior space" is *primarily* the concern of the architect, not the sculptor; though I disagree with Bruno Zevi who claims that the creation of inner space is the *differentia* of architecture *vis-à-vis* sculpture (and painting).[32] For some sculpture does—and by its use of ponderable masses, sculpture can always—create inner spaces in the usual sense. Whether or not the sort of inner space created in each case is similar, remains to be seen.

What I think Read primarily means, or should mean if D_2 is to stand any scrutiny, is either (d) that sculpture usually creates "filled" three-dimensional spaces as a perceived quantity, spaces *created* by the three-dimensional solid mass which constitute the sensible medium of sculpture, and/or (e) that sculpture usually creates relief *as a perceived quantity* or provides (visual) "sensations of depth."[33]

Starting with (d), it is noteworthy that in ordinary language we say that a body fills or occupies (three-dimensional) space; but by the same token this space itself is an object of thought, not perception. What is perceived is the three-dimensional surfaces of the space-occupying bodies. But for Read's and our purposes, i.e., as far as space as a perceived quantity in architecture, sculpture or painting, etc., is concerned, what is essential is something other than this filled space that we ordinarily talk about.

Now sculpture *is* distinguished from painting in terms of (d) above; for one thing, we get different three-dimensional views or perspectives in moving around a sculpture; whereas in many cases there is no such thing as "moving around a painting" in the first place. Of course, paintings in the round can be made, mounted on a revolving drum or sphere, say, or on a stationary cylinder round which the viewers can walk. Even then we cannot get different three-dimensional views or perspectives of the painting, unless it happens to be in relief. In that case some but not much of this sculpture-like visual quality can be had. The trouble is that this distinguishes architecture as well as sculpture from *most* painting. The same is true of (e) above, viz. relief in sculpture as a perceived quantity. Read, following Rodin, rightly emphasizes the importance of this for (certain kinds of) sculpture; and it is true that this kind of "real" as opposed to pictorial or "illusory" depth distinguishes (for Read, it distinguishes Rodin's and post-Rodin) sculpture from most, i.e., "flat" paintings. This feature also occurs in architecture. It is true that given the specific ways in which relief is created, its perceived quality and so its effect differ significantly with the two arts. But the difference is, I think, not one of kind but of degree, and no sharp lines are actually drawn at this point, in people's usual classification of certain artifacts as sculptures or as works of architecture.

To sum up, it appears that any possible sense of "creates a three-dimensional space as a perceived quantity" in which this phrase applies to sculpture, also applies to architecture—and vice versa. Thus D_2 does not serve or suffice to distinguish sculpture uniquely from painting. Nor can D_1 and D_2 together do so.

(2) "*Sculpture creates primarily touch-space (whereas painting creates sight-space*") (D_3)

This is really the heart of Read's thesis about sculpture, and what he regards as the most important near-differentia or differentia of that art. What Read means by this can perhaps be summarized as follows. (1) Touch-space is the apprehension of (a) the volume or bulk of objects, and (b) their mass and ponderability. The former comes from touching the object, the latter from handling it. (2) Tactile associations—memory or sensory motion connections—are involved in visual perception. For instance, "we may have an intuition of ponderability without actually lifting the objects, merely from our generalized knowledge of the relative weights of such materials as merble, clay, bronze, and lead."[34] (3) "Sculpture owes its individuality as an art to unique plastic qualities, to the possession and exploitation of a special kind of sensibility."[35] This specifically plastic sensibility involves three factors: (a) a sensation of the tactile quality of surfaces, (b) a sensation of volume as denoted by plane surfaces, and (c) a synthetic realization of the mass and ponderability of the object.[36]

In evaluating these claims, I should say right away that I completely accept propositions (1) and (2) above. But this, rather than helping Read's thesis (3), only helps to show that it requires various important qualifications which restrict its application. The mass and ponderability of a painted canvas, say, is admittedly irrelevant to it as a painting, or as art in general, in a way in which they are not irrelevant to *some* sculptures as such and so as art. But the three-dimensional surfaces of a "relief" painting can provide some sensations of three-dimensional touch-space, though considerably less than sculpture in the round.[37] (Note that "flat" paintings can provide an apprehension of a two-dimensional touch-space. But this is immaterial for Read's thesis.) Further—to show that (3) is not quite true in another direction, i.e., with respect to sculpture *vis-à-vis* other kinds of art utilizing three-dimensional substances or bodies as their media—various kinds of art, or artifacts that sometimes rise to the level of art—*can* exploit the plastic sensibility that Read wrongly thinks is uniquely associated with sculpture. Thus Delft or Chinese ceramics, Corinthian vases, and artistic jewelry, leatherwork and metal work not normally classified as sculpture, can provide, just as much as some sculpture, the three types of tactile sensations described in (3)(a)–(c) above. Persian rugs and Gobelin tapestries do so too; though it can be plausibly argued that as in the case of paintings, the sensations of mass and ponderability provided by them are almost always irrelevant to them as putative works of art. But what about sculpture itself? Clearly, only some sculptures can satisfy condition (3c), because of their size or weight (think of e.g. Michelangelo's *David* or *Moses*); while others cannot satisfy (3b) or even (3a) either; e.g., the gargoyles and the statues of saints on the exteriors of medieval European cathedrals, which are far beyond the physical reach of most people! Again, some statues are placed in such positions that going around them is impossible. Now we may well deplore this; and I would agree that in the case of *some* sculptures we get only part of the aesthetic pleasure they can provide, if we are unable to touch or handle them. But the fact remains that an "object" of a certain kind does not cease to be (what we call) a sculpture just because we are unable to enjoy it tactually. What is more important here, although *all* sculpture (but also rugs, tapestry, ceramics, jewelry, etc.) can *in principle* provide tactile sensations of types (3)(a)–(c) by virtue of utilizing a physical body or substance as a medium, this capacity does not, I think, constitute a *condition* for employing the word "sculpture" in ordinary or even professional artistic discourse. Sensations described under (3) (a)–(c) are only (factually or synthetically) "consequential" upon something's being what we call a sculpture, not a logically necessary condition of it. Thus it is false that

(i) the satisfaction of conditions (3)(a)–(c) is logically necessary for the normal application of "sculpture," and also false that (ii) all sculptures do satisfy that condition, though all can in principle do so.

My general line of argument against proposition (3) finds further support when we turn to proposition (2) above. I agree that tactile associations evoked visually are quite important with respect to some or all sculptures. Also, I am willing to hold that they can be more expressive in the case of sculpture than in the case of painting, because of the greater variety of physical materials at its disposal. But this does not warrant the conclusion that sculptures are primarily "intended"[38] (*qua* called sculpture?) to provide tactile sensations.

Again, in distinguishing from visual perception the alleged unique "plastic sensibility" involved in the enjoyment of sculpture, Read says that: "The sensibility required for this effort of realization [or the plastic sensibility] *has nothing in common* with ... the visual impression of a three-dimensional form on a two-dimensional plane."[39] But this defines "visual perception" too narrowly, making Read's positive thesis [(3)] quite trite—a truism or a tautology. For he ignores the patent fact that tactile associations of the qualities of surfaces and of volumes, or even of mass and ponderability, can also be provided by, among other things, the visual impressions of a skillfully executed three-dimensional form on a two-dimensional plane.

Finally and perhaps most important of all, what Read essentially does in his essay is to propose a *criterion or standard of excellence* in sculpture, under the guise of describing the nature of that art. Indeed, this is the way in which we have interpreted him so far, in order to put his thesis logically in as strong a position as possible or, at least, in compliance with his ostentive intention. In emphasizing the importance of this putative good-making feature, he unnecessarily though quite predictably demotes a traditional criterion-feature of merit in sculpture[40], involving visual sensations and therefore visual qualities. The latter is seen in his astounding denigration of what he claims to be "painterly" sculpture—which means, for him, practically the whole of classical and much of pre-Rodin modern Western sculpture! But he does not go as far as to propose, in effect, an honorific redefinition of the concept of sculpture, in the way Morris Weitz defines this activity, or even propose a nonhonorific redefinition of it. He does not refuse to apply the label "sculpture" to "painterly sculpture," and does not explicitly condemn it as poor sculpture; but he certainly regards it as inferior to sculpture that exploits the tactile resources of its three-dimensional medium. Thus he really tells us what he believes sculpture *should* do or be like in order to be sculpture *at its best*.[41] For instance, he quotes with approval Worringer's following statements: "The Egyptian relief is from the very first complete in its pure surface character.... The third dimension, the dimension by which we are actually aware of depth, from which all that is more profound in the drama of artistic creation draws its inspiration, is not present at all as a resistant in the artistic consciousness of the Egyptian."[42] It is clear that Read thinks of the third dimension as the source or condition of artistic value in sculpture, not merely as a condition of something's being a sculpture, good, bad or indifferent. (But the two are connected). Again:

> For centuries the Western world has admired this kind of sculpture [the kind in which "the palpability of the sculptured object" is ignored and the senses are confined "within a pictorial framework"]. Must we now be robbed of our simple pleasure? Of course not; as one kind of sculpture, giving a specific though limited pleasure, the typical reliefs of the Renaissance are justified.... There are other qualities that can be conveyed *only* by the art of sculpture, but by an art of sculpture completely emancipated from painterly prejudices.[43]

IV

Finally, is it advisable to adopt Trapp's views considered as revisionary recommendations? Reclassification of empirical phenomena is a frequent practice in the physical and social sciences, in the light of newly discovered uniformities or as called for by new hypotheses or theories, supplanting earlier classifications based on superficial resemblances or real or imagined common characteristics. Consequently it may be argued that essentially the same thing occurs in the cases under consideration; that instead of merely criss-crossing family resemblances, which result in all sorts of doubtful or borderline cases and lead to protracted disputes among writers on art and even the art-loving public, the acceptance of these proposals would provide more precise concepts defined in terms of certain common and peculiar features. But whatever the theoretical or practical advantages, if any, of scientific classifications or reclassifications of groups of phenomena in terms of necessary and sufficient conditions, this procedure appears to have no practical or theoretical advantages but only drawbacks in the present type of case. For the proposed restriction and/or extended employment of "painting" in fact makes not for greater semantic exactness but for confusion in practical and theoretical discussions of art. The current ordinary employment of "painting" is so well entrenched that, at best, only professional artists, critics and aestheticians would want ot adopt the new way of talking in question. Thus the existence, side by side, of the current and proposed usages would lead to unnecessary ambigutties and other verbal issues. Indeed, this may also infect the theoretical discussions of professionals on painting. Moreover, what theoretical gain are these putative essentialist recommendations supposed to provide? The main theoretical advantage that essentialist concepts in general have is that they are closed and *in that sense* more precise than open concepts; consequently no *theoretical* problems, and no hard semantic decisions are involved in any attempt to ascertain whether a particular essentialist and closed concept applies or does not apply to any newly encountered—discovered, invented or created—thing. But to extend to the various less general art concepts a point which Morris Weitz emphasizes in "The Role of Theory in Aesthetics" with regard to the concept of art as a whole, the openness of these concepts is an important advantage given the essentially creative character of art in the West. Further, as I pointed out in Section II, Trapp's recommendation does not really succeed in fashioning a closed concept. So he cannot claim for his proposal the putative advantages of closed as opposed to the ordinary, open-textured concepts, as well as being saddled with the practical drawbacks mentioned earlier.

There are special reasons for my rejection of Read's position concerning sculpture. I see no valid grounds for assigning to tactile sensations the preeminent position he assigns to them; particularly as he tends to downplay their visual qualities, including the "visual" associations of tactile sensations. Both types of qualities can be important to the same or to different extents; in the latter case, not always to the advantage of the tactile qualities. Some works are good because of their satisfaction of the tactile criteria; others for their satisfaction of the visual criteria, or both types of criteria. Indeed, the harmonious interplay or visual and tactile qualities is in my view more important than their separate satisfaction of vision and touch. For instance, a sculpture that mainly or wholly satisfies the sense of sight may be a better work than one which satisfies both sight and touch in a high degree, but whose visual qualities conflict with its tactile qualities, or vice versa.

It is clear that in saying the foregoing I accept with qualitifications the basic assumpiton underlying Read's evaluation of sculpture, viz. that *generally speaking* the more senses a work of art stimulates in a *satisfying* manner, the better it is as art assuming that it is the kind of object or activity, etc., that is by nature capable of stimulating two or more senses. The following are two main relatively specific qualifications we must add in order to render this "principle," as I abstractly qualified it in the preceding italicized passage, more acceptable.

(1) In some of the greatest art the stimulation of more than the characteristic sense or senses can interfere with and so diminish the work's effectiveness. Alternatively, it may be simply irrelevant to it as art, adding nothing to though also taking nothing away from the work's effectiveness. This can be clearly seen, I think, in the case of such supreme works of art as J.S. Bach's "Mass in B Minor" and "St. Matthew Passion," Beethoven's Ninth Symphony, 14th and 15th quartets, and Piano Sonatas Nos. 30, 31 and 32, *King Lear*, the *Divine Comedy*, Michelangelo's *David* and *Moses* and his *Pietà di Palestrina* in the Gallery of the Academy in Florence, and the *Laocöon* group in the Vatican Museum.

(2) A "law of diminishing returns" probably operates in the case of sense perception. We cannot assume that the more senses are involved in the perception of a work of art the richer or deeper is the resulting experience of qualified perceivers bound to be, particularly if we include smell and taste among the senses. For instance, imagine the effect of inhaling incense (or perfume?) while grazing at Michelangelo's *David* and listening to live music being performed on an instrument or a chamber ensemble in the towering shadow of the statue. Real or imaginary examples can be multiplied almost indefinitely. This raises the whole issue of the relation of different kinds of art to one another, as objects of aesthetic perception and enjoyment: the subjective and objective conditions under which they reinforce or enhance one another's impact by their coexistence, and under which they do the very opposite. But we cannot go into this matter here.[44]

NOTES

1. *The Journal of Aesthetics and Art Criticism*, Vol. XXVIII, No. 1 (Fall 1969), pp. 79–90.
2. Cf. also *The Concept of Art*, Chapter 2.
3. "On the Nature of Painting," in *Art and Philosophy*, edited by W.E. Kennick (St. Martin's Press, New York, 1964), pp. 214–225.
4. "The Art of Sculpture," *op. cit.*, pp. 226–238.
5. What Read does is logically different in important respects. See Section III.

6. This does not mean, nor do I maintain, that no modifications of any kind in these concepts are ever warranted; e.g. broadening them in various directions with the creation of new kinds of artifacts utilizing physical surfaces or bodies as (or as among their) media, and claiming to be paintings, sculptures of works of architecture. The only essential proviso is that all such modifications should preserve the open and nonessentialist character of these concepts. It is the particular kind of modification — broadening or narrowing down—of these concepts effectd or in effect proposed by the aestheticians in question or by other "traditional" aestheticians, that I find uncalled for. It is hoped that the discussion of the latter kind of modification in this essay will help us see more clearly the difference between the two kinds of change, their implications, and the reasons for them.

7. It is this thesis, or at least the first of it, with refinements, that Wittgenstein denies (in *Philosophical Investigations*) respecting many ordinary expressions and concepts. In "Family Resemblances and the Classification of Works of Art" and here, my view is that Wittgenstein's view applies, with certain important qualifications mentioned in that essay and in *The Concept of Art*, to the art names or art concepts we are concerned with.

8. Actually this thesis goes—must go—further, and claims that all things which *in future* are (*correctly*?) called paintings, or sculptures, etc., *would* possess these putative features. This predictive (or prescriptive?) element in the putative universal synthetic statement "All paintings (sculptures, etc.) possess such and-such qualities" often goes unnoticed when aestheticians defend the present, empirical essentialist thesis regarding a particular art form as a whole. For one thing, it is difficult to justify without falling back on the semantic thesis, (1), stated above. The same is true with regard to other nontechnical concepts, in other universes of discourse, which are considered essentialist concepts.

9. Trapp. *op. cit.*, p. 214.

10. I shall pass in silence over the difficult problem of which A-features, if any, are (a) perceived by sense as opposed to mentally, and (b) which of the former, if any exist, are perceived with the eye as opposed to tactually.

11. Cf. *op. cit.*, p. 217.

12. *Ibid.*, p. 218.

13. *Ibid.*

14. *Ibid.*

15. We also say "X lacks all meaning," though I think not "X is a meaningless" painting.

16. Cf. the analogous distinction relating to music, discussed in "The Identity of a Work of Music–I", in this volume.

17. *Op. cit.,* p. 216. Cf. also pp. 216 ff. on paintings, pastels, sketches, studies, mosaics, collages, etc.

18. *Ibid.*, p. 216.

19. *Op. cit.*, p. 226. Italics in original.

20. *Ibid.*, p. 227.

21. *Ibid.*, p. 228. Italics in original.

22. *Ibid.*, pp. 231–232. Italics in original.

23. *Ibid.*, p. 231.

24. *Ibid.*

25. *Ibid.*, p. 235.

26. Actually, he is not perfectly consistent in this respect, since at one point (ibid.,

pp. 231–232) he thinks of the third characteristic of sculpture, namely the provision of tactile qualities (or D_3 as I shall refer to it) as distinguishing sculpture from painting. This shift or vacillation is significant from the standpoint of my nonessentialist view of painting and sculpture.

27. Cf. my remarks in Section II respecting the relation between Trapp's putative differentiae, (a) and (c), of painting.

28. But as I said before, he is uncertain about this.

29. *Op. cit.*, p. 232.

30. *Ibid.*, p. 230.

31. *Ibid.*

32. "Architecture as Space," in Kennick, *op. cit.*, pp. 239–247.

33. See *op. cit.*, p. 234f., in relation to Read's discussion of Rodin's sculpture.

34. *Ibid.*, p. 232.

35. *Ibid.*, p. 233.

36. *Ibid.*

37. The same is true of collages, but these we may not wish to classify as paintings though they are not sculptures either.

38. Read does not explicitly say this; but his general position appears to imply it. Cf. *Ibid.*, p. 232.

39. *Ibid.*, p. 233. My italics.

40. This phenomenon has been widely commented on by linguistic philosophers, in relation to traditional attempts to offer real definitions of this or that art form. Cf. e.g. Beryl Lake's discussion of Croce's and Bell's putative definitions of art, in *Aesthetics and Language*, edited by William Elton (Oxford, 1954), pp. 100–113, and W. B. Gallie, "Art as an Essentially Contested Concept," *Philosophical Quarterly*, Vol. VI, No. 23 (Basil Blackwell, London, April 1955), pp. 97–114, as well as Morris Weitz's "The Role of Theory in Aesthetics," *passim*.

41. Cf. *Ibid.*, p. 232.

42. *Op. cit.*, p. 229, cf. also p. 232 and pp. 236–237.

43. *Ibid.*, pp. 231–232.

44. I have discussed this matter briefly, with regard to visual art, in my "Optimum Conditions of Visual Art," *Dianoia* (1973).

PART FOUR

Chapter 10

Art: New Methods, New Criteria

I

The unprecedented developments in Western art in this century have posed acute, even unprecedented problems for the aesthetician, critic and art public. The question (A) "Is X (an artifact, activity, etc.) art (or music, painting, etc.)?"[1] and the related question (B) "Is X good or poor art (or music, painting, etc.)?" have echoed down the corridors of the 20th century. The unfamiliarity of the new art does not alone explain the acute bewilderment with which people tend to react to it; or rather, the important question is why much new art strikes people as so puzzling, and so, what makes some new art so radically different from anything that has gone before. At least part of the answer is that art has never moved away from tradition so radically, and in so many directions at once, as in this century; though it is commonplace that in the past Western art has constantly moved in new directions in use of media or materials, techniques, subject mattter, form or effects. The most essential point is that perhaps for the first time in history art has been moving in *new kinds* of directions, and thus contemporary avant garde art is revolutionary in a perfectly literal sense. The most avant garde art challenges, and so requires a drastic modification, of the traditional *concept* of art as a whole and a host of related concepts; e.g., those of the artist and the creative process; the relation of the artist to his society, including his audience and the performers (or the performance) of his art and the aesthetic role or function of the latter; hence also the criteria for evaluating art that involves considerable collaboration between artist, performer and audience; the relation of art to Nature, fiction to fact; and so on. This is signalized by, e.g., (1) the progressive eroding, not to say breakdown (as in *art trouvés* and especially in, e.g., John Cage's "4 Minutes and 33 Seconds"[2]) of the traditional distinction between art—i.e., artifacts, man-devised activities, etc.—and Nature,[3] and between (2) fiction or imagination and reality (e.g., in Truman Capote's *In Cold Blood* and in some of Norman Mailer's work), as well as (3) the increasing intrusion of randomness or chance into art, and its gradual displacement of the notions of control and purposiveness in the creative process. Another feature (4) is the highly dynamic, even ephemeral character of some new art (kinetic art, happenings, self-destructive art, etc.) challenging the idea of relative durability or stability of plastic works of art and the idea of repeatability, sometimes of the more or less faithful reproduction, of temporal works of art. This is sometimes accompanied by (5) a shift of emphasis from the work of art as a "product," to the process or experience of creating it and the alleged intrinsic value of the latter, irrespective of the quality of the product. The hippie's motto, "All men are artists"[4] epitomizes this. Finally (6) the use of electronic tapes and computers in music or even the admission of animal painting into the domain of art has also eroded the view that art is (must be) a purely or peculiarly human creation. The continued challenge to the traditional Western concepts of art and the traditional concepts of the various art forms is accompanied by the tendency to challenge traditional criteria of artistic worth (A-criteria). The uncertainty as to whether something X that "looks" or "sounds" very different from accepted art *is* art_1, entails a corresponding uncertainty concerning X's valuation if it is judged to be art_1. It raises doubts as to whether the old criteria apply to it in any manner or degree, or what new criteria must be employed instead. For instance, there is little doubt that the traditional ideas of unity or coherence, completeness, and beauty—at least in their classical formulations—are inapplicable to some new art.

The basic conceptual source of questions (A) and (B) above in relation to all art, both classical and contemporary, is what I believe to be the fact that the ordinary generic concept of art_1 and its species are "family resemblance" (or "cluster"), hence open-textured, concepts, in the sense that *they are not employed on the basis of any determinate or relatively determinate common and/or peculiar phenomenological or affective features*.[5] If the opposite were the case, no theoretical uncertainty would exist regarding the classification of an artifact, activity, and the like, X, as art_1 or $nonart_1$, even—indeed, especially—when we are confronted with extremely novel artifacts and occurrences. The question would be settled by ascertaining whether X exhibits the defining features of all art_1 (or all $paintings_1$, etc.). Of course, this itself may often be more difficult to do than it sounds but it would be a practical, not a theoretical problem. Again, on the traditional account E-criteria would be provided, *once and for all*, by the common, and, especially, the peculiar features of art_1, $music_1$, etc. More correctly this would be true if (1) these features admit of degree or can be exhibited in a striking manner, and (2) X's possession of one or more of these features in an unusual degree or in a striking manner is taken as a (or the) standard of X's worth as a painting, poem, and so on. Given these things, there would be no theoretical problems regarding "new criteria." In point of fact the most basic reasons for the uncertainty relating to (A) and (B) appear to be conceptual. I should add that in the past, only question (B) was, generally speaking, a critical practical issue; and this probably helped conceal the theoretical problems that question (A) poses. Correspondingly, it probably helped conceal the inadequacy of any essentialist conception or definition of art.

II

The foregoing, if true, confronts us with the following situation. If we decide to keep the traditional concept(s) of art open, we have the option of (1) admitting every new activity or artifact whose author claims is art[6], or (2) selectively admitting certain things and excluding others. If we choose (2), which I believe is the more reasonable course, we need a general principle of selection. Such a principle is familiar to us all, since it has been in general lay and professional use probably since the history of art began. In its most general from it is in constant everyday use with respect to open-textured, hence many or all ordinary, concepts. I refer to the "Principle of Extension by Resemblance or Analogy," or "Principle E" as I shall conveniently call it. If, as I believe, the ordinary art concepts are cluster concepts, this principle provides the only rational procedure for deciding whether something X should or should not be counted as art_1, or $music_1$, etc. Theoretically speaking, it simply involves a ascertaining whether X shares any qualities with or has any qualities appreciably similar to the A- and N-features of what the judge regards as paradigms of art_1, $music_1$, etc.; and (b) "balancing" these 2 features[7] against X's dissimilarities to the latter's A- and

N-features. Further, if someone judges X to be art_1, this principle calls for his assessing its aesthetic worth in terms of the degree and the artistic significance of its similarities—with respect to its putative *A-features*—to the A-features of paradigms of good art_1, the so-called classics of painting, sculpture, music, etc. Consequently the judge's choice of paradigms, in any given case, is of crucial importance: his evaluation of X's worth so largely depends on it. Ideally, those paradigms must be chosen solely for their excellence and relevance to X; though in practice, the goodness of the paradigms chosen in particular cases may be a matter of dispute; and various subjective factors, such as the judge's predilections and tastes, may unconsciously influence his choice. As a consequence, the criteria of relevance are of paramount theoretical and practical importance. The general and obvious criterion is that a work of music must be judged by reference to paradigms of good music; poems by reference to paradigms of good poetry; and so on. But this process should not be carried to extremes, for rather obvious reasons. For one thing, a work may strive to combine in a new way, two or more conventional art forms or genres, i.e., to create multi media art; for another, the artist may be attempting to extend the scope of a conventional art form or genre by utilizing techniques or methods borrowed from or inspired by some other conventional art form or genre. In these cases, what is aesthetically most significant about the works, namely their originality, may well work against them if the frame of reference is the traditional novel form or the classical sonata form, and so on, while those that get the palm would be the most conventional or hackneyed works. This danger must also be guarded against[8] whenever we employ, as criteria features, various clusters of general or relatively general N- and A-features which we believe good classical poems, plays, or novels, or paintings, sculptures, etc., exhibit, rather than directly appealing to actual paradigmatic works. These clusters of good-making qualities are, or at any rate should be, arrived at by conscious or unconscious inductive generalization from the qualities of works we admire; while the ultimate rational ground of what we admire can only be the nature of their impact on us under optimum environmental conditions. But as would be expected, these generalizations, hence the nonexhaustive "check-lists" we arrive at, show the influence of our individual tastes and preferences, values, and the like, and so (to a greater or lesser extent) the influence of our society's or age's attitudes, values, and the like. For this reason the criteria features we employ tend to change as our attitudes, values, and experiences change with time—or, at least, they should do so if we are to avoid turning our criteria into straitjackets. Apart from the inescapable element of subjectivity and individual and collective bias I mentioned, the employment of clusters of good-making qualities we discern in past art as criteria-features of goodness of new art, involves other dangers. One of the chief of these—probably a chief reason why some aestheticians, such as Stuart Hampshire and Margaret Macdonald, reject the notion of general standards of aesthetic valuation—is that the interrelations of a work's features are essential to their good-making quality (or to the degree in which they are so). And this means that the interrelations of a work's N-features are of the essence; since the latter features-in-relation are what give rise to the former type of features. *This is true in proportion as the works in question are organic unities, hence, to that extent*, are good art. Thus ironically but not surprisingly, the best new art tends to suffer most from its mechanical and atomistic evaluation in terms of an abstract list of good-making qualities. The remedy is not the rejection of all general criteria or standards of aesthetic goodness, as Hampshire and Macdonald do, but their judicious, i.e., "contextual" use; or their intelligent adaptation to—hence their extension or modification to fit—the character and circumstances of the individual work to be evaluated. This is true, to some extent, of works in the well-worn tradition of some particular school, movement or age and not just the most revolutionary new works.

I said that a person's adventurousness or conservatism in employing Principle E to ascertain whether something X is or is not art_1, is partly determined by the paradigms selected, partly by the significance he attaches to X's similarities or dissimilarities to them. These in turn may be determined or conditioned by all sorts of extra-aesthetic, including moral or general axiological factors. Further, this adventurousness or conservatism in dealing with question (A), in relation to specific artifacts or occurrences X, Y, Z, etc., logically determines, in effect, his readiness or reluctance to adopt new E-criteria. But his enjoyment or lack of enjoyment of what he wishes to classify or judge may also play a dominant role here. If a person P derives pleasure from looking at or listening to something X which purports to be art_1, I think he will be normally disposed to accept it as art_1; for, *other things being equal*, something which pleases by the way it looks or sounds, or by its intellectual or imaginative qualities, tends to be regarded as *good* art, *a fortiori*, art_1. Obviously, things are often unequal; and this makes the present situation a fertile source of dispute. Certain kinds of things are generally regarded as incapable of being art, e.g., perfumes. (Also compare the problem of what is "merely decorative" or "merely entertaining" as opposed to what is "art_1.") If P's acceptance of X as art_{12} requires his modifying the concept of art that he has hitherto employed, as contemporary avant garde art often does, consistency demands that he do so. The same applies if P dislikes the way X looks or sounds, etc., since if he judges it to be poor art he must logically admit it into the domain of art, thereby modifying if necessary the concept of art_1 he employs. As we know, things often work out differently, and for good reason, I think. Unless P happens to be a philosopher of a certain kind, chances are that his desire not to "tamper" with the concept of art_1 generally overcomes his tendency to classify X as art_1 because he finds it dull or positively unpleasant to listen to, look at, etc. I think he would rightly think it unreasonable to modify a whole concept—especially a concept that has the weight of a long tradition behind it—spurred by a single case. This conservative tendency may be strengthened if P finds a whole group of other artifacts or occurrences, W, R, S, etc., resembling X in what appear to be significant ways, equally boring or unpleasant as phenomenological objects while the opposite tends to happen if P judges them to be pleasing (as X is here assumed to be). The validity of the reasoning involved here depends on whether P is a qualified judge. But whether or not this is so, his discovery that his reaction to X, W, R, S is typical of his particular community or society would normally instill greater confidence in his taste and appreciation of it, and so make him more willing or unwilling to modify, if necessary, the accepted concept of art.

Principle E, as applied to art, is double-barreled. We employ it in relation to (a) X's *phenomenological* (N- and A-) features, and, correlatively, (b) its *impact* on putative qualified perceivers under putative optimum environmental conditions. The latter is a logical consequence of what I believe is the fact that the concept of art includes an open and essentially contested set of *aims* which provide the ultimate regulative principle in determining whether or not any bona fide poem, painting, sculpture, etc., is good or poor art_1.[9] This procedure has been repeatedly exemplified in the history of art, as new artifacts or activities necessitated decisions regarding their admission into the domain of art_1 or their exclusion from it. Ultimately, the answer to question (B) must be determined by reference to X's *impact* on qualified perceivers in the appropriate circumstances; while the answer to question (A) is ascertainable on the strength of this as well as X's phenomenological features. (We have already met the reasoning involved in the latter case: if X can be correctly judged to be good art, it is, *a fortiori*, art$_1$. (This indicates one way in which "honorific redefinitions," as Morris Weitz describes them in "The Role of Theory in Assthetics," may be born.)[10] Ultimately, however, X can only be judged art$_1$ or not art$_1$ by the impact it has, if any, on qualified perceivers under optimum environmental conditions. This means that artifacts and occurrences that do not have a marked impact, whether pleasant or unpleasant, favorable or unfavorable, on putative qualified judges, cause the greatest uncertainty in relation to both (A) and (B). One is hard put to decide whether they should be regarded as poor art or not art$_1$ at all.

I said that the answer to question (A) is ascertainable on the strength of the impact the particular artifact, process, etc., X has on qualified perceivers under optimum conditions, as well as on the basis of its phenomenological features. Nevertheless, I do believe that the former *takes precedence* over the latter, whenever X's phenomenological qualities as such do not enable us to ascertain, with a fair degree of assurance, whether X should or should not be classified as art$_1$. I mean if X is or appears to be exceedingly different from things conventionally called art$_1$ (or music, paining, literature, etc.). In this type of case, the appeal to X's impact rather than to its phenomenological features as the final court of appeal has distinct advanteges. For though the specific impact of particular works, if any, is highly variable, there is a certain *general kind* of complex impact which art *aims* at *qua* art. This, I believe, is true of much if not all contemporary art, as well as of the art of the past. For it is my belief that, as traditionally conceived in the West, art has probably always aimed at the stimulation of the sudience's intellect, the broadening of its imaginative horizons, and the broadening and deepening of its emotional experience. In fact, these features *are* exhibited in a considerable number of contemporary productions whose creators claim for them the status of art (even though, I might add, these works include some of the most unusual productions in the history of Western art). Whether avant garde art generally aims at providing enjoyment to its audience by virtue of its nonaesthetic and expressive features, as traditional art does, is perhaps debatable. But much contemporary art, I believe, does so. Moreover the generality of the aims of art I enumerated, permits an immense variety and range in the kinds of phenomenological N- and A-features that, say, contemporary productions can have, hence permit extremely great phenomenological *differences* between them and the art of the past. The appeal to impact as the final arbiter has, therefore, the great advantage of not forcing new art into a straitjacket by suppressing and even destroying all creativity. In short, it helps prevent Principle E from turning into a conservative, even reactionary tool in the hands of narrow-minded and prejudiced audiences and critics.

A serious difficulty arises in attempting to apply Principle E in (A) above, in the case of productions whose dissimilarities, with respect to N-features, seem to be much more pronounced than their similarities to accepted art. For instance, this seems to be the case with regard to the Italian artist who sold, as samples of his art, ordinary balloons filled with his breath, or Christo Javacheff, whose "art" consists in his "wrapping" fountains, buildings and craggy inlets with polypropylene plastic. A more radical example is provided by the American artist who periodically changes his name, and regards the legal procedures involved in doing so, as well as the name-change itself, as part of his artistic activity and output. Example can be multipled. In the case of Javacheff's "works" as perhaps in the majority of other cases of experimental art, the sensory, imaginative and emotional impact of the putative art on sensitive, discriminating and open-minded audiences is the final—and in many cases the only—court of appeal. But neither this nor the closest "scrutiny" or "analysis" of the air-filled balloons or the closest scrutiny of the legal procedures involved in the artist's changing his name can help us decide whether to call either art$_1$. For these "far out" things other types of considerations are pertinent, for instance, (a) whether their maker intends them to be primarily or wholly treated as phenomenological objects, i.e., as something primarily or wholly to look at, listen to, etc., e.g., for the enjoyment of their visual or auditory, as well as intellectual, emotional or imaginative qualities, if any. But this is not sufficient to make them art, any more than the maker's desire to have them treated as mere utilitarian or practical artifacts, processes, etc., prevents them from being art, or even good art. Once again, (b) the way they impress sensitive and discriminating perceivers is what really matters here. A further factor that must be considered in conjunction with (b) is (c) whether any human or other sentient beings are involved in their production, arrangement or placement in the particular setting. On the basis of factor (a), the fact that there is no perceptual activity that may be observed or enjoyed, entails that the artist's changing his name cannot be art; and the same conclusion follows from factor (b) with regard to the legal documents and procedures that changing one's name involves in this country or elsewhere.

The foregoing is also true, in the last analysis, with regard to the goodness or badness of something that is extremely novel, such as, once again, the air-filled balloons or Javacheff's wrapped objects, if accepted as bona fide art_1.

But apart from the difficulties that revolutionary art poses in the attempt to apply Principle E to them, there are dangers inherent in the general attempt to appeal to accepted art as a basis for conceptual extrapolation. For instance, the nature of the latter itself may be misconceived. When this happens, the frame of reference used in judging a new production would not be traditional art as it really is but a misrepresentation or even, possibly, a caricature of it. What is more, the very idea of Principle E can be challenged as utterly conservative, even reactionary. In other words, even when the art critic, say, is extrapolating from extant art (or rather, that limited portion of it that he is acquainted with) "as it really is" (assuming that there is such a thing in the case a work's A-features, or that anyone can claim to know, definitely and once and for all, what this nature is) rather than from a distorted view of it, is not Principle E more honored in the breach than in the observance? For would it not unquestionably stifle their creativity or originality, if this "principle" is observed by practising *artists* as a practical principle? Indeed, is not creativity bound to die in the long run, however much good artists may resist it or protest against it, if the art public and especially the professional critics constantly and consistently use this alleged principle to accept or reject certain productions, as good or poor art, respectively, or even as art_1 at all?

My reply is that these dire consequences need not follow from the employment of Principle E, provided that those who employ it know how to apply it properly, and are fully cognizant of the pitfalls they may fall into if they are not careful. This means that the problem of answering questions (A) and (B) hinges on (1) the criterion for a *qualified judge* of $art_{1,\ 2}$ (or a qualified judge of a particular kind of $art_{1,\ 2}$), and on (2) the nature of the physical factors that constitute optimum environmental conditions for the perception and enjoyment of something of a particular description that purports to be $art_{1,\ 2}$. In fact, (1) and (2) contain in a nutshell many of the basic problems posed by the attempt to understand and enjoy modern art. In a lesser degree, the same is true of the new art of any other period. For questions (A) and (B) and related questions can be reformulated in terms of (1) and/or (2). Fortunately, the latter are theoratically soluble by extrapolation from the history of art, i.e., by using Principle E itself; though they are in fact difficult to solve in proportion as the art$_{1, 2}$ in question is noval. The noncircularity of this procedure, especially with regard to (1), cannot be shown here[11] but it is partly accomplished by appeal to general axiological, psychological and other extra-aesthetic factors which help determine a person's or group's acceptance or rejection of a new artifact or activity as art$_{1, 2}$, and which in fact partly determine the new E-criteria that critics or general audiences utilize.[10] The appeal to these cultural factors, which reflect the society's conservative or liberal temper or its mood at a given time, helps place provisional practical limits on the process of extension by resemblance. But even if not checked in this way, there is rarely any danger that it will do away with all boundaries. The problem is more often the opposite, stemming from the usual reluctance of many professional critics and older audiences to extend the concepts art_1 and art_2 to anything that does not sound or look or read very much like what they have been accustomed to calling art, and which has been familiar to them since their childhood or youth. I have observed that the younger set, on the whole, is considerably more adventurous.

III

Having sketched in general terms two chief types of problems confronting us in trying to understand and evaluate modern art, let us examine more closely a basic problem connected with the application of Principle E to actual cases, viz. the difficulty of (1) *recognizing* resemblances, or sufficient resemblances, between a noval artifact X that purports to be art$_{1, 2}$, and a paradigm or group of paradigms of art$_{1, 2}$; and of (2) ascertaining the artistic *significance* of these resemblances *vis-à-vis* the significance of the dissimilarities between them and these paradigmation objects. The latter is particularly important but especially vexing in the case of contemporary avant garde art, precisely because the dissimilarities between it and traditional art$_{1, 2}$ are, or at any rate seem to be, so much greater and more fundamental than their similarities. And it is precisely because of these differences that basic modifications in the concept of art$_{1, 2}$ are or would be necessitated by its classification as art$_{1, 2}$. It is clear that unless problems (1) and (2) can be resolved, Principle E cannot be adequately utilized so far as the *phenomenological* features of such radically novel artifacts and occurrences are concerned. But precisely because of these and related difficulties, the only criterion we can ultimately fall back upon is, as I said earlier, the impact of these productions on qualified audiences. For to generalize from what T. S. Eliot says about good poetry, good art in general can have an impact (he says good poetry can communicate) before it is understood.

The extreme novelty and consequent unfamiliarity of many of the N-features or gestalts of highly unconventional art make it extremely difficult for the perceiver, even after repeated encounters with it, to *recognize* anything like the A-features with which he is familiar, in classical art or in nature, persons or animals. It is even difficult for him to ascertain whether these N-features give rise to any A-features at all, including emotional qualities such as sadness, cheerfulness, joy, or melancholy, as phenomenological-*cum*-affective features of the particular artifacts or occurrences. Try if you will to characterize a piece of electronic music by Stockhausen or a work for "prepared piano" by John Cage as "sad," "cheerful," "gay," and the like; or try to apply it to such conventional A-terms as "delicate," "graceful," or "flamboyant," which are descriptions we unhesitatingly apply to the music of a Bach or even to a Bartok, to the sculptures of a Michelangelo or even the paintings of a Picasso or a Braque (including, to some extent, their cubistic paintings), as well as to human beings and animals. To a considerably lesser extent this is true of the visual forms of some recent or contemporary paintings and sculptures, especially nonobjective art, which have little or no resemblance to how sad or gay, melancholy or cheerful 19th century or even early 20th century art looks, let alone how sad or cheerful animals, or sad or cheerful people, normally look or behave.[13] (However, it is significant that the *colors* and *color schemes* of geometrical abstractions are readily describable in familiar emotional terms.) Our frequent inability to do so is partly due to the apparent lack of sufficient kinship between the new sounds and images and the sounds, melodies, harmonies, rhythms, and images we are accustomed to calling cheeful, sad, etc. This is partly true of works that utilize materials or forms derived from the inorganic, especially the complex and impersonal, world of modern technology, rather than from everyday human life or the organic world as a whole. But this difficulty is clearly relative. I have no doubt that American and other Western audiences find the forms, images and sounds of modern urban technological society that occur in much current

Western art considerably more comprehensible and assimilable than audiences in the so-called underdeveloped countries of Asia and Africa. There is probably also a significant difference in this respect between the younger and older generations in the Western World itself. (See later.)

An additional reason for the above difficulty is the increasing involvement of machines in the construction or composition of modern art objects. The use of technological products or ready-made artifacts—including the litter of what *Time* magazine called our "disposable civilization"—or other ingredients or facets of contemporary urban life, is clearly reflected in contemporary painting and sculpture. Pop art as well as constructivism in sculpture are two such types of art that here come to mind. On the other hand, one must not forget the very considerable use of organic forms, animal, human and plant, in contemporary visual, including abstract, art. Some of the paintings of Duchamp, Miró, Picasso and Stramos, and some of the sculptures of Archipenko (e.g., "The Boxers"), Henry Moore, and Leo Amino (e.g., "Creature of the Deep"), are but a few examples of this. With regard to the appreciation of works of this type, a different problem tends to arise in those instances in which the artist conceives of the forms he has utilized as purely abstract designs completely dissociated from the organisms which exhibit them and with which they are naturally associated in the spectator's experience. For the spectator, unaware of this, is tempted to treat them as representational or descriptive, rather than as pure abstract designs—at best, only symbolic of some objective reality, state of affairs, and the like. Further, apart from the artist's own intentions,[14] there are contemporary works whose phenomenological features proclaim their nonobjective character. But it is not uncommon to see spectators, including some art critics, treating them as though they were representational. The NBC "Today Show" recently provided a good example of this danger. A certain New York art critic who appeared on the morning program to talk about a retrospective Miró show that had just opened there, thought he saw definite representational elements in the abstract organism-like shapes, in several of the abstract canvasses. One could not but admire the ingenuity and imagination with which he transformed the webs of delicate lines into spiders and other animal forms, including duck-like fowl with funny bills! This is not to deny, of course, that Miró may have been "inspired" by the organic forms of these or other animals.

Avant garde music provides many examples of sounds (some

produced by unusual sounding devices used in addition to the conventional instruments of the orchestra) that are quite unrelated to our everyday personal emotional and imaginative life, in contrast to the pitched tones of violins, cellos, harps, or bassoons, which for Western ears, are imbued with associations, connotations and symbolic meanings, and with familiar feelings or emotions. This is also true to some extent of the music produced on Cage's "prepared piano." To be sure, the natural, unpitched sounds produced by wooden or metallic objects, electronic or nonelectronic machines, and the sounds which constantly bombard us from our environment in our busy, noisy daily life, do have familiar associations and connotations. Yet even they sound strange to our ears, seem to shed these associations and connotations, in the totally "alien" environment of the concert hall, auditorium, and so on. The same may be observed with regard to "visual art" resulting from placing familiar and utterly banal practical utensils or appliances, such as a toilet seat or a kitchen sink, in the totally different environment of a museum or an art gallery—particularly if these objects are not spatially insulated from the more conventional art objects housed within its walls. This process of placing familiar objects in unfamiliar settings, or of juxtaposing familiar or unfamiliar objects that do not normally occur together, tends both to divest them of part of their normal meanings and to exploit their conventional character and meanings, in order to set up an interesting dynamic tension between them and their settings or surroundings, hence between their conventional meanings or associations and those of their new environment.

Again, many listeners still find serial music forbiddingly cerebral; but "live aleatory electronic music, though not nonelectric aleatory music, is frequently more "depersonalized" or "dehumanized" than carefully planned and structured cerebral music. This is one reason why avant-garde music, when wedded to the dance, as in Cage's compositions for the Merce Cunningham Dance Company, tends to become considerably more palatable. For then it becomes associated with familiar human forms, ideas, emotions and meanings. However revolutionary a modern dance may be, it cannot differ from its classical antecedents half as much as, say, present avant garde music differs from the music of, say, Gustav Mahler or Richard Strauss, or Cubism differs from Impressionism. On the other hand, some of Cage's recent aleatory works for conventional instruments, e.g., carillon, are readily comprehensible even on a first hearing, and remarkably pleasing; but then they differ much less from traditional music than many of the works of Schoenberg or Bartok, not to mention Webern, Berg, Orff or Boulez. Moreover, even electronic aleatory music is not—indeed, cannot be—completely random. In this respect the difference between it and conventional music is one of degrees, not of kind.

Just as the look or sound of much of the new art makes its general appreciation a matter of great difficulty, the effect that this art has on general audiences is often one of perplexity or bewilderment. The latter's inability to perceive any, or at any rate, an appreciable number of A-features in it, is but one facet of their failure to respond to it in anything like the way they usually respond to familiar artifacts and occurrences which they consider good art. Because of their inability to "relate" to it or relate it to themselves, to recognize familiar expressive qualities in it, to respond to it with any pleasurable feelings, they tend to be irritated or bored with it; at best (or worst) it leaves them untouched. If they could only respond to it significantly like the way in which they respond to what they take to be paradigms of good traditional art, they would be gradually able to associate or correlate these affective states, usually unconsciously or semiconsciously, with the new N-features and gestalts that arouse them. This may proceed to the point that, on subsequent encounters with it, they would be gradually able to recognize the A-features to which these N-features give rise, for audiances in their particular culture. Indeed, this process itself would gradually *generate* these A-features for them.[15] Eventually, they would be able to attain this apprehension even when the particular circumstances prevent them form responding to them with the appropriate feelings. The young, borne and bred in the new sounds and forms, have the edge over their elders: not least because the new art objectifies and amplifies what they feel and think, and reflects their life styles. For the most avant garde art is often a crystalization of present trends as well as a catalyst for forces that might otherwise remain dormant. This, together with other factors, gradually leads to the adhesion of intellectual, imaginative and emotional associations and connotations to them, giving them dimensions of meaning they seldom or never have for the older generations. Thus they would be "relevant" for the young in degrees or ways in which they could never be for their parents and especially grandparents.

But all art lovers, young and old alike, must guard against two common dangers, though probably none entirely escape it, for rather obvious reasons. The first is the error of imposing their personal or communal prejudices and misconceptions as to what art is, or even what art must be, on current productions. The second danger, touched on earlier, is people's failure to recognize, or even their reluctance to try to recognize, genuine artistic qualities (A-features) in artifacts and occurrences that seem to be, especially superficially, radically unlike what they are accustomed to calling art. This danger stems from the failure to perceive the aesthetic relevance of the dissimilarities between the new and the old, familiar productions.

All too often people untutored in the arts, and, to some extent, artists and professional critics, make an insufficient effort to see a work for what it is, and to appreciate it on its own terms. They make no effort to adjust to it or to change their mental perspective to fit it; instead, they tend to force it into a procrustean bed.[16] For instance, even at this late date, I sometimes encounter people (though I must admit that they are usually older or even elderly persons, and generally lacking in sesthetic sophistication) who expect all painting and sculpture to be representational. Consequently they either tend to see representation where none exists or is intended, or alternatively, throw it overboard as "trash" or "junk" because they despair of giving it any coherent representational character. Likewise if they think that the creation of all art does, or should, involve the greatest degree of control possible, and are then confronted with an "action painting" by Mathieu or a painting by Jackson Pollock utilizing the "drip" technique; or if they are convinced that great architecture is synonymous with, say, the American colonial style and then stumble on the houses or buildings designed by Le Corbusier or Frank Lloyd Wright, or (worse), the visionary designs of Paolo Soleri.

To sum up: there is no general rule for resolving the essential tension between the demands of tradition and the demands of creativity, between the conceptual need to take into account the extension and intension of the generally accepted concept of art (or the concepts of its various species) and the need to allow for evolution and even revolution. The golden mean between hidebound traditionalism and the outright rejection of the past and its aesthetic catagories, as in the case of the moral golden mean, varies with the individual case and the circumstances. But the need to resolve this tension, to make conceptual decisions, as well as to judge what is thus brought into the domain of art as good or poor art, is unavoidable. This essay was designed to dramatize these facts, as well as some of the basic problems encountered in the attempt to do so.

NOTES

1. Where "art," "music," etc., are used in a descriptive sense (or as "art_1," "$music_1$," etc., in my notation) as opposed to an evaluative sense, i.e., as shorthand for "good (poor) art (music, etc.)" or "art_2," "$music_2$," in my notation.

2. Which consists of four minutes and thirty three seconds of silence. If complete, unbroken silence is counted as "music," the whole concept of music breaks down. However, I have reason to believe that Cage intended the "work" to be the total envirommental sounds in, e.g., the concert hall, together with the silence at the keyboard. This callenges the traditional concept of music much less than the former.

3. Cf. Christo Javacheff's "wrapping" of such natural things as the craggy inlet, Little Bay, near Sydney, Australia, with polypropylene plastic.

Morris Weitz is, I think, wrong in supposing that a natural object as such, e.g., driftwood exhibiting a striking form, would be ordinarily said to be sculpture, etc., in a literal, unextended sense of "sculpture," etc.

4. "The manifesto [of the hippie] is: 'All men are artists, and who cares that some are better than others; we can all have fun';" "The Hippie Revolt Against Middle-Class Morality," in *Philosophy For a New Generation* (The Macmillan Company, New York, 1970), A. K. Bierman *et al*, ed. p. 159. See also p. 160, on the hippie's concern for "expression over performance, impulse over product." Cf. also Jean Dubuffet's rejection of the distinction between artists and other people.

5. Cf. my *The Concept of Art* (New York University Press, New York, 1971), Chapter 2, and "Family Resemblances and the Classification of Works of Art," *The Journal of Aesthetics and Art Criticism*, XXVIII/1 (Fall 1969), pp. 79–90. However, I believe that, as conceived in the Western World, art has an open and contestable set of *general aims*—intellectual, imaginative and emotional—and that certain kinds of art have more specialized aims. These give the concepts in question an appreciable degree of unity. (See later.)

6. "John Hollander says that a poem is whatever purports to be one." [Van Meter Ames, "Is It Art?", *JAAC* (Fall 1971), p. 39.] The entire essay is relevant to our discussion in this paper; particularly in relation to the "powerful drive to bring art and life together in the continuity that Dewey wanted" (*ibid.*, p. 39). The conceptual implications of this are important for our discussion, but must be left for another occasion.

7. I use "A-feature" and "N-feature" as shorthand for "aesthetic feature" and "nonaesthetic feature," respectively. These terms are used in the way Frank Sibley does in "Aesthetic Concepts," in *Art and Philosoply* (St. Martin's Press, New York, 1964), W. E. Kennick, ed. Examples of aesthetic features are gracefulness, delicacy, flamboyance, dynamism, melancholy, cheerfulness, and piquancy.

8. Or, at least, the tension between the pull of tradition or the demands of continuity, and the pull of the present or the demands of creativity inherent in the very application of our aesthetic categories, must be resolved to the best of one's ability in any given instance.

9. See *The Concept of Art*, Chapter 3. See also Chapters 10–12.

10. The problem with honorific redefinitions, however, is that they actually restrict the concept of art to what the judge (aesthetician) really considers to be good art. But honorific redefinitions are not necessary consequences of the above procedure.

11. I have dealt with the problem of defining the concept of a qualified judge in *The Concept of Art*, Chapter 7.

12. Cf. *op. cit.*, Chapter 13.

13. This is relevant to, e.g., O.K. Bouwsma's and John Hospers' answer to such questions as "What makes sad music sad?" and "What makes a cheerful painting cheerful?", in "The Expression Theory of Art" (in Willian Elton, ed. *Aesthatics and Language*, Oxford, 1954), and "The Concept Of Artistic Expression," John Hospers, ed., *Introductory Reedings In Assthatics.* (Basil Black Well, New York, 1969), respectively.

I should add that the opposite of the above is true of pop art and current forms of New Realism. Likewise in the latest, very different paintings of, e.g., Picasso. The problems which the former two types of art pose for appreciations are in a way the opposite of those described above, since the uncertainty of some viewers as to whether paintings of soup cans, American flags, neckties, or giant hamburgers are art_1, or whether they are good art, rests on the commonplacaness, even triteness of their ostensible subject matter and the apparent banality of their treatment.

14. In this connection, it is interesting to note that, by his own admission, a painter such as Chagall uses representational or pictorial—e.g., human and animal—elements primarily for formal reasons; whereas an "abstract" painter such as Mondrian, who uses no representational elements at all, does not (by his own admission) wish to exclude life values from his art. This is why Chagall says: "I feel myself more "abstract" than Mondrian or Kandinsky in my use of pictorial elements. 'Abstract' in the sense that my painting does not recall reality." [John Hospers, "Meaning in Painting," Lee A. Jacobus, ed., *Aesthetics and the Arts* (Mcgraw-Hill Book Company, New York, 1968), p. 218.

15. Vide *The Concept of Art*, Chapters 5 and 6.

16. Indeed if one can hazard a generalization here, artists have tended to do so in proportion to their own originality and excellence as artists. Some of the most daring artists have been most remiss in this. The same is perhaps true of the most original critics.

Chapter 11

Artistic Freedom and Social Control

The first part of this essay defends the artist's right to create, unhindered by society, on two main grounds: first, on general ethical grounds, i.e., considering the artist as a human being; and second, by reference to the nature of art and artistic creativity. The second part outlines briefly the artist's basic responsibilities toward other artists and society as a whole.

THE ARTIST'S RIGHT TO CREATE OR SOCIETY'S RESPONSIBILITY TO THE ARTIST

Prima facie, society's *coercive* control of art, e.g., censorship or even the punishment of dissident artists, seems to be justified it one accepts (1) an instrumentalist—e.g., moralistic or political—theory of art, and (2) the view that society's essential function is furthering the general good. For with regard to (2) it may be said, following Plato, for example, that the function of society is to provide the conditions that foster the creation, growth, and conservation of all possible values; and since *good* art is a great positive value, furnishing the artist with optimum conditions for artistic creativity is one of society's basic responsibilities. Likewise it may be thought that society has the responsibility to discourage the creation of poor art, which is as undesirable as good art is desirable.

Now suppose we agree for the sake of argument (and indeed, I firmly believe this to be true) that society has the responsibility to furnish optimum conditions for the flourishing of good art (proposition *p*). From this it does *not* follow that society has the further responsibility to discourage poor art (proposition *q*). Indeed, proposition *q*—or even whether *society's* discouraging of poor art is desirable (proposition *s*)—remains a wide-open question, if we accept *p*. Independent grounds for proposition p and for proposition *q* (or for *s*) must be sought by anyone wishing to maintain them. What is more important, there is a great difference between accepting proposition *q* itself and supporting societal coercion of art, as I shall stress in what follows.

What has generally exercised and what currently exercises those who would place the artist under society's control is not so much aesthetically bad art as what they consider to be morally, socially, or politically unhealthy, dangerous, or subversive art—which very often is not the same thing at all. Sheer formal imperfection, such as lack of composition, proportion, or harmony in a symphony or a sculpture; technical or artistic flaws in the construction of a novel's or play's plot or in characterization; artificiality, dullness, mediocrity of invention in a poem or a painting and the like, often fail to raise a ripple of concern or indignation in the minds of those who call for or practice censorship. Only if we adopt an instrumentalist theory of art—particularly moralistic theories such as those of Plato or Tolstoy, or political theories such as those of Marxist theoreticians or aestheticians—would a logical connection exist (be established) between aesthetically good and putative morally, socially, and/or politically desirable art, on the one hand, and between aesthetically poor and putative morally, socially, or politically undesirable art on the other. In the absence of such a theory of art, it would be difficult to establish even a contingent connection between them. There appears to be no empirical correlation between aesthetically good art and art that supports the Estabishment, and between poor art and anti-Establishment art. History shows that frequently the reverse has been true.

I stated earlier that propositions (1) and (2) above do not jointly entail that society has the responsibility (and we may add, or the right) to exercise coercive control over art. For all that follows is that society has the responsibility to encourage good art—and *perhaps* to discourage poor art—*in some hitherto undefined sense or way*. I shall now argue that the same would be true if we hold, together with proposition (2), the proposition [(3)] that art *actually has* salutary or harmful moral or political effects on society, whether or not one also holds proposition (1). For from the supposition that society has the responsibility (or the right) to protect its members from the subversive influence of certain kinds of art, it likewise does *not* follow that society has the responsibility (or the right) to coerce the artist for the putative general good.

The basic question therefore is: Are there any valid grounds, in addition to or different from propositions (1)–(3), capable of justifying society's coercive restriction of the artist's freedom to create? My unequivocal answer is No. I maintain that all the moral evidence goes entirely the other way; hence it is society's moral duty to provide the artist with the maximum freedom possible. I shall now outline some of my main moral reasons for this view.

First, I believe that all persons have a right to self-actualization; and that this includes the artist's right freely to create, as a condition as well as a form of his self-actualization as a human being. The right to self-actualization can be regard as a main form of freedom, considered (as for instance with Sartre) as the foundation of all values. Either way, the artist would have the right to create freely; since the creation of good art actualizes the artist *qua* artist, and his actualization as a human being includes his self-actualization as an artist.

But no human or other right is exercised in a vacuum: the actual exercise of the right of self-actualization is limited or qualified by the right of the individual to exercise his other rights, and the right of others to exercise theirs. The theoretical limitations on the exercise of the artist's right to create freely may be of two general sorts. First, it is limited by the right of all other persons, artists an nonartists, to exercise their own freedoms or rights. For example, and artist has no right to indulge in a particular way of life that he considers to be necessary to or congenial for his artistic creativity, in a manner that hinders or prevents other artists from creating—or creating in a way and in circumstances they find congenial. Second, the artist's own striving for creativity must not interfere with the way of life elected by the other members of society. For example, it is morally wrong for prestigious artists to use their influence to harm artists they envy or disapprove of, either because of the latter's superior ability or because of their unorthodox ideas or productions. The harassment of such dissident Soviet writers as Alexandr Solzhenitsyn by the Secretariat of the Writers' Union is a glaring example of this.

In actual fact, these things are relatively rare; and when they happen, their undesirable effects are limited. History shows that the exact opposite is far more prevalent. Non-artists, especially the inartistic Establishment, have generally frowned on and sometimes tried to force artists to create according to their own prejudices and misconceptions about good and bad art, or what is or is not art. In this century the suppression of dissident artists in totalitarian and other dictatorial regimes, such as Nazi Germany and Fascist Italy and Spain, Portugal, and the Communist World, is the most extreme, systematic, and pervasive form of this in human history. Even the harassment of Solzhenitsyn by the Secretariat of the Writers' Union is an example of this. For the members of that body were and are—whether by choice or through intimidation—nothing but docile puppets of the regime.

If we accept the principle that a person is innocent until proven guilty, the onus of proving, in any given instance, that a particular work of art subverts a *good* social order falls squarely on the shoulders of the particular community or society. It is not the artist's responsibility, either *qua* person or *qua* artist, to prove that what he is doing is innocuous or positively good, whenever he sets pen to paper or brush to canvas. Nor should he be called upon to defend his past work at the government's whims. Moreover, the putative good or bad effects of art on the audience's moral or social behavior is, as far as I know, far from empirically known; though it has been assumed by a long line of philosophers, critics, educators, and others, from Plato's and Aristotle's time on, that art has considerable powers for well or ill. Until this matter is empirically resolved, fairness dictates no other course of action than giving the artist all the freedom he needs in the pursuit of his art. To quote a statement from the much-quoted Mao Tse-tung, "Let a thousand flowers bloom!" (Of course, we all know what happened to this judicious injunction in the People's Republic of China during the "Great Leap Forward." But that is one of history's many poignant ironies.) Anything else violates the principle of justice and fairness and penalizes the artist in advance of evidence of wrongdoing on the basis of little more than a theoretical possibility. The portrayal of the myriad evils of society, as in the novels of Charles Dickens or of the American muckrakers in the 1920s and 1930s, has sometimes roused an otherwise lethargic government or people to positive action. But I know of few work of art, not excepting works of literature proper,[1] that have caused a revolution or a war, or led to political assassination or other forms of violence. The reasons are intriguing and worth investigating by social scientists; but the fact remains that few if any works of art can be categorically called dangerous—rather than the attitudes and actions of those who fear art, or fear particular works, as allegedly subersive and who proceed to suppress what they dislike. Further, history shows that countries which oppress nonconformist artists in the name of the general good generally identify the latter with the special interests of the tiny minority in power, or the Establishment which supports and is in turn supported by it. Moreover, this has usually been true in porportion as the countries in question have been undemocratic; and the opposite with the relatively open societies we call democracies. Ironically, those countries in greatest need of gadflies such as artist-rebels, where the real public interest requires the unhampered criticism of an oppressive status quo, are precisely those in which that opportunity is most strenuously denied to the people. The opposite is usually true of more open societies. It is practically an axiom of history that nations which stifle freedom of thought and expression are those which fear these freedoms most, since they have the most to fear from them. The suppression of freedom is really the outcome not of a desire to preserve what is good in a society (however much the oppressors would like to think so), but of a desire to preserve what is in fact bad in them. Good countries or societies need not fear freedom of thought and expression, for these freedoms include the freedom to dissent from any "subversive" ideas thay may be expressed, in art and outside art. Good ideas have no need to be protected by censorship, any more than good political systems need Iron Curtains or Berlin Walls to keep their citizens within their confines.

The matter can be stated somewhat differently. The artist, like everyone else, has the right—indeed, the duty—to speak out against what he rationally considers to be evil in his country or the world. And he should be perfectly free to do so through his art if he so chooses. Certainly the best artists, inasmuch as they create deeply moving art, can be very effective critics of society through their art if their artistic genius lends itself to polemical social, political, or moral ideas and they have the necessary social, political, or moral insights, and, finally if they choose to express the latter in their art. (It is commonplace that in poetry or even in prose literature, good moral and political writing is hard to come by.) Paraphrasing Socrates at his trial, society should reward as a benefactor the artist who has the moral courage to act as its conscience—rather than jailing, exiling, shooting, or crucifying him, sending him to the Gulag Archipelago, or placing him in a mental asylum. After all, to lionize him would be merely to treat him like a "celebrity": an athlete, entertainer, "jet setter," or (until recently, in this country) politician. That the artist's fate has usually not been the latter is a commentary on the general badness of the world in which we are presently incarcerated, rather than on the alleged dangerousness of some art.

Finally, as I have stated in another essay,[2] the arts have a number of major humanistic functions in today's world. One of them lies in their helping us to know ourselves and the human condition—or to know them better—by tearing off the masks of appearance, illusion, self-deception, or delusion, about ourselves and the world, that as human beings we find so difficult to avoid. For these multifarious forms of appearance and make-believe appear to be the mirages which all human societies, civilized and uncivilized, appear to be endlessly pursuing or practicing. The best art penetrates to and reveals the naked lineaments of reality and in that sense "holds the mirror up to nature." The profound and sweeping insights of the greatest artists in their art are among the most valuable contributions of art to the human spirit. It would be most tragic for us as human beings, no less than as art lovers, if the artist is not permitted to contribute to the world in this way.

The preceding discussion naturally leads to a particularly interesting aesthetic question. The question is whether originality (which is an essential part of creativity in an *honorific sense* or is generally regarded in the West as indispensable for artistic excellence[3]) *logically* requires artistic freedom. A positive answer would clearly strengthen the case for artistic freedom, within the theoretical bounds imposed by the considerations outlined earlier.

It may seem that a certain well-known theory of art and the creative process (*in a descriptive sense of the latter*), viz. the 19th century Romantic or canonical Expression Theory of art, makes artistic freedom a *sine qua non* of artistic originality. That theory holds that the creative process (in the descriptive sense) is in essence a form of "self-expression": the expression of the artist's feelings or emotions, psyche, or individuality; consequently, a work of art is an expression of these phenomena. If we now characterize originality the way Vincent Tomas characterizes *creativity* in an *honorific sense* in "Creativity in Art," i.e., as an activity which "always issues in something that is different in an interesting, important, fruitful, or other valuable way," and if every person is unique or possesses an element of uniqueness in his feelings and emotions, personality, etc, it would follow that, other things being equal, a work is good art in proportion as it expresses fully or adequately its creator's feelings, emotions, or personality. But adequate self-expression clearly requires artistic freedom, at least within the bounds I drew earlier.

One problem with his reasoning is that the canonical Expression Theory is essentially untenable, as has been convincingly shown by a number of contemporary aestheticians.[5] The question is whether a more adequate account of the creative process, together with the proposition that originality is a good-making quality, would entail the desired conclusion. The answer is, I think, "No." The creative process in the descriptive sense—which is what concerns us here—is by definition independent of the aesthetic goodness or badness of the art resulting from it. It is not creativity in this, but in the honorific, sense that is relevant to the question of artistic freedom, for this includes originality as a good-making quality. Does the honorific concept of originality then presuppose the concept of artistic freedom? I think the answer is qualified "Yes." Only a bare *minimum* of artistic freedom appears to be logically presupposed by a modicum of originality. Even extreme imitativeness—which, by the very meaning of "imitativeness," involves a bare minimum of "difference," though not necessarily aesthetically interesting or significant difference—is logically impossible without a minimum of freedom to deviate from the model imitated.

However, this conclusion does not take us very far in the defence of the maximum artistic freedom. History does show, I think, that given the Western concept of originality, freedom to experiment has been generally requisite (though not sufficient) for the most original art. The artist cannot discover exactly where his artistic talents lie, the optimum conditions for the full exercise of those talents, and what sort of art he is best suited to create unless he is free to explore different ideas, styles, and techniques, and has at his disposal the practical means or tools to apply them in his productions. Unless he is free to experiment, he is unlikely to hit on the best means for creating his best art. Any good art he produces would be a fortunate accident.

Further, if creativity in the descriptive sense involves "difference" in some way or degree, it is unpredictable by definition; though this does not entail (*pace* Tomas[6]) the falsity of the view that the activities involved in the production of art are invariably goal-directed. The argument for artistic freedom is independent of whether the creative process is or is not goal-directed. But the concept of creativity does entail that an artist cannot know beforehand what kinds of results he will actually end up with in any given instance: though he may—and sometimes does—have a preconceived plan or goal, varying in degree of clarity or vagueness, specificity or generality, and certain beliefs about the outcome he hopes to get. This is particularly true if he employs new methods or styles, as in the case of avant garde artists. To a lesser extent this is also true of more conventional techniques.

On the other hand, restricting the artist's freedom is an excellent way of forcing him underground, into slavish imitation or sterile silence. Such consequences are amply exemplified in Soviet and East European art since the Communist takeover. We cannot do much more than speculate as to whether such dissident artists as Pasternak, Shostakovich, Solzhenitsyn, and Amalrik would have been able to produce good art had they chosen (in Shostakovitch's case, chosen throughout his musical career) to comply with the restrictions imposed by the government. Though it is conceivable that their genius would have partly triumphed over these restrictions, it is, I think, unlikely that Pasternak would have produced works of the same caliber as *Dr. Zhivago*, or that Solzhenitsyn would have produced *One Day in the Life of Ivan Denisovich, Cancer Ward*, or *The First Circle*. On the other hand, we know that Eugene Zamiatin wrote his finest work—the devastating satire *We*—in the Soviet Union before he went into voluntary exile forever. Likewise, Mikhail Bulgakov's hilarious and highly original satire, *The Master and Margarita*, was written in the Soviet Union. Zamiatin, as a matter of fact, never wrote anything approaching the quality of *We* after his self-exile. This does not contradict the view that a controlled society is not conducive to the creation of good art, for both Zamiatin's and Bulgakov's masterworks, as well as Pasternak's *Dr. Zhivago* and Solzhenitsyn's major novels are, or contain, powerful *criticisms* of the abuses and injustices of the Stalin era and, with the sole exception of *One Day in the Life of Ivan Denisovich*, were written in defiance of official harassment and in the face of actual or potential punishment.

THE RESPONSIBILITY OF THE ARTIST

I shall conclude with a few observations concerning the artist's responsibility as an artist. First, the artist has the primary responsibility to bend all his creative energies, throughout his life, to the fashioning of the very best art he can create, hence to realize as fully as possible his potentialities as an artist. This follows from the principle that a person who has a special ability or talent is obligated to try to actualize it, or from the more general principle that whoever is capable of creating a particular value has the duty to do so. At the very least, if a person chooses the "artistic way of life," he is committed to actualizing it as fully as possible, as long as that choice lasts. However, I do not think that the artist has the responsibility to instruct or edify (Plato), communicate morally good feelings and (hence, allegedly) help unite mankind in love and brotherhood (Tolstoy), or help the cause of some political movement or ideology (Communism). This, apart from whether or not art does, or can, have morally good or bad effects on people's lives. To give the artist such a responsibility is unfair to him and not calculated to help the cause of art, even supposing that is advances a particular social, political, educational, moral, or religious cause. As I said earlier, there appears to be no hard evidence that aesthetically good art has salutary moral effects, and the opposite with poor art. If the two happen to coincide, it would be purely coincidental. Indeed, there is historical evidence that artists who have made social, moral, or other extra-aesthetic goals their objective, have tended to produce the reverse of good art. Or when they did produce good art, they did so by ignoring or opposing the society's putative moral, social, or other goals. Tolstoy's novels and stories (with the exception of his relatively inferior later moralistic tales) are a classic example.

A corollary of the foregoing is that the artist has the obligation—perhaps the moral obligation—not to prostitute art for passing popularity, money, or other self-serving goals. An outgrowth of this, I think, is his obligation to help others, especially other artists, to resist the foregoing temptations.

The artist—particulary the successful and influential artist—has the further obligation to help and encourage other less fortunate artists. He also has the duty to defend the rights of other artists and the artistic way of life. Collectively, artists have a similar obligation to other artists within and without their various organizations. Jean-Paul Sartre and Simone de Beauvoir, Rostropovich and David Oistrakh (the latter two in their defence of Solzhenitsyn) are shining examples of artists who have courageously defended artistic freedom, sometimes at grave personal risk.

NOTES

1. In saying "works of literature proper" I exclude straightforward revolutionary or other activist material that is merely presented in a pleasing literary language or style.
2. "The Humanistic Functions of the Arts Today," *Proceedings of the International Congress of the Humanities* (Atlanta, August 27–September 1, 1974).
3. I say "generally regarded in the West" because it is not evident whether originality is (a) considered to be a good-making quality in all present-day cultures but that the term means different things in different parts of the world, or whether (b) the term has essentially the same meaning in, e.g., Far Eastern as in Western countries but that they do not uniformly regard it as a good-making quality.

4. In W. E. Kennick, ed., *Art and Philosophy* (St. Martin's Press, New York, 1964), p. 286.

5. E.g., Susanne Langer, O. K. Bouwsma, Margaret Macdonald, and John Hospers. Cf. also my "The Expression Theory of Art: A Critical Evaluation," *Journal of Aesthetics and Art Critcism*, Vol. 23, No. 3 (Spring 1965), pp. 335–352.

6. In Kennick, ed., *Art and Philosophy*, pp. 283–294.

Chapter 12

Humanistic Functions of the Arts Today

I

Because of limitations of space as well as the vastness of the subject under consideration, I shall concentrate on art in the contemporary west—and even then will only consider some of the main humanistic functions that art can have in it. I shall not attempt to assess the extent to which Western art has actually served any of the putative functions I shall discuss. Further, I shall not explore the crucial question of the ways in which art can be made to function in the manner described, or to function more effectively than heretofore. A prescription for making art more effective in the desired ways through education, e.g., by making the general public more responsive to it, would constitute an important part of the aims of education in general and of art education in particular. But I hope that the discussion following this essey would bring out some of the facets of humanistic education in the arts.

I shall now indicate how I shall use the terms "humanism" and "humanistic" in this paper, before I pass to the main part of my discussion.

II

Western culture exemplifies different sorts of humanism: Classical Greek, Renaissance, 19th Century humanism (including the humanisms of Auguste Comte, Karl Marx, and Friedrich Nietzsche). and finally, various brands of 20th century humanism, in the writings of, e.g., Aldous and Julian Huxley, Bertrand Russell, A.J. Ayer, J.P. Sartre, Albert Camus, André Malraux, etc. Such Christian scholars as

Étienne Gilson also speak of "Christian Humanism," pre-eminently in Medieval Christian philosophy and theology, particularly in the thought of the angelic doctor. Yet these philosophically diverse forms of humanism have one essential feature in common. This feature is well described by Nicola Abbagnano in the article "Humanism" in the *Encyclopedia of Philosophy*, as follows: "Humanism is . . . any philosophy which recognizes the value or dignity of man and makes him the measure of all things or somehow takes human nature, its limits, or its interests as its theme."[1] This fits well (though some better than others) the forms of humanism I enumerated, except "Christian humanism" on the one hand and Sartre's humanism on the other, for reasons which will become evident. It is also, *with qualifications*, the way I use the term "humanism" in this essay. Tlhe preceding characterization of humanism does fit the Christian ontology and cosmology if we leave out "makes him [man] the measure of all things," and change "somehow takes human nature, its limits, or its interests as its theme" to "somehow takes human nature, its limits, or its interests as *one of its main* themes (the other being the divine order itself)."[2]

It is noteworthy that even in Abbagnano's characterization humanism is not restricted to atheistic philosophies (and this, again, is part of my understanding of humanism). But as suggested above, it does entail the ontological and axiological subordination of any deity or deities that a humanist may believe in, to man's life and concerns on this planet. Thus I regard Aristotle's philosophy as a whole and certainly the life and thought of Socrates, as well as the philosophy of Epicurus and his followers, as major examples of Hellenic and Hellenistic humanism, respectively, notwithstanding the theistic element in all of them. In particular, Aristotle's and Epicurus' metaphysical naturalism[3] makes these philosophers decidedly more humanistic in our sense than, say, Plato.

Finally, the humanism I have described should be distinguished from what I regard as an untenable form of humanism; viz. the anthropocentric view that in Hamlet's immortal words sees man as the "paragon of animals, a little lower than the angels," as the king (by divine or "human" right) of Nature, or which declares (as Sartre puts it in *Existentialism and Humanism*) "Man is magnificiant!" Art as humanistic is not a form of (or at least those works we might call "humanistic art" are not examples of) this self-centered, provincial human idolatry or "human racism."[4] Sartre describes the latter as a humanism which "takes man as an end and as superior value."[5] He adds: "The existentialist will never assume man as an end; for he always remains to be made."[6] But as Robert Champigny notes. "The philosophy of Sartre does appear to be proposing not only a human ideal, but an ideal of the human, as an end."[7] Again: "It remains theoretically possible, however, to distinguish this humanism from a humanism which would also take the human as an end and value, but as an idol to be worshipped. Sartre rejects such a worship of man, a kind of worship which is expressed in such ecstatic sighs as: 'How human!'."[8]

Although the foregoing passage largely expresses my own view, I do not agree with Sartre (1) that we have complete freedom of choice, and (2) that human beings have no nature ("essence"); though I believe that there is always a future, including a human future, to be made. Consequently my reasons for rejecting "human racism" are different. I can find no objective grounds—be they metaphysical, logical or empirical—for assigning to man a pre-eminent axiological status. Certainly man's considerable domination over nature is neither itself a natural moral right nor evidence of his putative axiological superiority to the rest of nature.

1. Modern man, especially modern Western man, having in many ways conquered the world, is in dire danger of losing his soul. In this as well as other respects, Faust remains the arch-symbol of Western man. In advanced technological society in general (with the possible exception, for very special cultural reasons, of contemporary Japan) man is becoming increasingly mechanized, dehumanized and alienated. To quote Herbert Marcuse, he has increasingly become "a mere instrument, . . . a thing."[9] We are becoming brutalized by a technological monster that the Dr. Frankenstein of modern Western society has created and is now in danger of being destroyed by. The life of the vast majority of man has become more devoid of meaning than perhaps ever before, by being progressively cut off from nature and from other men in man-created jungles of steel and concrete, or, better, in steel and concrete cells, sentenced to a life term of almost solitary confinement. Art is one of the few remaining creations of man which can help maintain or restore his humanity against these vast destructive forces, which can help restore a wholeness to men's bruised and battered psyches, for art can keep alive and nourish the inborn human capacity to feel and imagine, to dream beautiful dreams, and to be or remain sensitive to order and beauty in the human world and in nature—or what has remained of the latter after man's centuries-long rape and depredation of it.

2. Fiction, theatre and the best cinematic art can play an additional humanistic role here; viz. preserving our capacity to form human relations, transcending our limited self-centered universes, our isolation, on the deepest levels to which men are capable; in short, they can help us establish or reestablish what Martin Buber calls "I-Thou relationships." By sharing the profoundest insights of the great writers of the past and present and the greatest film makers, into the human mind and heart, and especially by imaginative empathy with the characters and situations they create, our capacity for inter-subjective experience may be quickened and extended. We may then become more sensitive to ourselves and others, and so, perhaps, better equipped to exist on the deeper human levels. We may be better able to communicate on the existential level, to overcome our solitariness, which is so much part of the human condition. Thus once again, we may perhaps become more fully human than we could be without art.

How much of contemporary fiction, theatre and film—including some of the best art of these types—as well as much contemporary painting and sculpture, hold up a most unflattering mirror up to human nature and society! Like the images in the distorting mirrors we take pleasure in viewing ourselves in fun fairs or in Disneyland, this art shows man as horribly funny, ridiculous or even grotesque. The myriad masks and illusions of decency, integrity and altruism are brutally stripped off, and we flinch as we try to confront ourselves as thoroughly perverse, irrational, infantile, sadomasochistic, unspeakably inhuman. Marquis de Sade's writings, Dostoevsky's *Notes From Underground*, Sartre's *No Exit*, the Theatre of the Absurd and Genet's Theatre of Cruelty or Hatred, Solzhenitsyn's *One Day in the Life of Ivan Denisovich* and *The Gulag Archipelago*, Golding's *Lord of the Flies*, are but a few of the remarkable works that sear our minds and hearts with this flaming image of fallen man.[10] In visual art we may recall the savage paintings of George Grosz and Francis Bacon. Again, a good deal of contemporary avant garde music, particularly electronic music, is frightening in (what I feel is) its eerie presentation of the depersonalization and dehumanization of advanced technological society.

The fact that a good deal of the best art, both classical and modern, confronts us with the unvarnished truth about ourselves rather than shielding us from it, brings us to the next point, namely, that I do not claim that art, even the best art, can make us morally better human beings, or even that it is an aim of art to do so, à la Plato, Tolstoy and other moralistic philosophers of art. That is why, throughout this essay, I generally talk about art in general, whether "idealistic" or "realistic," "edifying" or the opposite, whether "good, bad or indifferent." It is clear that being more fully human is not necessarily identical with being more moral. In fact, being more fully human necessarily carries within itself the seed of the malevolent, even diabolical in man; if man is, as often conceived, a most curious cross between the angelic and the demonic. Think for instance of the blame which is commonly heaped, rightly or wrongly, on murder stories, and on films and television programs portraying assorted types of crime and violence, for the increasing rate of violence and crime in the United States and elsewhere.

The preceding brings home other dangers inherent in the humanistic uses of art. There is always the danger that, like Madame Bovary in Flaubert's celebrated novel, the reading public will feed its fantasy on romantic nothings that idealize human beings and relationships (e.g., romantic love) beyond recognition—thereby becoming less rather than better equipped to face the complexities of actual human relationships realistically. One cannot help but think here not only of a great deal of the pulp literature but also of the many crassly sentimental but wildly popular Hollywood films in circulation. We must therefore add the important proviso that at least generally speaking, the present function is limited to good, especially the best literature and films (in the latter case, particularly the best of the New Wave Cinema).

A further pitfall is dramatized by the following passage from Miguel de Unamuno's essay "Ibsen and Kierkegaard":

> Most people go to the theatre to see and hear what they see and hear every day dressed up a bit with literary and aesthetic trimmings, to see themselves in the mirror of daily reality, and it is for that reason that I do not go there. The characters portrayed there are the same ones that continually are embittering and harrassing my life. Neither in life nor in our theatre do I find either the tormented heroes or souls of Ibsen. They would be thrown from the theatre by our honored middle class in the name of "good taste," that repugnant, nauseating "good taste."[11]

In other words, people may (as often happens) only go to see those films or plays, or read those novels that portray the kind of people they themselves happen to be. But even when they do otherwise—as for example, when they wander into a play of Ibsen's or Strindberg's (perhaps better, a play of Genet's) they may find in it only what they had expected to find: a carbon copy or mirror image of themselves (or their illusions of themselves). They may project themselves bodily into the characters or situations portrayed, and so put themselves (or have the illusion of putting themselves) into the shoes of these characters, rather than becoming transformed into them. Thus they may "live in possibility" (in Kierkegaard's phrase) in a way they would be ineapable of in actual life; but the broadening of their inner horizons may be much more circumscribed than if they "became" Hamlet, Lady Macbeth, Ivan Karamazov or Ivan Denisovich. The result is that they may miss what is truly original, profound, exceptional in these characters—precisely what they must perceive and experience in order to grow inwardly in the manner I sketched above.

3. There is a third possible function of art, which is closely connected with the preceding function. I mean that art can help bring human beings together *communally*, as distinct from helping them achieve or maintain unique personal "I-Thou relationships" [second function, above]. The present "social" as opposed to the preceding "existential" use of art would lie in its helping us realize our social nature—which is, indeed, something that a great deal of European art did in the past and which art still does to varying extents in so-called underdeveloped countries. I am thinking chiefly of the performing arts—especially of folk music (instrumental and vocal), folk dancing, and folk theatre. In the Middle Ages, even religious architecture (e.g., the great cathedrals of Chartres and Reims) had the collaborative, communal, as well as anonymous character of folk songs, dances, and theatre. Again, if certain historians of art are to be believed, we are reminded of the manner in which folk literature—such as the folk epic, the ballad, and the romance—was created in the Middle Ages and earlier and of the communal character of the audience's imaginative participation in the superhuman exploits of the great epic heroes or the plight of the lovelorn damsels, while the folk epics were being chanted or recited. The sense of belonging to a larger, more meaningful and abiding human whole—the village, country town, rural district—was and is shared by performers and audiences alike.

In this kind of art and its enactment we find the best examples of Tolstoy's ideal of (good) art as uniting all mankind through an audience's emotional union with the artist and, through him, with the emotional (artistic) heritage of mankind. In Europe, one of the most extraordinary surviving examples of the communal activity of creating (or recreating) and enjoying art is the Passion Play performed once every decade by the entire village of Oberammergau in Bavaria. The most remarkable thing about this unique phenomenon for our purposes is not merely the entire's village's active participation in the enactment of the Passion Play but the fact that this and the long and painstaking preparations for it occupy the center of the villagers' entire life. They literally live (and live together) from year to year for that glorious event that occurs but once every ten years!

Contrast this with modern theatres in Europe and the United States—even so-called theatre in the round[12]—and especially film theatres. In the latter case the audience's experience of the film is perhaps the limit of "noncommunality," not least because of the enveloping darkness, all but reducing the audience psychologically to anonymous shadows or to nothingness. The image of each viewer in his separate seat, psychologically isolated from the rest of the audience, eyes glued to the silver screen, is a telling metaphor of the "desocialization" or "decommunalization" of modern man in advanced technological society. The source of this "solitary confinement" in the experience of a film lies only partly in the nature of film itself, and in the absence of feedback from the audience. (Contrast the legitimate theatre, which thrives on the spellbinding influence of good, especially great, actors and actresses on the audience.)[13] For it is also partly due to the dehumanization and alienation which Western audiences bring with them to the film theatre and which remains with them during and after the screening. We see this, for instance, if we compare it with the warmer, more congenial atmosophere of the movie theatres in, e.g., the Middle East, where in a much more closely knit society, entire families or groups of young men and women frequent the movies to have a pleasant time together. No wonder going to the movies is one of the most popular pastimes there!

It is worth noting that philosophy—philosophy of man—cannot achieve any of the foregoing ends as such, by virtue of its generally abstract, highly intellectual portrayal of man's nature and condition. What art does, instead, is to present vibrant images of lived and liveable human nature, human nature in the flesh, so to speak. In fact, the artistic presentation of the transmuted intellectual insights of philosophy about man and the human condition constitute one of the main creative powers of art—this, apart from the remarkable fact that, with a few notable exceptions, the truest insights into the deepest recesses of the human heart and mind have been hitherto provided by the great artists, not by philosophers or even psychologists. Perhaps in a hundred years empirical psychology will catch up with the insights of a Shakespeare, a Tolstoy or a Dostoevsky into the murky depths of the human psyche.

4. In a relatively young and radically future-oriented society such as the United States, art can provide, like science and philosophy, a certain degree of temporal continuity and tradition. This, together with other cohesive cultural forces, can serve as an antidote to the damaging psychological or existential sense of temporal discontinuity, of radical separation from the past. The emotional belonging to a time and place, so important for psychological well being and happiness, requires a certain degree of identification not only with some contemporaneous community or society but with a personal and communal past. This country's greatest source of continuity so far is, I think, its social and political history. American art, and even American literature of the past, have played a relatively minor role in providing a sense of community and cultural unity to this country (to the extent that this sense exists).

In the highly traditional cultures and subcultures of Asia and Africa, art needs to effect the opposite goal. It needs to become a spearhead of change, a major rallying point of progress. This it can do by continuing imaginatively to chart out hitherto unrealized or even unthought of possibilities of individual and collective human existence. Utopian and contra-Utopian literature and science fiction (some of which is also Utopian) provide, of course, the best examples of this. But various other types of literature as well as film can do so too, e.g., problem plays or novels, such as the works of Ibsen, Shaw, and the American muckrakers of the 1920s, to mention only a few examples. In this way these arts, and, to a lesser extent other arts, can serve as "the historian of the future."[14] What is more, the concrete imaginative portrayal of these possibilities and alternatives can make them more comprehensible as well as more attractive or more repulsive. Examples are Utopias and contra-Utopias, respectively.

In highly traditional societies art has too often been the tool and instrument of reaction or conservatism, rather than of intellectual, aesthetic or spiritual renovation, even revolution. There it has tended slavishly to hold up a mirror—and a distorted, deceptively idealized mirror—to a really defunct past. But I think it is an illusion to suppose that the rare original artist can singlehandedly lessen or break the stranglehold of a dead tradition. The right social-political, economic, intellectual, and often, religious forces must lend a great helping hand.

5. A further function of art, stressed by such writers as E.M. Forster and Wallace Stevens,[16] is to bring order into the chaos of the world. In this respect too we have art that we may not perish from the

truth. Art can do so in different degrees by creating sensuous, imaginative and intellectual forms, which, in Susanne Langer's terms, are "expressive of human feeling," i.e. of some segment of man's psychic life. The not infrequent disorder we encounter in our lives is imaginatively and emotionally metamorphosed by good art into an order that is often "expressive" of that disorder.

A good work makes a particular order (or type of order) an object of the audience's imaginative, intellectual and emotional as well as sensuous apprehension. But this is only half the picture (*pace* Langer). For the sensuous, imaginative and intellectual qualities of (good) art that are expressive of order are also, essentially, objects of possible (and at least in the case of qualified perceivers, under optimum environmental conditions, actual) experience. The order created by good art thus becomes lived or felt and not merely perceived order. In this, art introduces previously nonexistent dimensions of order into the objective world, and concomitantly, into the *Lebenswelt* of human cognition and experience.

To the extent that art brings some type of order or other into the universe and into human experience, it serves to counteract or mitigate the disruptive and destructive forces in nature and society. And this is no mean achievement; especially in a century that enjoys the dubious distinction of being one of the most chaotic in history. In this mad and ugly age it brings at least a modicum of sorely needed sanity, beauty and harmony into our lives. But this is considerably more true of the art of the past (perhaps most notably Renaissance and Baroque art) than of contemporary art. On the contrary, the latter is often a frightening, sometimes literally nightmarish reflection and extension of the disorder and disruption of the contemporary world itself. I have already mentioned such painters as Grosz and Francis Bacon; and we can not add to the list many New Wave films, such as Resnais' *Hiroshima Mon Amour*, Fellini's *Satyricon* and *La Dolce Vita*, Antonioni's *Lavventura*, Godard's *Weekend*, and much of the work of Bergman. The exploitation of randomness in literaturo and music (aleatory music), including taped and live electronic music, dramatically reflects this—in this case, *through the artist's deliberate abandonment of the maximum possible control with regard to both form and content*. The same is true to a lesser extent of surrealist art. But this does not imply the abandonment of all *form* (structure, organization), and so, of all *order*. Randomness (chance) resulting from either deliberate or accidental relinquishment of conscious control must not be confused with absolute disorder, whatever that may mean, or, in the case of temporal phenomena, with the absence of all order. Indeed, absolute disorder (as opposed to relative disorder[17]) is logically impossible, both objectively and in experience. Every possible configuration of any cluster of elements constitutes some (kind of) order. What we ordinarily call disorder is either some undesired or unexpected organization or temporal order, or an organization or order that exhibits minimal patterning or temporal ordering.

Still, not *all* groupings or even organization of elements constitute an *aesthetically pleasing* or effective form (an aesthetic form). Note the fact that, in this sense, we speak of disorganized or formless (or even chaotic) paintings, poems, works of music, etc., as flawed by a basic poor-making quality. Conversely, being well-organized or unified (the opposite of being aesthetically formless) constitutes an important good-making aesthetic quality. It presumably corresponds to or is part of what Clive Bell calls "significant form." More clearly, it is part of what Langer calls "expressive form."

The preceding should be distinguished from the fact that much contemporary avant garde art consciously or unconsciously reflects the chaos of the contemporary world. The ability to reflect and to convey a vivid sense of chaos is the mark of *good, particularly great art*, not the opposite. For conveying a sense of chaos, and being chaotic, are utterly different things. Thus I am convinced that only nonchaotic, or, positively, well-organized or highly unified works can portray chaos effectively, and so, convey a sense of chaos. Finally—and this is another way of saying that at least some aleatory and other sorts of "indeterminate" art *are* good art—the absence of total control or purposiveness is utterly different from a work's being disorganized or chaotic.

6. The final function of art for our purposes is more general than any of the preceding functions, since it involves all men all times. It consists in the artist's giving his and his audience's existence a meaning it would otherwise lack. This is true whether or not some deity exists and gives human existence a cosmic meaning (purpose), unless man's creation and enjoyment of art are part of this deity's putative divine purpose! Consequently, the question of whether the creation or the enjoyment of art gives human life (a) a purpose, or (b) some other sort of significance or value, does not depend on one's metaphysical views respecting the origin and putative purpose of reality. The nonexistence of God does not deprive the creation or enjoyment of art—or any other human activity for that matter—of any significance it may have.

Nor does it follow that art will have value (or greater value) if God does exist and if human existence has a cosmic purpose; likewise with the existence or nonexistence of personal immortality. For I believe that whether the origin and the ultimate end (termination) of human existence, the activity of creating *good* art gives the artist a quality and density of experience he would otherwise be deprived of and consequently the poorer for not having; likewise with his audience. I believe that these experiences—and good art itself—have objective value however brief and ephemeral a person's life may be, or in the face of his inescapable mortality; similarly if the human race and the civilization it has so painfully created over innumerable centuries *are* one day wiped off the face of the earth.

However, *starting from the fact or assumption that art, and the creation and enjoyment of art, are values*, it does follow[18] that the latter would have had greater value if human life were not bounded by death, or if the human personality is (or were) immortal and capable of creating or enjoying art in the afterlife. But this is obviously quite different from the common view, held by Dostoevsky and existentialist philosophers and writers, that no objective values can exist without God and personal immortality.

Yet I would agree with Camus and Malraux that if God and immortality are only (noble) illusions, the experience of creating and enjoying art endows life with great value, at the same time as it provides it with a highly desirable goal. Even in an absurd universe, art would not be a Sisyphusian enterprise; though Camus imagines Sisyphus to be happy (this, without necessarily conceiving of art, as Camus does, as a form of rebellion against an unintelligible and axiologically meaningless universe). Living—if possible, even living solely—for the creation or the enjoyment of good art, is a noble form of existence even when (or if) it does not lessen the horror of annihilation or shield us from the agonies of living and of dying.

NOTES

1. *Ibid.*, pp. 69–70.
2. It can be plausibly argued, however, that this change would rob the definition of precisely what is essential to humanism; viz. the primary emphasis on man and his existence, here and now.
3. Cf. *Ibid.*, p. 70 on naturalism and humanism in general.
4. I borrow this phrase from Robert Champigny, *Humanism and Human Racism, A Critical Study of Essays by Sartre and Camus* (Mouton, The Hague, 1972).
5. *Existentialisme est un Humanisme* (Les Editions Nagel, Paris, 1946), p. 90.

6. *Ibid.*, p. 92.

7. *Ibid.*

8. Champigny, *op. cit.*, p. 37.

9. *One-Dimensional Man* (Beacon Press Boston, 1970), p. 33.

10. Many works of literature, as well as films and other kinds of art, are also impassioned gestures of rebellion or protest against man's dehumanization of man. The works of such writers as Solzhenitsyn and Amalrik, Evtushenko's "Babi Yar" and Picasso's "Guernica," are only a small but significant part of this type of art.

11. *Perplexities and Paradoxes* (Greenwood Press New York, 1968), p. 56.

12. Which creates to some extent a sense of togetherness and involvement with the performers and perhaps with the rest of the audience.

13. Likewise with musical performances.

14. I borrow this phrase and this idea from a paper by Professor George Linden of Southern Illinois University, read recently at the University of Wisconsin-Milwaukee.

15. "Art for Art's Sake," from *Two Cheers for Democracy* (Harcourt New York, Brace, 1951).

16. "Two or Three Ideas," Opus Posthumous, Samuel French Morse, ed. (Knopf New York, 1957), pp. 206–69.

17. Meaning (a) disorder merely to some extent, or (b) relative to some envisaged organization, sequence, etc.

18. If we add that the duration of a worthwhile activity—here the activity of producing or enjoying art—partly determines its value.

Chapter 13

The Need for Art in the Modern World

I

Throughout his checkered career as *homo sapiens*, or at least from the time he made his first cave paintings to the present, man has never ceased to need art, and in more ways than one. The sheer fact that art has stayed alive, and frequently well, during all that time testifies to a deep-rooted impulse or need to create and to enjoy art. The need for art is ubiquitous, universal.

The need for art takes various forms, and touches man's emotional, intellectual, imaginative and volitional nature. Of the forms it takes I shall consider only four, specifically in relation to the contemporary world, for I believe that among other things, we need art (1) for insight into the reality of man and his world, and their everchanging appearances. This I shall call man's need for truth. (2) Man also needs art to provide ever-fresh visions of himself and the world ideally speaking, and so, what man ought to strive to be. This I shall call man's need for the ideal and the longing for perfection. In the creation and the enjoyment of some good art, "the desire of the moth for the star, of the night for the morrow" that Shelley speaks of, comes into full play. It is closely related to and can be regarded as part of (3) a further need for art. I mean the need to provide man with dreams and visions in general, enabling him to "live in possibility" (in Kierkegaard's graphic phrase); to give free rein to his imagination and the contemplative intellect; to make him "dream of before and after, and . . . for what is not." In familiar Leibnizian terms, it is the need to imagine and intellectually to entertain as many of the infinite Leibnizian "possible worlds" as one can; while need (2) is more restricted, being confined to imagining and entertaining, and perhaps striving toward, a happier world of perfect harmony, peace and "good will toward men." (4) Finally, and connected with the preceding, man needs art for that happy state of inner peace and tranquility, that blessed delight, which comes from the experience, in ourselves or in other things, of order, coherence, unity and completeness—or "form" in general. Good, but especially great, works of art satisfy in some degree or other (in some respects, uniquely) one or more of the foregoing major human needs. In fact, a single great work can perhaps satisfy all those needs and more; though much excellent art satisfies only some. The essential things is that good art satisfies these needs in a significantly different way from religion, science or philosophy. In fact, each of these main human endeavors does so, wholly or in part, in its own distinctive way, not duplicatied by the others. That is one main reason why, despite the ancient quarrel of poetry (art) and philosophy and the modern quarrel of science and religion, they are all absolutely essential for human civilization; that is, for man's full humanity or, at least, for his approximation to it.

I claimed that the foregoing needs are common to all mankind, though not in the sense that every single human being actually *feels* every one of them. That would go well beyond the facts. Further, the intensity, depth or persistence of these needs tends to vary in different times and places. Special circumstances tend to give prominence to one particular need, or to a certain subset of these needs, relative to others. Because of the mind-boggling and perhaps unprecedented degree of destructiveness, savagery and depredation systematically practiced in our mad and sad century, and because of the snowballing accumulation and exacerbation with time of worldwide economic, sociopolitical and human problems, I feel that our need is perhaps greater than any previous time, for (1)–(4) above, and so, perhaps, for that which good art can offer. Our need for science, especially for more developed human sciences, and in general, for a humanized and humanistic science, is very great. Even greater if possible is our present need for a moral and humane and far wiser management and application of the discoveries of modern science. Good philosophy too continues to be needed: not least a sustained quest for wisdom in the usual sense, which, except for Existentialism, post-Greek Western philosophy has tended to ignore. In this as well as in other ways Western philosophy can learn from Eastern philosophy. As for religion, the question whether a need for some form of it still exists is more difficult to answer, and I shall put it aside.

I shall now enlarge, as space permits, on each of the four needs I enumerated, in relation to the need for (good) art today.

II

One of the most striking characteristics of man, I believe, which perhaps helps distinguish him from other animals, is his profound propensity to delusions and self-deception as well as to make-believe, hence his tendency to indulge in fantasies and illusions. Human history as a whole, I believe, amply bears this out. In fact it can be convincingly argued that individual human life would be very hard or impossible to bear in the absence of assorted types of fantasies and illusions concerning ourselves and others, and the world; and that human society would be at best shortlived without collective illusions and some form and degree of make-believe or other. But whether or not this is true, I believe that the effort and the longing to escape from reality into a shining illusory world, evident in much of the present world, is particularly acute. This is not surprising in the sad and terrible times in which we have been thrust or in which we have thrust ourselves. As far as it goes, it bears our Freud's findings that unsatisfied persons are prone to fantasizing.

Although the impulse to shut one's eyes to unpleasant realities is a human,—all too human—impulse, it is also dangerous to the extent that it prevents one from facing up to and trying to improve one's lot. The need for positive action is especially great in our troubled world, and promises to become still greater in the future, precisely because of the immensity of the problems we are facing and will certainly continue to face. Much good past art, and much good Western art today, tears away the masks of deception and the veils of appearance behind which we hide from the world and from one another, on even from ourselves. It forces us to gaze on reality and experience it in imagination as much as we are able to without going stark mad or committing hara-kiri. In this art has a powerful ally in modern science, especially in astronomy and cosmology, evolutionary biology, psychology (in particular, depth psychology), and the other human sciences. The names of Copernicus, Darwin and Freud clearly stand out in relation to man's slow but sure fall from his self-erected pedestal as "the paragon of animals, a little lower than the angels." As far back as the Renaissance, in Montaigne's essays and in Shakespeare's *Hamlet*, man was already perceived as that "quintessence of dust."

Much of the truth art provides is "human" or "lived" truth. But a significant amount of good art (e.g., some good fiction and drama) poses such questions as whether human truth is attainable, and whether it is relative. A considerable amount of good art also provides insight into the tantalizing and often tragic but invariably ambiguous interplay of appearances and illusions, among themselves, and with reality. *King Oedipus, Hamlet, Othello* and *King Lear*, Dostoevsky's later novels and Tolstoy's *The Death of Ivan Ilych*, much of Ibsen, Pirandello, Sartre, Genet, Robbe-Grillet as well as Kurosawa's *Rashoman*, Bergman's *Magician*, and Fellini's *8½* are only a few of the titles and names that come to mind in relation to the manifold forms and interfaces of appearance and reality, illusion and truth captured in art—confining ourselves to "dramatic" literature and narrative film. Existentialist philosophy has some way to go and psychology a still longer way to go to catch up with literature and the other arts in plummeting the murky, terrifying lower depths and scaling the spiritual heights of the human psyche.

Perhaps equally important, the mirror that in Shakespeare's words art holds up to nature is polished in such crafty fashion that the human faces we see in it seem tantalizingly familiar yet strange, having "suffered a sea-change, into something rich and strange." One of the most potent devices by which art conveys its insights, namely indirection, is particularly suited to subtly overcoming our defenses, our natural tendency to recoil from unpalatable truths about ourselves. Art insinuates its most effective truths into our psyches largely unaware of us, helping to open our eyes to the deeper parallels between ourselves, our experiences and our lives, on the one hand, and the characters, experiences and lives portrayed on the other: parallels that we would be most reluctant to see or acknowledge were they between us and our experiences and lives on the one hand and other real people, experiences, etc., on the other. This neither science nor philosophy as such is normally equipped to do. For this reason too didactic art, or in general, art with an explicit "message," so often fails in its intent, in addition to being quite frequently dull and hence poor art. Such "instruction" as art may provide must never be divorced from its ability to delight. The aesthetic delight is indeed instrumental in its success (if it is successful) in "instructing." In that sense the former is a "forepleasure" but not, as for Freud, a prelude to the release of the audience's subconscious tensions, the vicarious fulfillment of their repressed subconscious urges. However, the latter too may perhaps be sometimes true.

Two points remain to be made here: first, that illusions and make-believe are not necessarily undesirable, that they sometimes play a salutary role in human life and society. Thus I am not advocating—what is really impossible—the doing away with all our life-supporting personal and social illusions and make-believe, but only those that hinder us from tackling our urgent individual and collective problems. Not just the well-being but the survival of the human race demands, on our part, not less than the whole attainable truth concerning these problems and the possibility or impossibility of solving them. Mankind must grow up and face up to reality or go the way of the dinosaur and the saber-tooth tiger. Yet we must also remember that the ability to live in the light of the truth is not only nobler than the ability to perceive it, it is more difficult and more rare.

Second, the preceding does not contradict the truth of Nietzsche's dictum that we have art that we may not perish from the truth. (Good) art, as Nietzsche clearly saw, enables us to withstand the "slings and arrows of outrageous fortune" through its imposition of form—order, coherence and unity, sometimes also aesthetic completeness—on the chaotic complexity of life and experience: in Classical art, through its Apollonian transformation of the irrational Dionysian impulses in man into things of beauty. But this is not—it is the farthest from—illusion and self-deception. Good art is not an escape into a cheap never-never land, a tinsel Disneyland. That, along with psychedelic drugs, is the domain of bad art, time-murdering television shows and movies, and supermarket best-sellers.[1] But this brings me to the next section, to the visions of ideal realms that some good art paints before our eyes and minds.

III

Classical Greek art was and is a far cry from a deception or an illusion, offered by a "skillful liar," as Aristotle, following Plato, wrongheadedly speaks of the poet.[2] On the contrary, it is (leaving aside certain important aspects of Tragedy) largely a glimpse of a magnificent idealized or even ideal world of perfact harmony, order and beauty. But the good artist who idealizes Nature or man does not intend to make the audience mistake the imaginary, idealized world for the real world; nor is the discerning audience likely to be deceived by his vision. Similarly, the Neo-Classical ideals of beauty (e.g. in Michelangelo) inherited from the Greeks cannot be called on illusion or deception; rather, they are the artist's conception of an ideal of human form, human existence, Nature, etc. In this type of art (which I shall call "idealistic" art) we get visions not of what reality is perceived by the artist to be but as it might or could be were it more harmonious or orderly, unified, morally good or beautiful.[3] Or that type of art provides various conceptions of how reality ought to be. An ancient Chinese saying has it that "The lotus rises unsullied above the muddy pond." Good "idealistic" art is the lotus that rises unsullied above the world's muddy pond.

Man has always needed, and I believe will always need, a star to which to hitch his wagon. Note for example the wealth of Utopian writing in world literature. He needs it to give him hope for a better life for himself and his fellow men and women, and an incentive to strive to improve his life and the life of others. As Underground Man says in Dostoevsky's *Notes From Underground*, "man is a creative animal, doomed to strive consciously toward a goal, engaged in full-time engineering, as it were, busy building himself roads that lead *somewhere—never mind where*."[4] Or, as Zamiatin graphically portrays in his Kafkaesque dystopia, *We*, the way to ensure man's acquiescence in the *status quo*, however horrible or inhuman it may be—or an effective way of destroying his individuality and humanity—is to excise his imagination, his tendency to dream dreams. I shall return to this.

Man is a self-deluding animal. But he is so because he is first and foremost a purposive being and often lusts after his goals so passionately that he confuses his dreams with reality, or deliberately hoodwinks himself and others into believing that he has attained them or is on the verge of doing so, when in fact he is as far from them as ever. But unless he strives toward something, no matter what, he will atrophy and die.[5] Herein lies the satisfaction of a basic human need by good "idealistic" art. For unless man is armed with visions of some ideal, including visions of perfect things, he would be like a blind man groping in the dark, not knowing where to go. The quest for God or some other all-perfect Ultimate Reality, which is a mainspring of most of the religions of the world and has inspired the sublimest religious art, including mystical poetry of the highest aesthetic order, is a prime example of this yearning for the Ideal. In short, man is set apart from the other animals, in considerable part, by his ability to dream dreams and to work toward their realization. Moreover, much of human progress would have been all but impossible but for his dreaming dreams—and then striving to realize them. There are no great awakenings without great dreams.

But do we ourselves need dreams, ideals, less than our ancestors? Hardly. If anything, I believe that our need is especially great today not only because of the awesome and in some ways unique problems we face, but also because of our disconcerting unwillingness or inability to date to wrestle with them. At the same time, as part of these problems themselves, the unremitting pressures and tensions of modern life in the highly industrial urban Western countries are making it increasingly difficult to "stand and stare"—and dream dreams. Many of us are forced to lose sight of ideals by being increasingly immersed in the daily rat race of survival. For what Wordsworth wrote in the 19th century is even truer today: "The world is too much with us."

IV

The Classical—e.g. the ancient Greek—artist enabled himself and his contemporaries to withstand the truth largely through his visions of an idealized or even ideal world. In that world where balance, order, proportion, harmony and unity reign supreme—the sensuous and mental counterparts of the Greeks' moral ideal of the Golden Mean—man tamed or sublimated the terrors of his breast and of the world, and transcended them. Likewise, generations of men since then have found in these values of art so sorely lacking in the actual world an inner peace or a deeply soothing quality as well as an aesthetic delight which great beauty generally bestows on the perceiver. These qualities are of course ingredients of well-being. We are here reminded of the analogous role that Plato assigned to the philosopher's contemplation of the perfect Forms, and of the similar role that Schopenhauer assigned to the contemplation of the Platonic Forms in his *The World As Will and Idea*.

One of the special ways in which good contemporary art can contribute to the emotional well-being that is so hard to come by in daily life is by its humanizing the machine and the Machine Age. To the extent that it is successful it makes us feel psychologically more at home, more secure in the otherwise frightening impersonal world that technology has created. Rather than, as many do, merely decrying or naively trying to conjure away Blake's "dark, satanic mills" by taking refuge in illusory Rousseauesque–Thoreauesque dreams of a return to a simpler, pastoral part, many contemporary artists in Europe and the United States have been wisely harnessing technology in various forms to creative and humanistic aesthetic ends. In that way their art, whenever aesthetically successful, imaginatively counteracts and helps overcome the profoundly depersonalizing and dehumanizing tendencies and effects of modern technology as well as the other familiar aspects of modern urban blight.

V

The craving for happiness appears to be a universal human want. In addition—or perhaps as part of the craving for happiness itself—we find a passionate desire in many people to give free rein to their imagination. Whatever truth the "play-theory" of art has as an account of the creative process in art I think rests on this. Moreover, although the desire for the imaginative exploration of unrealized possibilities may be limited to some persons, I see a basic need for it throughout man's existence: at present and the future no less than in the past. In fact the forces in contemporary culture which tend to blunt men's senses and sensibilities also tend to deaden their imagination. Some good art, by stimulating and nourishing the imagination as well as our other faculties, helps ensure the aliveness and humanity of man. In the case of children good art can help ensure that their vital imagination will not atrophy, as it often does, as they grow older.

The need for a lively imagination that good art (and science as well) can satisfy is closely related to the need for man imaginatively to enjoy contemplating, in their own right, the endless panoramas of unrealized possibilities of our world and the inexhaustible possibilities of imaginary worlds. The exquisite pleasures that the contemplation of these manifold possibilities can provide need no elaboration. Apart from that, it makes for human survival and well-being, just like the unflinching confrontation of reality. Imagination, if not absolutely essential for the full awareness of and the ability to explore fully the various alternatives of action open to a person from moment to moment, is very useful in these respects. Consequently it is crucial for right moral action. In fact, as the American philosopher Brand Blanshard has observed in one of his writings, human evil is often a result of inability to put oneself in other people's shoes. Moreover, life would be utterly dull and uninteresting, and practically shorn of hope, without the enticing vistas of possibilities and opportunities opened by imagination.

Finally, the rather rare quality of imaginativeness is a fountain of invention, not only in art but in science and technology and in private and public affairs. It is a source of creative thinking in general, not just of artistic creation. It is a quality common to or at the root of both intellect and imagination, for imagination need not involve imagery. And imaginativeness, fertile imagination, is nourished both by science and good art. On the other hand, thinking is not necessarily abstract and general; nor is it always about what is the case. Like imagination it can be concrete and specific, and concerned with what is merely possible.

Utilizing Leibniz' concept of possible worlds, every good but, especially, evey great work of art, as a work of imagination, can be profitably envisaged as a sketch of a Leibnizian possible world or a segment of such a world. Living such a "world" or a segment thereof in imagination can be immensely exhiliarating and liberating. It can also provide a vantage point from which one gains new and rare understanding of the actual world and into oneself and the human condition. This is one of the chief ways in which, obliquely or implicitly, art can have immense relevance to our life and world, however visionary or fantastical it may be on the surface. The same is true of visions of the ideal. They too provide a deeper understanding of what is, by throwing into sharp relief its limitations and deficiencies.

NOTES

1. Compare this with what Abraham Kaplan, in "The Aesthetics of the Popular Arts," *Modern Culture and the Arts*, 2rd ed. (Mcgraw-Hill Book Company New York, 1972), James B. Hall and Barry Ulanov, eds. pp. 48–62, says concerning so-called popular art.

2. In this they were followed by, among others, David Hume and, with qualifications, Oscar Wilde.

3. The following passage from Firdausi's *Shahnama* is a delightful example of this:

> Such a spot as the heart delighted in,
> where day lingered long and never diminished.
> No blazing July was ever seen here, nor icy December;
> its air was all perfume, its rain fell as wine.
> All the year round its climate breathed springtime
> and its blossoms were lovely as rosy-cheeked maids.
> Hearts remained far removed from pain, grief, and care;
> a Demon's body was there to suffer all ill.
> Day's head there sunk down in slumber,
> having taught a lesson of goodness and right.

(Quoted from Reuben Levy, *An Introduction to Persian Literature* (Columbia University Press, New York, 1969, p. 71.)

5. In *Man's Search for Meaning*, Viktor Frankl develops the profound truth that man is a meaning-seeking being; that the essence of man is the will to meaning. But the quest for meaning is tantamount to the pursuit of positive values (or at least what the seeker believes to be positive values), and presupposes man's essential purposiveness.

Index

www.ingramcontent.com/pod-product-compliance
Lightning Source LLC
LaVergne TN
LVHW010550100826
845148LV00013B/2686

* 9 7 8 1 6 0 8 9 9 5 7 2 1 *